Workplace Dispute Resolution

Workplace Dispute Resolution
Directions for the 21st Century

Edited by Sandra E. Gleason

Michigan State University Press

East Lansing

All Michigan State University Press Books are produced on paper which meets the requirements of the American National Standard for Information Sciences—Permanence of paper for printed materials ANSI Z23.48–1984.

Printed in the United States of America

Michigan State University Press
East Lansing, Michigan 48823–5202

Library of Congress Cataloging-in-Publication Data

Workplace dispute resolution : directions for the twenty-first century
    / edited by Sandra E. Gleason.
        p.   cm.
    Includes bibliographical references and index.
    ISBN 0-87013-436-1 (alk. paper)
    1. Arbritration, Industrial—United States. 2. Labor disputes—United States
    3. Dispute resolution (Law)—United States.
    I. Gleason, Sandra E.
    KF3425.W67   1997
    344.7301'89—dc21   97-25092
                                                                    CIP

BONNIE LEE GLEASON

my mother and best friend
with thanks for her unfailing support and encouragement

and

the memory of
EDMUND HALL GLEASON

my father
whose gift to me of a sense of humor helped me finish this book

Contents

Perspectives from Japan and Western Europe

New Perspectives on Negotiation

Epilogue: Relevance and Communication

ACKNOWLEDGMENTS

The idea for this book initially emerged during a research project with Karen Roberts that investigated procedural justice issues in the processing and management of workers' compensation claims. As a consequence of this research I saw the need for a volume that would provide a multidisciplinary introduction to workplace dispute resolution as presently practiced and identify the emerging directions of change that will guide the evolution of these dispute resolution systems into the 21st century. Discussions with Karen Roberts and Joel Cutcher-Gershenfeld provided many ideas for the design of this volume.

Much of the work on this book was completed while I was the Planning Director in the Office of Planning and Budgets (OPB) of Michigan State University. The Directors of OPB, Robert M. Lockhart and his successor David Byelich, were very supportive of my work on this volume. My secretary, Elaine Richard, assisted in a variety of ways, as did Cheryl Serra, Jean Barrows, and Richard Jacobson. The secretarial and computer assistance of these staff helped bring this project to fruition more quickly than would have been possible otherwise.

This section would be incomplete without also thanking three other sets of people. First, Richard N. Block, Peter Feuille, and Karen Roberts provided many helpful comments on the introductory chapter. It was much improved as a consequence of their assistance. In addition, the authors who participated in this volume worked hard to write interesting, insightful and stimulating chapters. As a consequence of their efforts this book is a rich collection of perspectives on workplace dispute resolution. Finally, I would like to express my appreciation to the staff of the Michigan State University Press, particularly the editor in chief, Julie Loehr, for the advice and guidance provided as this book developed.

Sandra E. Gleason, editor

ABOUT THE AUTHORS

Max H. Bazerman (Ph.D. in Organizational Behavior, Carnegie-Mellon University) is the J. Jay Gerber Distinguished Professor of Dispute Resolution and Organizations in the Kellogg Graduate School of Management at Northwestern University. His research focuses on decision making, negotiation, fairness, social comparison processes, and the natural environment. He has published over 100 research articles and written or co-edited eight books, including several on management and negotiation. Also, he has been a consultant to over thirty different companies including IBM, McKinsey, Merrill Lynch, Allstate, and Johnson and Johnson.

Deborah I. Chapman is the administrative director of the School Leadership Program at Dartmouth College. Before that she was an administrator, researcher, and teacher at the Amos Tuck School of Business Administration. She did graduate work at Pennsylvania State University. Her research interests concern the evolution of relationships, particularly as a function of gender and developmental experiences.

R. Oliver Clarke is a visiting professor in the School of Labor and Industrial Relations at Michigan State University. His research focuses on comparative industrial relations. He has taught at universities in Australia, Belgium, Britain, Canada, Taiwan, and the United States. For 18 years he analyzed industrial relations developments for the Organization for Economic Cooperation and Development (OECD) in Paris. Before joining the OECD he was the Secretary of a major British employers' association. He also has worked as a management consultant.

Joel Cutcher-Gershenfeld (Ph.D. in Industrial Relations, Massachusetts Institute of Technology) is a visiting associate professor at Babson College and MIT's Sloan School of Management, and co-directs the Negotiations in the Workplace Initiative at the Program on Negotiation at the Harvard Law School. He has co-authored or co-edited seven books and multiple articles on negotiation, training, dispute resolution, labor-management cooperation, and global diffusion of knowledge-driven work systems. Also, he has consulted extensively with public and private sector employers and unions on the design and implementation of a variety of workplace systems for continuous quality improvement, team-based operations, employee involvement, and dispute resolution.

Kristina A. Diekmann (Ph.D. in Organizational Behavior, Northwestern University) is an assistant professor of Management in the College of Business Administration at the University of Notre Dame. Her primary research interests are in negotiation and decision making, with a focus on fairness, impression management and interpersonal perception. She is the author of several refereed articles on these topics. In addition to teaching negotiations and management at Notre Dame, she has conducted several negotiation training sessions in various executive programs at the Kellogg Graduate School of Management and at the University of Notre Dame.

Peter Feuille (Ph.D. in Industrial Relations-Organizational Behavior, University of California-Berkeley) is a Professor of Labor and Industrial Relations at the University of Illinois at Urbana-Champaign, where he also serves as Director of the Institute of Labor and Industrial Relations. He has published widely on various industrial relations topics, with a special focus on labor-management dispute resolution procedures. He has taught various industrial relations courses to university students and to union and management practitioners. In addition, he is an active arbitrator and mediator, and a member of the National Academy of Arbitrators.

Sandra E. Gleason (Ph.D. in Economics, Michigan State University) is a Professor in the School of Labor and Industrial Relations and an Assistant Dean in the College of Social Science at Michigan State University. Previous positions included Planning Director in the Office of Planning and Budgets and Associate Director for the Academic Program of the School of Labor and Industrial Relations. She has published articles on procedural justice in workers' compensation claims and the decision to file a sex discrimination complaint. Her current research interests include procedural justice in workplace dispute resolution, with particular attention to the employee perspective.

Leonard Greenhalgh (Ph.D. in Management, Cornell University) is a Professor of Management at the Amos Tuck School of Business Administration at Dartmouth College. While at Cornell, he worked with Robert B. McKersie conducting research and programs for a labor-management committee working on job security and re-employment issues. His current research focuses on the dynamics of working relationships.

Timothy Hedeen is the Executive Director of the Dispute Resolution Center in Saint Paul, Minnesota and is completing his Ph.D. in Social Science at Syracuse University. He is on the board of directors of the National Association for Community Mediation. Hedeen previously was the Director of the Onondaga County Dispute Resolution Center in Syracuse, New York, and has conducted extensive research on the New York State Unified Court System's Community Dispute Resolution Centers Program. His research interests include mediator style and evaluation, and the study of factors determining whether various groups accept mediation as a dispute resolution process.

Thomas A. Kochan (Ph.D. in Industrial Relations, University of Wisconsin) is the George M. Bunker Professor of Management in the Sloan School of Management at the Massachusetts Institute of Technology. His research covers a variety of topics related to industrial relations and human resource management in the public and private sector, with attention focused in several recent books on the transformation of American organizations and industrial relations. He has served as a third party mediator, fact finder, arbitrator, and consultant to various government and private sector organizations and labor-management groups. From 1993 to 1995 he served on the Commission on the Future of Worker/Management Relations that investigated methods to improve the productivity and global competitiveness of the American workplace.

Deborah M. Kolb (Ph.D. in Management, Massachusetts Institute of Technology) is a Professor of Negotiation and Dispute Resolution at Simmons College and the Director of the Simmons Institute on Leadership and Change. From 1991-1994, Kolb was Executive Director of the Program on Negotiation at Harvard Law School. She is currently a Senior Fellow at the Program where she co-directs the Negotiations in the Workplace Program and is faculty editor of the *Negotiation Journal.* Her research looks at how current negotiation practices affect women and men negotiators in different fields and how these different experiences may lead to alternative models of problem solving and conflict resolution. She has published numerous articles and book chapters on conflict in organizations, mediation and gender issues in negotiation, and is the author or co-editor of several books on these topics.

Michio Nitta (Ph.D. in Economics, University of Tokyo) is a Professor of Industrial Relations in the Institute of Social Science at the University of Tokyo. He has been a Visiting Fulbright Scholar at the Sloan School of Management, Massachusetts Institute of Technology, and a visiting professor in the School of Labor and Industrial Relations, Michigan State University, and the East Asian Institute, Free University of Berlin. His research interests include comparative industrial relations and human resource management, including the cross-cultural diffusion of innovative work practices. He recently published a book on worker participation in the Japanese steel industry.

Linda L. Putnam (Ph.D., University of Minnesota) is Professor and Head of the Department of Speech Communication at Texas A & M University. Her current research interests include communication strategies in negotiation, organizational conflict, language analysis in organizations, and groups in organizations. She has published many articles and book chapters in management and communication journals and is the co-editor of several books. In 1993 she received the Speech Communication Association's Charles H. Woolbert Research Award for a seminal article in the field and was elected a Fellow of the International Communication Association in 1995.

Karen Roberts (Ph.D. in Urban Studies, Massachusetts Institute of Technology) is an Associate Professor in the School of Labor and Industrial Relations and an associate in the Institute for Public Policy and Social Research at Michigan State University. Her research interests include workers' compensation and workplace disability, medical cost containment, procedural justice, career paths of scientists and engineers, and comparative labor markets with particular emphasis on the United States and Canada. A current project involves the establishment of shop-floor dispute resolution systems in various firms in Michigan. She trains both labor and management on disputes arising from a disability in the workplace and dispute resolution techniques.

Mary Rowe (Ph.D. in Economics, Columbia University) is an ombuds-person at the Massachusetts Institute of Technology and Adjunct Professor of Negotiation and Conflict Management at the MIT Sloan School of Management. She has written many articles in the field of conflict management and serves on the Editorial Policy Committee of the *Negotiation Journal* and the Steering Committee of the Program on Negotiation. Rowe co-founded and served as the first President of The Ombudsman Association. She has helped to set up ombuds offices in several hundred corporations, government agencies and academic institutions and has helped to design a number of major, integrated conflict management systems.

Sylvia P. Skratek (Interdisciplinary Ph.D. with an emphasis on public sector labor relations, University of Michigan) is Vice President of Mediation Research and Education Project, Inc., a not for profit corporation that promotes the mediation of grievances arising under collective bargaining contracts. She is President of Skratek and Associates, an organization that provides conflict management and problem solving strategies at the workplace. She has over twenty years of experience in negotiations and dispute resolution with an emphasis upon labor-management disputes and public policy disputes. Her experience includes implementing organizational dispute resolution systems and facilitating cooperative labor relations programs within unionized work environments. She has published several research articles on mediation and arbitration. Dr. Skratek also is an arbitrator actively practicing in six western states.

Ann E. Tenbrunsel (Ph.D. in Organizational Behavior, Northwestern University) is an Assistant Professor of Management in the College of Business Administration at the University of Notre Dame. Her research interests focus on decision making and negotiations, with a specific emphasis on ethics. Tenbrunsel is the author of several refereed articles and has co-edited two books on these topics. In addition to research and teaching, she also acts as a negotiation consultant to executives from a variety of companies and industries.

1

MANAGING WORKPLACE DISPUTES
OVERVIEW AND DIRECTIONS FOR THE 21ST CENTURY

Sandra E. Gleason

I. Introduction

The concept of employee "voice" at the workplace has become more important in recent years; this concept "refers to any means by which employees express their views and provide firms or other interested parties . . . with information that pertains to their employment condition."[1] Although this concept was developed initially with respect to unions serving as the voice of their members, it has been expanded to include both union and nonunion institutions and activities that provide voice for employees as individuals and as groups.

One important category of voice mechanisms is dispute resolution systems. These systems are created to provide a structured approach to identify, discuss, and resolve workplace conflicts that have been transformed into disputes. The disputes that are managed by such systems include a broad range of issues from interpersonal conflicts such as some forms of sexual harassment to the discontent of union members with some feature of their contract.

The systems used to manage workplace disputes have their roots in collective bargaining between unions and management. The contracts developed have defined mutually acceptable grievance procedures in the unionized workplace. Some systems, including complaint systems and grievance procedures, have been initiated by nonunion employers.[2] In addition, a variety of employee-management cooperative initiatives have emerged in both union and nonunion firms to facilitate teamwork and develop modes of cooperative work that attempt to either prevent disputes or deal with disputes in their early stages. Some of these initiatives in the United States have been influenced by Western Europe and Japan.

Examples include works councils mandated by law in Germany and joint labor-management committees in Japan.

Workplace conflicts must be analyzed as social phenomena. As discussed below, this social context means that conflicts are caused by a wide variety of factors. The focus in this volume is on how these forms of social conflict are managed at the work site, with particular attention to innovative perspectives that facilitate better understanding of dispute resolution and improve approaches to dispute management.

Approaches to dispute management have varied during the twentieth century. In the present era the type of management mechanisms employed reflect the stage on the dispute continuum to which a dispute has progressed and whether it is based primarily on interests, rights, or power. These factors determine whether a preventive or remedial approach can be used for a given dispute. This volume continues the tradition of a multidisciplinary approach to understanding the challenges faced by those responsible for the ongoing management of workplace disputes. While building on this tradition and extending it, each chapter also identifies important directions for future research.

II.   Workplace Conflicts as Social Phenomena

The study of workplace conflict is a highly interdisciplinary activity. Whatever their disciplinary perspectives, scholars generally agree on at least three major conclusions.[3] First, conflict is a pervasive element of social life in the workplace. It occurs at all levels from the interpersonal to the interorganizational.

> . . . disputes are cultural events, evolving within a framework of rules about what is worth fighting for, what is the normal or moral way to fight, what kinds of wrongs warrant action, and what kinds of reme-dies are acceptable . . . these perceptions and conceptions influence behavior in ways which cannot be described as rational choice-making. . . . Dispute behavior, like other aspects of informal social life, contains aspects of both rational and non-rational behavior; it incorporates the dimension of choice as well as habit, convention, and affect.[4]

A second major conclusion reached by scholars about workplace conflicts is that most conflicts involve parties who have both cooperative and competitive interests, i.e., most conflicts are "mixed-motive." A useful definition of conflict, therefore, ". . . is an expressed struggle between at least two interdependent parties, who perceive incompatible goals, scarce rewards, and interference from the other party in achieving their goals. They are in a position of opposition in conjunction with cooperation."[5]

The final conclusion is that conflict can be constructive if managed well, but destructive if unmanaged or managed poorly. Management

efforts, however, are affected by the attitudes and behaviors of disputants. Sometimes the disputants themselves are the primary contributors to
the conflict outcome, regardless of how the dispute is managed.

The positive benefits of conflict include the airing of problems that an
employer needs to address and the resulting beneficial changes in such areas as
policies, procedures, programs, organizational structure, and productivity. It
can be a constructive force for innovation. A sense of solidarity can be created
among those engaged in a conflict as well as a stronger sense of enthusiasm
and purpose. Negative consequences can include reduced productivity and job
performance, psychological or physical injury,[6] emotional distress,[7] inability to
sleep, the disruption of social relationships, interference with problem solving
activities, the escalation of differences into antagonistic positions, and increased hostility.[8]

III. Sources of Workplace Conflict

Since conflict between employees and between employees and management is
the result of social interaction and high interdependence at the workplace, it
can reflect a wide variety of causal factors. These range from the structural
features of the workplace, job frustration, and personality characteristics to
differences in culture, race, values, gender, personal preferences, and social
status.[9] The complexity created by multiple factors means there is virtually an
infinite number of sources of conflict. As a consequence, conflict can vary
substantially in such features as the scope, intensity, number of participants,
the objective being sought, and ultimate outcomes.

Gmelch and Carroll [10] identify the following ten sources of conflict
based on the structure of a complex organization: the levels of the
bureaucratic hierarchy; the rules and regulations influencing job structure and role clarity; the degree of departmental specialization; the
demographic and psychosocial similarities and differences among the
staff and the degree of staff stability; the degree of use of close supervision; the degree of employee participation in decision making; the type
of power used by a manager to achieve goals (e.g., rewards and recognition, punishment, personal persuasion); the type of reward and
recognition systems in place and their implementation; the degree of
staff interdependence; and conflicts in the roles and responsibilities of
managers. They argue that these sources may generate conflicts between
employees and management, independent of whatever interpersonal
conflicts may be occurring between employees.

Bergmann and Volkema [11] studied the sources of interpersonal
conflict at work. They found that about 62 percent of the issues underlying conflict between subordinates and supervisors included goal conflict, rejection of employee input, vague task assignments, unfair
performance evaluations, downgrading a coworker, poor work scheduling, unrealistic workloads, and misuse of power. In the area of conflict
between coworkers, about 61 percent of the issues that generated con-

flict included coworkers not carrying their workload, personalities, different work ethics, downgrading coworkers, and goal conflict.

In addition, their research showed that conflicts were handled in a variety of ways. An employee who was in conflict with a supervisor was more likely to talk with the supervisor about the conflict. In contrast, a conflict with a coworker was more likely to be handled by avoidance, i.e., the employee would stop talking to the person. A tracking of the response pattern indicated, however, that the most frequent responses to conflict were problem solving activities.

Their analysis of how interpersonal conflict is handled shows that conflicts must be transformed by individuals into disputes to become actionable events. This transformation requires three sequential, subjective processes labeled "naming," "blaming," and "claiming." [12] Naming refers to the recognition that an experience has been harmful in some way. Blaming turns this perceived harmful experience into a grievance by assigning fault or blaming another person, group, or institution. This transformation implies that a norm has been violated and that the person believes something can and should be done to correct the situation. This also implies some notion of fairness. In the final transformation, the claiming process, the grievance is expressed to someone or through some mechanism with responsibility for the situation or environment and a remedy is requested. Thus, when an employee decides to stop talking to a coworker with whom there is a conflict, the conflict stops at the blaming stage. But when a conflict is discussed with a supervisor, the conflict has been transformed by "claiming." If a claim is rejected, either partially or totally, it is transformed into a dispute.

IV. A Continuum of Disputes: Prevention and Remedy

Given the complexity of causes of conflict and the subjectivity of the dispute transformation process, disputes typically involve a mixture of concerns related to interests, rights, and power. Consequently, determining the appropriate method of resolution depends on whether the dispute is based *primarily* on interests, rights, or power. Which of these factors is relatively most important in a given dispute is often linked with the stage to which that dispute has progressed. To illustrate the impact of dispute progression, it is useful to think of a continuum of dispute stages and to compare two polar extremes of that continuum.

At one end of the continuum is the dispute that begins as an interpersonal conflict between two employees and is transformed into an actionable event. Examples would be some forms of harassment by a coworker or a dispute over how a task should be completed. This is the stage in which the dispute remains the closest to the parties and therefore is relatively easy to resolve. It has the potential to be resolved by the parties involved, perhaps aided by some objective or neutral person such as an ombudsman of the employer. Employees trained in conflict management skills such as active listening and interpersonal communications skills who work in an environment that encourages proactive intervention are empowered to self-manage a dispute close to the source of the conflict. This can prevent the dispute from escalating and requiring a more complex and formal dispute resolution mechanism. This type of dispute remains relatively private and inexpensive to settle.

In this situation solutions can be more readily based on the interests of the parties identified through negotiation aimed at joint problem solving. When a dispute is based primarily on interests, the best approach is to address the sources of the conflict and the needs of the parties in a straightforward manner to work out a mutually satisfying result. This approach is based on four basic guidelines: keep the people involved separate from the problem; focus on the interests of the parties rather than on their positions; identify a variety of ways to resolve the conflict before making a decision; and base the resolution on objective standards. The end product can be a "win-win" resolution. The focus here is on "preventive voice procedures" that allow the employee to provide input as decisions are being made.[13]

In contrast, at the other end of the continuum is the dispute that has moved without resolution from its source through the organization and required external intervention of some type. Such disputes often become relatively public, and include cases involving union grievances that proceed to arbitration or sex discrimination claims filed in the federal court system. The cost of resolving disputes at this advanced stage is typically quite high for both parties since it can require a lawyer or team of lawyers for litigation, and can impose substantial personal costs on the employee filing the complaint.[14]

Disputes that proceed to resolution systems outside the workplace are based primarily on the rights and power of the parties. When a dispute is based primarily on rights, there is often a legal precedent or a union contract that can be used to determine the outcome. For example, a variety of civil rights laws define employee rights to equal treatment at their place of employment, and contracts negotiated through collective bargaining specify employee rights on a variety of matters such as seniority and safety. The dispute based primarily on power involves one party exercising power to impose, or threatening to impose, costs on another party. Examples of the use of power that can be linked with disputes include a union threatening to strike or a supervisor using the power of the position to deny a promotion sought by a subordinate.

In these highly escalated disputes the solution or remedy to the problem is more likely to be dictated by an outsider to the process such as an arbitrator or judge. Consequently, the resolution is adjudicated or imposed rather than negotiated. The resolution is more likely to be "win-lose," reflecting the adversarial nature of the dispute resolution process employed. It may entail accepting a result but resenting the outcome. "Focusing on who is right, as in litigation, or on who is more powerful, as in a strike, usually leaves at least one party perceiving itself as the loser."[15] Hence, issues of fair treatment during the process, or procedural justice, are very important.

Procedures based on rights and power typically are "remedial voice procedures" that provide mechanisms to an employee to challenge a decision after it has been made.[16] Procedures designed to remedy or correct decisions can exist within as well as outside an organization. Examples of internal procedures include grievance procedures found in union and nonunion workplaces and grievance mediation used in some unionized workplaces as the stage prior to sending a grievance to an outside arbitrator.

The approaches available to resolve disputes in either the preventive or remedial mode generate different costs and benefits. The following four criteria have been suggested for use in evaluating the "best" option for a particular dispute: (1) the monetary and nonmonetary costs borne by the parties; (2) the durability of the resolution; (3) the effect on the relationship of the parties involved (does it improve, or at least not damage, the relationship); and (4) satisfaction with the outcome as judged by the perceived fairness of the resolution or the actual outcome achieved (distributive justice) and the fairness of the procedure used (procedural justice).[17]

V.   Employer Approaches to Managing Conflict

Managing disputes is one important dimension of the management of the employer-employee relationship. As discussed above, disputes are a natural result of the structure and operations of the workplace. Employers need efficient ways to resolve disputes quickly and fairly to avoid the many negative costs generated by unresolved problems. As the generally weaker party in the relationship, employees need the protection provided by both formal and informal dispute management systems aimed at achieving organizational justice.

Over time, three basic approaches have been used to manage disputes at the workplace.[18] The first or "traditionalist" approach was used from the 1890s through the middle of the 1940s. During this era, conflict was seen as destructive and largely reflecting bad temper and other personality behaviors, so the role of management was to eliminate it from the organization. Dispute management was largely a unilateral and reactive management activity that reflected the hierarchical structure of the workplace. While not widespread, the dispute resolution systems that did exist relied on remedial voice mechanisms that were largely adversarial.

This "traditionalist approach" was followed in the 1950s through the 1980s by the "behavioral approach." This perspective accepted conflict as natural in complex organizations with multiple built-in conflicts. The management of conflict was aimed at reducing the amount of conflict through preventive strategies, such as employee training to change attitudes and behaviors to support the acceptance of differences among employees and groups of employees, thereby reducing the sources of conflict. These preventive strategies were used in addition to remedial voice procedures.

Today the "principled approach" prevails. This approach also accepts conflict as a necessary part of organization life, but it differs from the behavioral approach in the belief that conflict management means viewing conflict as necessary and as an activity to be encouraged in a productive organization. This perspective became more widely accepted in the 1980s due to the influence of the Harvard Negotiation Project and books such as *Getting to YES: Negotiating Agreement Without Giving In.*[19]

The principled approach views conflict as a means of identifying problems that can interfere with the achievement of the goals and needs of both the individual and the organization. This approach requires the recognition of the nature and causes of conflict, the identification and investigation of effective response options, and the use of principled conflict resolution to resolve disputes. The goal is to find the optimal level of conflict that permits both individual and organizational goals to be achieved.[20] Thus, while both preventive and remedial voice procedures are used, increasing emphasis is being placed on the former. More attention is being given to the use of interest-based problem solving using negotiation and innovations to support this approach.

This latest approach to dispute resolution has been encouraged by four considerations. First, some employers have come to understand the positive benefits that can emerge from a well-managed and properly working dispute resolution system. Second, employers around the world are seeking ways to effectively handle disputes arising over the changes in employment practices required to survive in an increasingly global economy. Employer responses to competitive forces will continue to affect the introduction and use of new technologies and competitive strategies, as well as systems of compensation and patterns of skills and training to fit the new technologies. These changes also will raise a variety of issues related to labor force adjustments to the business cycle and structural changes, including job security, job mobility, and staffing.[21]

Third, employers have become increasingly concerned about finding more cost-effective methods of dispute resolution. As discussed by several authors in this volume, there is widespread discontent with the costs and delays of grievance procedures, arbitration, and litigated settlements. Less costly and faster alternatives with more satisfactory outcomes are being sought. This search for better methods has encouraged some employers to experiment with preventive approaches to empower employees to self-manage disputes, including a variety of forms of labor-management cooperative activities, and integrated conflict management systems.

Finally, this shift in approach to the management of disputes over time also mirrors the historical trend in workplaces in the industrialized countries toward more participation by employees and less coercion of employees. This is seen in the willingness to view dispute resolution as a decision making process based on the multilateral and interactive involvement of appropriate parties to a dispute. It is a nonadversarial, analytical approach that considers the concerns of affected parties before decisions are made, a form of problem solving that ensures a variety of values and world views are considered and multiple options explored as potential outcomes.[22] It also gives organizations the flexibility to respond more readily to employees and groups of employees with conflict and negotiation styles that vary by gender, ethnicity, and a variety of other factors.[23]

The dispute management systems actually used today in public and private sector organizations are quite varied. They may include only preventive voice procedures, only remedial voice procedures, a mixture of both, or have no clearly identified approach. Procedures may be informal as in many small and medium-sized nonunion organizations, highly structured and formal as in the grievance procedures of large unionized organizations, or some mixture of informal and formal.

VI.   Overview of Chapters

The chapters in this volume are set in the context of the principled approach to dispute resolution as it continues to evolve to meet the challenges that will be faced by the workplaces in the twenty-first century. A number of important emerging issues in the effective management of workplace disputes are discussed. These issues are explored from three viewpoints: perspectives from developments in the United States, perspectives from Japan and Western Europe, and perspectives on negotiation as a tool for successful dispute resolution.

A. Perspectives from the United States

Interest in dispute resolution in the workplace originally focused on the unionized workplace and this remains an important focus. But as the role of unions has declined since the 1950s, attention has shifted in new directions. Scholars and practitioners have become increasingly interested in dispute resolution in the nonunion workplace and in establishments experimenting with new organizations of work such as team-based production. The attention given to new workplace applications of dispute management also has focused more attention on designing systems from the perspective of the complainants, the users of the systems. Particular attention has been given to making systems more comfortable and easier to use while also considering the users' evaluations of what constitutes fair treatment.

Feuille provides an overview of dispute resolution activities in the unionized workplace. He argues that disputing is the key behavioral feature differentiating union and nonunion establishments. The roles of unions and management in dispute management reflect different interpretations of the collective bargaining contract and differential motivations and definitions of self-interest. But he believes both parties typically continue to view contract negotiations as power-based bargaining, i.e., a win-lose activity. He provides an assessment of the scholarly research and operational data on dispute resolution activities in the 1980s and 1990s. Particular attention is paid to three primary arenas for dispute activities: public policy, contract negotiations, and the handling of grievances as part of daily operations.

His chapter introduces and explains a wide variety of approaches to dispute resolution that are discussed from different perspectives in later chapters. He also identifies a theme revisited in other chapters: the multiple positive effects at the work site resulting from the development of cooperative/participative labor-management programs such as quality of work life (QWL) programs and team-based systems.

Skratek continues the focus on the unionized work setting as she discusses grievance handling in more detail. In this context she develops the concept of a "conflictive partnership" resulting from the movement toward more labor-management cooperation in the 1980s. This also has meant greater use of "problem solving" bargaining as the focus has shifted away from power and rights and win-lose bargaining toward interests and mutual gains bargaining. She provides an overview of the two basic innovative approaches developed: grievance mediation and grievance prevention. Based on her own practitioner experience, Skratek discusses the steps required to successfully implement these two approaches.

In contrast to Feuille and Skratek, Rowe discusses dispute resolution in the nonunion workplace. She notes that although dispute resolution procedures are standard components of the labor-management contract in the unionized sector, internal dispute resolution procedures have not been standard features of the nonunion environment. Even though there has been a marked expansion of internal dispute resolution procedures and systems in the nonunion sector in recent years, there is no reliable estimate of how pervasive these are. About 50 percent of large nonunion firms report having some form of grievance procedure.[24]

Rowe reviews the criticisms of these procedures in nonunion workplaces as inadequate protectors of employee rights. She discusses the innovations emerging in the nonunion environment to address these criticisms. Factors encouraging innovations include an increased concern for employee rights, interest in appropriate dispute resolution (ADR) focused on interests, cost control, and healthy organizational development.

Rowe discusses the importance of using a proactive focus to resolve disputes at an early stage. She argues from her experience as a practitioner that it is important to develop an integrated design that provides multiple options for users, with particular attention to the needs of women and people of color. This user-friendly design supports the use of approaches that allow employees to help themselves settle a dispute. This approach is referred to as an "integrated conflict management system." Rowe reviews the characteristics of a successful system, including the scope of the conflicts to be handled, the role of stakeholders, the provision of options responsive to the needs of complainants with varied demographic and other characteristics, the functions to be performed, and methods of dispute resolution.

The increasing use of teams is a fundamental change in how work is organized in all sectors of the economy. The use of teams means that new forms of workplace conflict within and between teams will develop, thereby creating new challenges for managing workplace disputes. While previous literature on teams has focused almost entirely on conflicts within teams, Cutcher-Gershenfeld and Kochan explore team conflict set within the broader organizational system in which a team operates. A six-step process improvement framework is used: (1) clarify the aim or goal being pursued; (2) understand what is actually happening; (3) analyze the root causes of any gaps between the aim and the present reality; (4) identify improvement options; (5) develop an implementation plan; and (6) evaluate results.

This analytical framework is used to reconceptualize dispute resolution in a team-based, mixed-motive work system. Based on their experience working with teams, they argue that there are four key features for managing conflict in this environment. These include helping employees develop comfort in dealing with conflict since conflict is pervasive, a commitment to resolving the conflict close to the source, seeking a resolution based primarily on interests, and developing the capacity to learn from conflicts. Like Rowe, they conclude that the best approach is to establish an integrated system with multiple options for resolving different types of disputes.

Employees in the United States want to be treated fairly by employers. This concern is explored by Gleason and Roberts who examine the fairness of the processes and procedures, that is, procedural justice, used in workers' compensation claims and disputes. They review the multiple and subjective dimensions used to evaluate the presence or absence of procedural justice. The reported perceptions of procedural fairness in disputes are based on their research on a sample of workers' compensation claims in Michigan. A survey of claimants identified substantial dissatisfaction with procedural justice in the handling of their claims and resulting disputes. Gleason and Roberts discuss the implications of this research for the creation of "fair organizations" and the design of dispute management systems perceived by users as procedurally fair.

B. Perspectives from Japan and Western Europe

Employers in most advanced countries today are facing a similar set of economic and workplace changes as discussed above. Whether unionized or not, they are experimenting with new strategies for managing their human resources. This experimentation inevitably overflows into dispute management.

As the U.S. economy becomes increasingly involved with the global marketplace, it becomes even more important to understand how disputes are managed in other countries for at least three reasons. First, studying comparative industrial relations helps us understand more fully our own system, its culturally determined features and philosophical basis for managing employees and disputes, and potential directions for change.[25] Second, as U.S. firms locate overseas they will have to adapt to the philosophies and institutions of other countries. Finally, we may learn about approaches that can be adapted to the United States to improve our dispute management systems.[26] An introduction to this cross-cultural perspective on managing disputes is provided in the chapters by Nitta and Clarke. These chapters help us understand the difficulty of transplanting dispute resolution innovations between countries with different histories and institutions.

Nitta uses two case studies to describe the plant level and work site dispute resolution system innovations designed to increase labor/management cooperation. He describes how the challenges imposed by the changing competitive environment reviewed above are handled by the innovations introduced in two United States-Japanese joint ventures in the steel industry. He reviews the Japanese and German systems based on the joint sharing of the responsibility for decision making on specified issues with their proactive focus on the prevention of disputes to support cooperation. The variations in innovations through the cooperative partnership at National Steel, a workplace with previously established employment relations practices, and participative management at L-S Electrogalvanizing (LSE), an entirely new facility, are explained. Both companies focus on preventing disputes or, when this fails, on settling disputes in their early stages as close to the source of the dispute as possible.

Clarke describes variations in dispute resolution systems in four nations in Western Europe that are heavily unionized: Britain, France, Germany, and Sweden. He reviews the industrial relations background of each nation and the structure of collective bargaining and related grievance procedures within organizations. In addition, he also explains the role of the state in managing workplace disputes and the laws on strikes. He discusses the differences between these four European countries and the United States due to differences in the recognition of unions, the extent of coverage of collective bargaining, the primary level at which collective bargaining is conducted, the availability of special public procedures for grievances, the use of arbitration, and the way the state handles disputes in essential services.

C. New Perspectives on Negotiation

As noted above, over time employers have moved away from relying solely on the traditional dispute management approach based on remediation toward greater reliance on more proactive prevention and problem solving activities. This has focused attention on the process of negotiation as an important tool to facilitate workplace dispute resolution through problem solving close to the source of the dispute.

Workplace disputes are not typically disputes between strangers, but rather involve people who know each other to some degree and who may have worked together for a number of years. In this context, the parties to a dispute must manage in their negotiations the tension between fairness and self-interest, the impact of the nature of their relationship on how they choose to handle disputes, and the impact of gender biases.

While fairness of treatment of the parties to a dispute is an important value supported by employee and employers, there often is a tension between acting in a fair manner and in pursuing one's own self-interest. In a negotiation the parties want to do as well as possible, but fairness is important in maintaining ongoing relationships, managing disputes, and influencing the outcomes of a dispute. Diekmann, Tenbrunsel, and Bazerman discuss the economic and behavioral decision theory perspectives on fairness in negotiation and the ambiguity and subjective factors confronted in efforts to define fairness. They argue that although people are constrained by fairness, they will maximize their own outcomes when they can justify doing so. Justifications and impression management are used to resolve the tension between self-interest and fairness. People manage the impression of being fair so they are perceived as being fair to gain social approval in the negotiation process.

Greenhalgh and Chapman argue that the characteristics of the relationship between the parties are the central determinants of the process and outcome of the dispute. They argue that the interpersonal nature of a relationship determines the choice of relying primarily on power, negotiation, or conflict resolution to handle disputes, as well as the process to be used to implement each option and the effectiveness of the implementation. Power is the ability to gain compliance with an outcome that benefits the person using power. They distinguish between negotiation, or getting commitment to a particular course of action to settle a dispute, and conflict resolution techniques used in a persuasive process to reframe the dispute as a mutual problem to be worked out jointly.

Consequently, they argue that it is important to understand how people think about and assess relationships. They report the findings of

their research which identify four sets of factors that determine the nature of the relationship between parties. These factors are attraction,
rapport, bonding, and the scope and time horizons of the relationship.
Attraction includes common interests, affection, whether the other person is stimulating, and romantic interest. Rapport covers trust, the
openness of the relationship, empathy, acceptance, and respect. Bonding
determines the degree to which parties see each other as allies or enemies, how competitive they are, and the benefits a person receives from
a relationship.

Kolb and Putnam use the "lens of gender" and feminist standpoint
theory to explore our understanding of negotiation as a social activity
for problem solving. They review the current theory of negotiation
analysis and discuss three factors that result in the "gendering" of the
theory. First, attributes associated with masculine worldviews are more
prominent than those associated with feminine perspectives. Second,
there is no recognition of how the different social and power positions
of negotiators influence the definition of the dispute and the options and
ability to participate in bargaining. Finally, certain "invisible" features
of the negotiation process, such as the creation of a comfortable context
for a good working relationship, are ignored. In addition, Kolb and
Putnam review the three major approaches used to frame gender issues
in negotiation. None yield straightforward answers about how to deal
with a man or a woman in a negotiation.

They discuss the impact of these gender biases by considering two
basic assumptions in the current theory of negotiation: the concept of
the negotiator as a purely autonomous individual agent and the view of
negotiation as primarily an instrumental activity, that is, a means of
achieving particular outcomes by selecting strategies expected to lead to
those outcomes. A focus on the autonomous agent ignores the connections built by interpersonal relationships and interests among the parties
to a dispute and how these connections are fostered during negotiations
to build a comfortable psychological and emotional context and working
relationship. Instead of a focus on the instrumentality of negotiation,
they argue that negotiation is a process of transformation that can
change the expectations, explanations, and understandings about the
negotiation process. It provides a forum for the parties to interact that
also can move the resolution of a dispute toward previously unconsid-
ered outcomes once interests, issues, preferences, and options are expressed openly.

D. Epilogue: Relevance and Communication

The previous chapters describe and analyze our current understanding
about managing disputes at the workplace and directions of change in
dispute management methods and systems, and identify directions for
future research. The final chapter shifts the focus of this volume to the

concern about how to reach a broader audience—practitioners in the dispute management community—to disseminate ideas about more effective ways to manage disputes. Hedeen discusses the need to study actual dispute processes and the people experiencing them in order to develop better dispute management systems. He argues it is important to identify research topics relevant to practice and thus of interest to practitioners, and use research methods in applied settings that reflect the real world. Hedeen also believes it is necessary to improve access to research findings and recommendations to improve dispute resolution practice based on research by paying attention to how and where research is published and presented.

VII. Conclusion

Disputes in the workplace can be created by multiple sources of conflict ranging from personality conflicts to structural problems in an organization. Employers must decide how they will handle these disputes. The authors in this volume provide a variety of viewpoints that help us understand why employers committed to effective dispute management will use a combination of preventive and remedial dispute resolution mechanisms. A dispute management system designed to effectively handle the challenges faced by public and private organizations in the 21st century will not only provide methods appropriate to the type and stage of the dispute, but also appropriate for the needs of those who use the system.

Notes

1.   D. Lewin and P. D. Sherer, "Does Strategic Choice Explain Senior Executives Preferences on Employee Voice and Representation?" in *Employee Representation: Alternatives and Future Directors*, ed. B. E. Kaufman and M. M. Kleiner (Madison, Wis.: Industrial Relations Research Association Series, 1993), 239.

2.   R. Feuille and D. R. Chachere, "Looking Fair or Being Fair: Remedial Voice Procedures in Nonunion Workplaces," *Journal of Management* 21 (1995): 27-42.

3.   M. Deutsch, "Subjective Features of Conflict Resolution: Psychological, Social and Cultural Influences," in *New Directions in Conflict Theory: Conflict Resolution and Conflict Transformation*, ed. R. Vayrynen (London: Sage Publications, 1991), 26-56.

4.   S. E. Merry and S. S. Silbey, "What Do Plaintiffs Want? Reexamining the Concept of Dispute," *The Justice System* 9 (1984): 157-58.

5.   J. H. Frost and W. W. Wilmot, *Interpersonal Conflict* (Dubuque, Iowa: Wm. C. Brown Co. Publishers, 1978), 9.

6.   T. S. Denenberg, R. V. Denenberg, M. Braverman, and S. Braverman, "Dispute Resolution and Workplace Violence," *Dispute Resolution Journal* 51 (1996): 6-16.

7.   It should be noted that relatively little attention has been given to emotions in organizations and the emotional labor required of employees on the job. For a variety of perspectives on emotional labor at the workplace see S. Fineman, ed., *Emotion in Organizations* (Newbury Park, Calif.: Sage Publications, 1993).

8.   T. J. Bergmann and R. J. Volkema, "Understanding and Managing Interpersonal Conflict at Work: Its Issues, Interactive Processes, and Consequences," in *Managing Conflict: An Interdisciplinary Approach,* ed. M. A. Rahim (New York: Praeger Publishers, 1989); H. Bisno, *Managing Conflict* (Newbury Park, Calif., Sage Publications, 1988); Frost and Wilmot, *Interpersonal Conflict.*

9.   Bisno, *Managing Conflict.*

10.   W. H. Gmelch and J. B. Carroll, "The Three R's of Conflict Management for Department Chairs and Faculty," *Innovative Higher Education* 16 (1991): 107-23.

11.   Bergmann and Volkema, "Understanding and Managing Interpersonal Conflict," 7-19.

12.   W. L. F. Felsteiner, R. L. Abel, and A. Sarat, "The Emergence and Transformation of Disputes: Naming, Blaming, Claiming. . ." *Law and Society Review* 15 (1980-81): 631-54.

13.   Feuille and Chachere, "Looking Fair or Being Fair."

14.   S. E. Gleason, "The Decision to File a Sex Discrimination Complaint in the Federal Government: The Benefits and Costs of 'Voice,'" *Proceedings of the 36th Annual Meeting of the Industrial Relations Research Association,* San Francisco (December 28-30, 1983): 189-97.

15. W. L. Ury, J. M. Brett, and S. B. Goldberg, *Getting Disputes Resolved: Designing Systems to Cut the Costs of Conflict* (San Francisco: Jossey-Bass Publishers, 1988), 14.

16.   Feuille and Chachere, "Looking Fair or Being Fair."

17. Ury, Brett, and Goldberg, *Getting Disputes Resolved.*

18. Gmelch and Carroll, "The Three R's of Conflict Management."

19. R. Fisher and W. L. Ury, *Getting to YES: Negotiating Agreement Without Giving In* (Ontario, Canada: Penguin Books, 1983).

20. F. C. Earley and G. B. Northcraft, "Goal Setting, Resources Interdependence, and Conflict Management," in *Managing Conflict: An Interdisciplinary Approach,* ed., M. A. Rahim (New York: Praeger Publishers, 1989), 161-70.

21. R. M. Locke, "The Transformation of Industrial Relations? A Cross-National Review," in K. S. Wever and L. Turner, eds., *The Comparative Political Economy of Industrial Relations* (Madison, Wis.: Industrial Relations Research Association, 1995), 9.

22. J. Burton, *Conflict: Resolution and Provention* (New York: St. Martin's Press, Inc., 1990).

23. Frost and Wilmot, *Interpersonal Conflict.*

24. Also see Feuille and Chachere, "Looking Fair or Being Fair," for more discussion of this point.

25. G. Strauss, "Industrial Relations as an Academic Field: What's Wrong with It?" in *Theories and Concepts in Comparative Industrial Relations,* eds. J. Barbash and K. Barbash (Columbia: University of South Carolina Press, 1989), 255.

26. This focus has been deemed important enough to justify committing one of the annual volumes of the Industrial Relations Research Association to it. See K. S. Wever and L. Turner, eds., *The Comparative Political Economy of Industrial Relations* (Madison, Wis.: Industrial Relations Research Association, 1995).

Part One

Perspectives From the United States

2

DISPUTE RESOLUTION FRONTIERS IN THE UNIONIZED WORKPLACE

Peter Feuille

I. Introduction

Employees and managers often have divergent views about workplace conduct, job performance, and the appropriate nature of workplace rewards. These different perspectives frequently result in disputes of one kind or another. In nonunion establishments, employees who disagree with their superiors usually express their differences on an individual basis, and they must do so from a weak power position. One result is that the amount of overt employee-employer disputing is relatively modest. In contrast, in unionized workplaces the disputing dimension is much more salient as a result of the union's presence as the collective agent of the employees. This collective voice may emerge at the public policy level as efforts to change the government's labor relations rules, at the negotiating level as threatened or actual strikes or boycotts in the quest for more favorable employment terms, and most often at the workplace level as grievances challenging managerial interpretations of existing employment terms. In this chapter we will examine a mix of scholarly research and operational data to assess the contributions made by each of these three sets of activities in the area of dispute management. Particular attention is focused on selected union-management dispute resolution (DR) developments of the 1980s and 1990s.

II. The Union-Management Relationship

The presence of a union in the workplace dramatically changes how employers and employees interact with each other, especially when they disagree about something. The justification for the union's existence, in the society and in any workplace, is that some employers will not treat employees as equitably as they deserve to be treated unless the union insists upon it. In other words, unions rely upon a "logic of equity" to challenge the natural (i.e., nonunion) order of things. Where they have representation rights, unions use the collective bargaining process to seek more employee-favorable terms than the employer would provide on its own. Unions persuade employers to agree to such terms as higher wages, better fringes, and increased job security by manipulating the employer's costs of disagreeing with the union via such tactics as threatened or actual strikes, slowdowns, boycotts, and so on.[1] As this implies, and as union and employer behavior confirms, the parties typically view contract negotiations as an exercise in power-based distributive, i.e., win-lose, bargaining.[2]

In unionized workplaces, these negotiated terms are written down in the union contract. Because the contract requires employers to provide employment terms that they would not ordinarily provide, the contract is the document that codifies the gains that the union has achieved at management's expense. Unions believe that these provisions are the desirable fruits of their valiant struggle with employers who are insufficiently attuned to the equity interests of employees, and thus these contractual provisions need to be protected and expanded. In contrast, employers are driven by a "logic of efficiency" belief that they must safeguard operating efficiency from encroachment by unions which are too little concerned with the competitive realities of the product marketplace. Therefore, employers tend to see contract terms as unwanted provisions whose impact on efficiency should be minimized. Union and management negotiators, however, are frequently not able to specify their contract terms with the breadth and precision that will cover all the workplace contingencies that may arise. Further, it is often easier in negotiations to obtain mutual agreement on generally worded provisions than on clearly specified terms.[3]

Opposing union and management negotiating perspectives mean that unions and employers usually have different perspectives on how to interpret and apply the contract on a day-to-day basis. In addition, the use of generally worded contract terms allows for differing contract interpretations as contingencies arise. Accordingly, union desires for employee-favorable interpretations may clash with management desires for efficiency-enhancing interpretations. When these interpretations conflict and an informal resolution is not possible, the usual result is a contract interpretation dispute which then becomes the basis for a grievance.

These disputing behaviors also confirm that the union-management relationship is motivationally asymmetric because the union is an eager participant in the relationship and the employer is reluctant. Unions work diligently to establish and maintain their union-management ties, while employers usually try to avoid becoming unionized and sometimes work to break off existing relationships with unions.[4] The research demonstrating that unions have used their bargaining power to obtain increased wages, fringes, and work rules, at the expense of reduced corporate profits and managerial flexibility, indicates that these conflict-oriented motivations and behaviors accurately reflect union and employer self-interests.[5] These motivations also explain why unions and employers, and the union and employer federations to which they belong, devote so much effort to enhancing their bargaining power by seeking favorable labor relations rules from the government.

This analysis suggests that disputing is the key behavioral feature that differentiates employment relationships in union and nonunion establishments. In the remainder of this chapter we examine the three primary dispute arenas in which unions and employers compete for favorable outcomes: the public policy (or societal) arena, the contract negotiation arena, and the workplace (or shopfloor) arena.[6] We pay particular attention to the noteworthy developments in these dispute arenas during the 1980s and 1990s.

III. Labor Relations Policy Dispute Resolution

Unions and employers see the statutes, regulations, and agency and judicial rulings governing union-management (U-M) relationships as objects to be manipulated in a continuing effort to increase one side's power at the expense of the other side. These public policy disputes usually are high-stakes battles, for their outcome can have a significant influence on (a) the establishment of new union-management relationships, (b) the amount and form of disputing that occurs in unionized workplaces, and (c) the ability of unions and employers to obtain self-favorable outcomes.

The U-M regulatory stakes are highest in the battles over labor relations statutes, for the content of these laws can have a very substantial impact on union and employer power at the collective bargaining table. At the national level, the most important postwar labor relations legislative battles were as follows: (1) the 1947 struggle over the passage of the Taft-Hartley Act and its many restrictions on union bargaining and strike activities; (2) the 1958-59 fight over the passage of the Landrum-Griffin Act and its regulation of internal union affairs; (3) the 1977-78 struggle over the proposed Labor Law Reform Act to modify the organizing and bargaining provisions of Taft-Hartley in a manner that would make it easier for unions to organize new workers and bargain contracts; and (4) the unions' 1988-94 effort to legislatively prohibit employers from permanently replacing strikers via the proposed Workplace Fairness Act. The unions lost all of these high-profile lobbying efforts, a track record that is consistent with the postwar decline in union political influence at the national level. On all four occasions, Congress either adopted new restrictions on union activities or declined to adopt union-favorable rules, with the result that all of these legislative efforts resulted in real or perceived reductions in union bargaining power. Moreover, the fact that these lobbying battles occurred primarily in Washington should not obscure the fact that the impetus for them resulted from the manner in which thousands of organizing and bargaining disputes were handled in workplaces across the country.

Unions, however, have scored a string of impressive victories in state legislatures during the past thirty years as they have sought and obtained, despite public employer opposition, the legislatively protected right to organize and bargain for millions of state and local government employees. By now at least thirty-five states grant some or all of the public employees within their boundaries the right to organize and bargain. Some of these states also have given some employee groups substantial impasse resolution rights, including either the right to strike or use compulsory interest arbitration.[7] Moreover, research indicates that the spread of these public sector bargaining laws results in increased unionization,[8] which in turn has resulted in the spread of negotiated grievance procedures patterned on the private sector grievance model as discussed below. In other words, these union legislative successes have made many public employees and employers much more familiar with formal U-M dispute resolution procedures than they were previously.

In contrast to the intermittent lobbying battles over new statutory rules, unions and employers routinely tilt at each other over how the existing rules should be interpreted. For instance, National Labor Relations Board (NLRB) figures show that between 1949 and 1979 there was almost an eightfold increase in the unfair labor practice charges that unions and employers filed against each other, though since then the number of these charges has declined somewhat.[9] Unions allege that during the Reagan and Bush administrations the NLRB administered the National Labor Relations Act in a blatantly promanagement manner. There is no question that the board issued several high-profile, employer-favorable unfair labor practice decisions during the 1980s, including some which reversed existing union-favorable precedents. But an analysis of 414 major board decisions during the 1981-89 period showed that unions won 54 percent of the decisions, which suggests that the board may have been something less than a complete captive of management interests during those years.[10] The continuing union complaints about board procedures and decisions reflects union frustration with the inability of these procedures, and the underlying statutes, to curb employer resistance to union organizing and bargaining efforts.[11]

Courtrooms also are the scene of frequent union and employer jousting over how legislative and common law DR rules should be applied. Research shows that during the 1971-83 period the number of lawsuits filed annually in federal district courts under the National Labor Relations Act, the Labor Management Reporting and Disclosure Act, and the Railway Labor Act almost doubled, but after 1983 these lawsuit filings tapered off considerably.[12] Much of this litigation involves the most contentious union and employer disputes over NLRB decisions and grievance arbitration arrangements, and these court decisions can have a very strong influence on how unions and employers deal with each other at the bargaining table and in the workplace.

For instance, over the years the U.S. Supreme Court has issued several decisions that provide very strong protection to the grievance arbitration procedures unions and employers have negotiated to resolve their most difficult grievances (which will be examined in more detail below). Beginning with the landmark 1960 Steelworkers Trilogy decisions and continuing through its 1987 decision in *United Paperworkers v. Misco*,[13] the Supreme Court has emphatically instructed unions and employers that they must abide by their contractual promises to use their arbitration procedures to resolve grievance disputes, and that they must abide by arbitrators' decisions even (and especially) when the results are not to their liking. These decisions have created a protective legal umbrella around these arbitration procedures, which in turn has directly contributed over the years to the resolution of millions of contract interpretation disputes without work stoppages or litigation. As another example, in its 1938 decision in *NLRB v. Mackay Radio and Telegraph*,[14] the Supreme Court explicitly protected the right of struck employers under the National Labor Relations Act to hire replacement workers to permanently take the jobs of strikers. This decision became increasingly controversial during the 1980s as private employers exercised this right more frequently than in previous decades.

The 1980s and 1990s have seen the continuation of the high "hostility quotient" level in the labor relations rhetoric offered for public consumption that developed during the 1970s.[15] Most of this rhetoric has been union-inspired, for the unions have seen themselves on the short end of a continuing power imbalance that developed during the 1970s, worsened during the 1980s, and has continued at a low ebb during the 1990s. The unions see this power imbalance as caused, in large part, by unfavorable labor relations rules that allow private employers far too much freedom to resist union organizing and bargaining efforts, including the ability to engage in serious unfair labor practices and then receive only modest penalties. Private sector employers agree that these rules favor them, for they vigorously resist every union effort to modify them in a union-favorable direction.[16] So far the unions have not been able to muster the political clout necessary to obtain new union-favorable rules. Further, it is readily apparent that the balanced analysis of workplace interests offered during 1994-95 by the Clinton administration's Commission on the Future of Worker-Management Relations (the "Dunlop Commission") has produced inadequate political support for rules changes in a direction that will enhance union organizing and bargaining power.[17] Accordingly, we should expect the political stalemate over these rules to continue, accompanied by repeated expressions of opposition to or support for the status quo from the competing sides of the bargaining table.

IV. Contract Negotiation Dispute Resolution

In the private sector the standard method of resolving negotiating disputes over new employment terms is the threat of a strike, followed by an actual work stoppage in a small fraction of the cases. As this implies, there is little reliance upon third party DR procedures. In the public sector the use of threatened or actual strikes is much less customary due to legal limitations imposed on the right to strike. These limitations reflect the belief that public employees should not be able to collectively withhold services from the public they serve. As a result, there is a much greater reliance upon DR procedures in public sector bargaining.

A. Strikes

Several decades of strike data support four conclusions. The first is that most strikes occur at contract negotiation time. The spread and use of negotiated grievance and arbitration procedures to handle grievance disputes have made contract interpretation strikes unusual.

Second, during the 1980s and 1990s the average strike propensity in the private sector declined substantially. For instance, research indicates that during the 1970s average strike rates in large bargaining units (those with 1,000 or more workers) were in the 12-14 percent range,[18] and then declined to about 9 percent in the 1980s.[19] Additional research indicates that strike rates in small bargaining units (those with fewer than 1,000 workers) generally have been much lower than in large units.[20] Because the typical bargaining unit is rather small, the average strike rate for the entire private sector almost certainly has been in the single digit range for a long time, and it declined noticeably during the 1980s and 1990s. For instance, negotiation and strike data from the Federal Mediation and Conciliation Service (FMCS) indicate that about 2.5 percent of the 1976-77 contract negotiations for which the FMCS received negotiation notices from unions and employers resulted in work stoppages. For the years 1991-92, this percentage declined to about nine-tenths of 1 percent.[21]

This downward trend in strike propensities is even more apparent in the strike occurrence statistics reported in table 1, which shows the dramatic decline in the annual number of strikes in recent years. Compared to the 1970s, annual strike levels have declined about 80 percent to a level unmatched since the early years of the Great Depression. This reduction in strikes is the result of the shrinking unionized sector and a reduced strike propensity in the bargaining units that remain.[22]

Table 1.   Work Stoppages in the U.S.[1]

Year	Large Stoppages[2] (BLS)	All Stoppages[3]		
	(BLS)	(BLS)	(FMCS)	(BNA)
1950	424	4,843		
1955	363	4,320		
1960	222	3,333		
1965	268	3,963	1,792	
1970	381	5,716	2,632	
1975	235	5,031	3,005	
1976	231	5,648	2,609	
1977	298	5,506	3,111	
1978	219	4,230	2,720	
1979	235	4,827	2,897	
1980	187	3,885	2,764	
1981	145	2,568	2,129	
1982	96		1,168	
1983	81		647	
1984	62		1,215	
1985	54		1,016	
1986	69		1,119	
1987	46		921	
1988	40		779	
1989	51		755	
1990	44		711	839
1991	40		589	706
1992	35		518	
1993	35		493	
1994	45		471	
1995	31		385	

Notes:
1. "Work stoppages" include strikes and a small number of lockouts.
2. "Large" work stoppages are those involving 1,000 workers or more. This information is collected and reported by the U.S. Bureau of Labor Statistics.
3. Data on "all work stoppages" come from three sources. The "BLS" column presents data on all stoppages involving six workers or more that were identified by the Bureau of Labor Statistics for each calendar year through 1981. The "FMCS" column reports the number of work stoppages identified each fiscal year by the Federal Mediation and Conciliation Service via the bargaining notices it receives from unions and employers. The "BNA" column specifies the work stoppages reported by the research division of the Bureau of National Affairs for the 1990 and 1991 calendar years. The data collection methods of these three agencies differ. However, the BLS figures are the most comprehensive.

Third, research has confirmed that there is a great deal of variation in strike rates across industries and firms and over time.[23] As a result, it is difficult to formulate a general explanation of strikes that allows us to predict strike occurrences in specific situations.

Fourth, the reduction in strike rates is a direct result of increased employer aggressiveness in bargaining. Research has confirmed increased employer negotiating insistence upon favorable outcomes, employer willingness to unilaterally impose final offers upon their employees, and employer willingness to hire replacement workers when their workers strike.[24]

Relying on strike data from the U.S. and several European countries, Arthur Ross and Paul Hartman in 1960 observed that the strike was "withering away."[25] Their observation, which initially attracted much favorable attention, fell into disfavor in this country when it was superseded by the increased strike levels of the late 1960s and the 1970s. But strike data from the 1980s and 1990s indicate that strikes indeed may be withering away, though for reasons that were not foreseen thirty-five years ago. Moreover, there is nothing on the horizon that suggests that the diminished level of strikes will reverse itself in the near future.

Perhaps the diminished role of the strike in U.S. union-management dispute resolution is most apparent in the manner in which the federal government handles "national emergency" labor disputes. During the 1940s and 1950s, one of the most hotly debated issues in the entire public policy spectrum was how society should handle strikes that created emergencies for others.[26] By the 1990s this topic had passed into the hands of the labor historians, for the federal government had long since adopted a much more laissez-faire approach toward strikes,[27] and industrial relations scholars shifted their attention away from them. A succession of federal policy makers, both Democratic and Republican, have come to believe that strikes rarely pose emergencies, either real or imagined, that need to be handled. This belief is the result, in part, of a substantially diminished union ability to deprive consumers of "essential" goods or services via a work stoppage. Accordingly, with the exception of the railroad industry, the federal government essentially has removed itself from the emergency strike intervention business.[28] For instance, the government has not attempted to invoke the Taft-Hartley Title II emergency dispute "cooling-off" procedure since 1978, and the Railway Labor Act's emergency board intervention procedure has been invoked only once since that same year. Moreover, the use of emergency boards in the railroad industry declined during the 1980s and 1990s.

As noted in the preceding section, employer hiring of permanent striker replacements has become the most contentious labor relations public policy issue during the past dozen years. Unions claim (a) that this phenomenon has frightened workers into remaining on the job, even in the wake of unfriendly employer behaviors, for fear of being replaced if they walk out, (b) that when strikes do occur the specter of permanent replacement generates increasingly confrontational behavior, and (c) that the increased use of this practice can be traced to President Reagan's 1981 decision to permanently replace 11,300 striking air traffic controllers. Recent research confirms that employers raised the replacement issue more frequently during 1980s strikes than during the 1970s, and the sharp decline in strikes shown in table 1 is consistent with worker replacement fears.[29] Recent research also confirms that employer hiring (or threatened hiring) of permanent replacements leads to a significant increase in the difficulty of resolving the strike.[30] Other research indicates, however, that employers have been using this tactic ever since the 1930s and that such use became more frequent beginning in the late 1970s.[31] This finding is not consistent with the claim that this is a post-1981 air traffic controller strike phenomenon. In any case, the continuation of the regulatory status quo means that this highly contentious subject will continue to occupy center stage in labor relations policy debates in the foreseeable future.

B. Strike Substitutes

As the balance of strike power has shifted toward employers, unions have sought other methods for pressuring recalcitrant employers. The two most visible strike substitutes to emerge during the past fifteen or so years are corporate campaigns and in-plant strategies.

Corporate Campaigns. A much-publicized union pressure tactic emerged in the late 1970s under the label of the "corporate campaign." This tactic received a huge boost in visibility and popularity when it was successfully used during the late 1970s by the Amalgamated Clothing and Textile Workers Union in its campaign to organize selected plants of the J. P. Stevens textile company.[32] These campaigns involve union efforts to use nonstrike tactics, such as financial pressure from investors and creditors, union-initiated regulatory investigations, and adverse publicity, to make it costly for employers to resist union organizing and bargaining efforts. Sometimes these tactics are used as part of organizing drives at nonunion firms, and sometimes as complements to or substitutes for strikes during bargaining at unionized firms.[33]

The track record of these campaigns is mixed, for they usually are very expensive and long-term undertakings that may strain the union treasury and the commitment of the workers involved. They appear to work best against employers that sell directly to consumers and that are sensitive about their public image, or that are heavily regulated by the government.[34] There is no question that these campaigns will continue, but their expense and uncertainty make it very unlikely that they will become a regularly used feature of the labor relations DR landscape.

In-Plant Strategy. The increased risk of striking has caused some unions to embrace what is called the "in-plant strategy,"[35] an approach that has its roots in the sit-down strikes of the 1930s and the increased use of permanent striker replacements in the 1980s. This approach eschews work stoppages in favor of having employees remain on the job, receive their paychecks while avoiding the risk of being replaced, and then disrupt normal operations from within the plant. These disruptions include a wide variety of behaviors: implementing work-to-rule efforts (whereby workers require extensive instructions and then follow all rules and directives very carefully [i.e., slowly]), not volunteering for anything, refusing to work overtime, filing large numbers of grievances, having group confrontations with supervisors whenever a worker is disciplined, filing charges with government agencies, calling in sick, wearing symbols of solidarity and resistance to management (caps, T-shirts, armbands, buttons, etc.), holding rallies outside the plant gate, and in general establishing a climate in which employer-employee cooperation and normal production do not exist. Employers claim that sometimes these efforts spill over into outright sabotage.[36]

This approach is believed to have been formulated in the early 1980s.[37] This approach has had many successes, for it can lead to seriously reduced output that creates pressure on employers to resolve the dispute on union-favorable terms. At other times, employers have responded by disciplining and/or laying off employees, shifting production elsewhere, or locking out employees and hiring temporary replacements. In some circumstances, unions have combined a corporate campaign with the in-plant strategy.[38] This can be a high-pressure combination with an employer that has no short-run options to cope with a production slowdown and a besmirched public image. There are no national data on these efforts, so it is not apparent how widespread the in-plant strategy has become. As with corporate campaigns, it will continue to be used, but it is not yet clear if it will become a standard part of the union-management DR repertoire.

C. Dispute Resolution Procedures

A separate category of strike substitutes are DR procedures that provide for the intervention of a third party into the contract negotiation dispute to help the parties reach agreement. The DR Holy Grail sought by labor relations scholars is a third-party DR procedure that will prevent strikes in contract negotiation disputes, that unions and employers will embrace with equal enthusiasm, and that will provide plenty of high-paying moonlighting opportunities for these scholars. During the postwar period there has been a continual search for a contract negotiation DR procedure with these features, but so far with a notable lack of success. As we will see, there continues to be a mutual reluctance among private sector unions and employers to involve third parties in contract negotiation disputes, though there is the occasional exception. In the public sector, state legislatures have imposed many DR intervention procedures upon the negotiating parties, though often over the resistance of one side or the other.

Mediation. Ever since the 1947 creation of the Federal Mediation and Conciliation Service, the federal government has provided mediation services to U-M negotiators in most private sector industries.[39] This FMCS intervention authority is limited, however, by two key factors. The first is that private sector mediation is voluntary, and thus either party's objection is enough to prevent a mediator from becoming involved. The second is that the mediator has no authority to impose any sort of settlement, which means that the dispute (including a work stoppage) may continue after mediation has concluded. The fact that private sector strike rates remained relatively high for thirty years after the FMCS's creation, and that the reduced strike rates of the 1980s and 1990s were not the result of changes in mediation procedures, suggests that mediation's overall contribution to private sector union-management DR has been modest.

Mediation has played a larger role in public sector negotiations, largely as a result of legislative mandates in many state bargaining laws that require that mediation be used when impasse is reached. The fact that many public sector jurisdictions prohibit strikes also gives the parties additional incentive to reach agreement with the aid of mediators.

Fact-Finding. Fact-finding is a misnamed process that has nothing to do with a search for lost facts and everything to do with the fashioning of a DR procedural compromise. Fact-finding is a mix of mediation and arbitration. It allows the union and employer to maintain the same control over the negotiating outcome as exists in mediation while at the same time imposing the structure and formality of arbitration. Fact finders hold hearings and issue written reports that analyze the issues and recommend solutions. The parties are free to accept, modify, or reject these recommendations. As a result, fact-finding sometimes is called "mediation in writing" or "advisory arbitration."

Fact-finding in the private sector has been largely confined to the government's emergency DR procedures. As we have seen above, these procedures have come to be used less and less often, and thus this kind of third party intervention has become quite rare. Fact-finding in the public sector has become more frequent as state legislatures have imposed it as a compromise between union efforts to obtain compulsory arbitration and employer efforts to require only mediation to resolve negotiating disputes. It has become the terminal impasse step in the public sector bargaining laws in twenty-one states.[40] Sometimes the use of this method results in a settlement of the negotiating impasse, and at other times the fact finder's recommendations are rejected by one or both parties. In both sectors it has received generally bad press because of its inability to guarantee to unions or employers their preferred outcomes and its simultaneous inability to prevent strikes. In short, it is a DR compromise procedure that often pleases nobody.

Interest Arbitration in the Private Sector. Interest arbitration can be used to resolve contract negotiation disputes. This process takes its name from the fact that the parties are negotiating to express their interests in the collective bargaining agreement (e.g., higher vs. lower wages, more vs. fewer work rules, etc.), and arbitration can be used to resolve negotiating stalemates over these competing union and employer interests. The federal government has never given itself the standing authority to require that private sector unions and employers arbitrate their contract negotiation impasses. Indeed, the last serious legislative proposal to adopt *compulsory* interest arbitration for use in private sector disputes was offered in 1970 and died quickly.[41] The government's unwillingness to legislate compulsory arbitration into existence reflects the sacred article of faith held by both unions and employers that they should be able to determine their own employment terms, even when they have great difficulty doing so.[42]

Once in a while private sector unions and employers have been willing to use *voluntary* interest arbitration when it is in their mutual interest to do so. For instance, occasionally a major airline and its unions will use arbitration to resolve a thorny negotiating dispute, as occurred between American Airlines and its pilots' and flight attendants' unions during 1993-95. Easily the most visible interest arbitration scheme in the country is major league baseball's salary arbitration arrangement for resolving salary disputes between players and clubs. This final-offer procedure, which is prominently featured in the nation's sports news each February, has become a major bone of contention between the two sides, and it played a major role in the dizzying escalation of player salaries and in the 1994 baseball strike.

The most ambitious effort to replace the strike-threat DR system with interest arbitration occurred in the steel industry during the 1970s. By the early 1970s there was a boom-and-bust production cycle in that industry that was tied to the three-year contract negotiation cycle: steel customers would stockpile steel in anticipation of a strike as the contract expiration loomed, and then when a new contract was reached without a strike customers would cut back their orders while they consumed their inventories. The steel companies and the union wanted to end this costly up-and-down production cycle, so in 1973 they adopted the Experimental Negotiating Agreement (ENA). This arrangement provided for arbitration instead of a strike if the parties could not reach agreement.[43] This procedure was in place for the 1974, 1977, and 1980 negotiations, though each time the parties were able to reach agreement without calling in the arbitrators. The ENA was quite successful in eliminating the boom-and-bust production cycle. At the same time, it contributed to some very expensive settlements. By 1982 the steel companies decided they could no longer afford this arbitration-threat procedure. Accordingly, they canceled it, and there has been no known effort to revive it.

The ENA is most noteworthy as a monument to the general unwillingness of private sector unions and employers to voluntarily embrace interest arbitration. At the time the ENA was adopted, it was seen as a wonderful example of "labor statesmanship" that other unions and employers hopefully would follow. This did not happen, and the ENA existed in splendid isolation as a union-management response to steel industry-specific problems. This isolation is consistent with 1961-62 government data that showed that fewer than 2 percent of private sector union contracts provided for interest arbitration to resolve negotiating disputes,[45] and that percentage probably is even smaller today. Moreover, the NLRB has ruled that interest arbitration is a permissive subject of bargaining, so there is not even a legally enforceable obligation to bargain over this subject.[46] When the scarcity of voluntary interest arbitration arrangements is combined with the absence of compulsory arbitration, the appropriate conclusion is that interest arbitration in the private sector has become almost a nonevent. Further, there is nothing on the horizon that warrants a change in this assessment.

Interest Arbitration in the Public Sector. Over the past twenty-five years, there has been a great deal of experimentation with compulsory interest arbitration in government. The public sector's historical antipathy toward strikes, when combined with the unions' emergence as possessors of formidable political and bargaining clout on behalf of their public employee members, has produced in the federal government and in about twenty-two states compulsory arbitration laws that prohibit strikes and mandate that arbitration will be used to resolve negotiating impasses involving selected groups of public employees. The usual public rationale for these laws is that they prevent strikes by vital groups of public employees, and the fact that these strikes are usually illegal is conveniently overlooked. At the same time, research has shown that arbitration is associated with fewer strikes than otherwise would occur, so it is an effective strike prevention mechanism.[47]

The real driving force behind the adoption of these laws is union lobbying to change the impasse resolution rules in a manner that will increase their power at the negotiating table. Public employers agree that the availability of compulsory arbitration procedures enhances union bargaining power, for employers routinely lobby against the passage of these statutes.[48] This shared perception is confirmed by research that shows that the presence of arbitration laws for police, firefighters, and teachers leads to more employee-favorable contract terms, such as higher wages and more generous fringe benefits, than would otherwise be the case.[49] As a result, arbitration's strike-prevention function does not come cheap.

The spread of compulsory interest arbitration was matched by concern that the availability of arbitration would reduce union and employer incentives to bargain. Instead of doing the hard bargaining necessary to reach agreement, it was feared that unions and employers would simply hand their difficult disputes to arbitrators. The experience under these laws shows that some unions and employers have abdicated their negotiating responsibilities in favor of arbitrated decisions, and there is no question that the interest arbitration usage rate is higher than the strike rate.[50] Most unions and employers, however, negotiate their own agreements even when arbitration is available, so the presence of compulsory interest arbitration does not eliminate the bargaining process.

Compulsory interest arbitration is a controversial DR method that is adopted and used because unions see it as providing them with a more advantageous bargaining arena than they would have otherwise. Experience shows that it is difficult for unions to lobby arbitration laws onto the books, but once they have done so legislatures are unwilling to repeal such statutes. It appears that most of the highly unionized Northeastern, Midwestern, and Far Western states that are likely to pass these laws have already done so, and it is unlikely that interest arbitration will be adopted in the parts of the country where union political influence is modest. As a result, public sector interest arbitration will continue to exist on an intermittent basis around the country.

In short, the public sector continues to be a natural laboratory where many different kinds of third party DR procedures have been adopted and used to resolve negotiating disputes. These procedures have been widely researched, and the results from these investigations have substantially expanded our knowledge of how union and employer negotiating incentives and outcomes are affected by different DR rules.[51]

V. Grievance Dispute Resolution

In contrast to the intermittent nature of U-M disputes over public labor relations policy and new contract terms, U-M disputes over existing contract terms are a part of the everyday landscape in unionized workplaces. These disputes usually involve a claim, or grievance, that an employee's rights under the union contract have been violated by the employer. Grievance procedures (GPs) exist in almost every union contract, and their nearly universal presence is a result of the voluntary negotiating decisions made by unions and employers. Grievance procedures tend to have the same key features across workplaces, including (a) a definition that limits grievances to claims of contract violations, (b) an emphasis on written processing, (c) a series of ascending steps up the organizational hierarchy to handle grievances, (d) arbitration as the terminal step, and (e) explicit time limits for filing and appealing. Most grievance procedures entail four or five steps. Step 1 is an informal or oral presentation of a grievance. Step 2 is a formal or written statement of the grievance presented to the immediate supervisor. Steps 3 and 4 reflect the movement of the written grievance to higher levels of management and the union. If the grievance is not settled, it goes to arbitration as the final step.

The fact that the union is the moving party, and the presence of an arbitration step that is controlled equally by the union and the employer, give the union a strong voice in the resolution of grievances. But these procedural characteristics tell us little about such GP operational features as the rate at which grievances are filed, the speed with which they are resolved, the procedural step at which settlement occurs, the arbitration rate, the prevailing party, the perceptions of outcome appropriateness, and so on. Accordingly, in the sections below we examine a growing body of research evidence about GPs in use.

A. Grievance Filing

The most notable feature of the grievance filing rate across workplaces is its variety. The standard filing measure is the number of formal (i.e., written) grievances per 100 employees per year. Of course, this measure excludes the river of oral complaints that are resolved informally and never enter the organization's recordkeeping system. A study of 1980-82 grievance activity across several dozen private and public organizations (steel companies, department stores, hospitals, public schools) found a fifteen-fold variation in grievance filing, with rates that ranged from 1.6 to 24.9 grievances per 100 employees per year around an average rate of about 11.[52] A more recent study of grievance initiation in 1,205 Canadian work groups found filing rates ranging from 0.6 (in education) to 48.2 (in railroads) grievances per 100 employees per year around an average rate of 17.[53] This huge variation in filing rates indicates that employers and employees in some workplaces are able to develop consistent views of how the union contract should be interpreted, but in other places the parties have inconsistent views. Expressed another way, this evidence indicates that formal grievance disputes may be inevitable in unionized workplaces, but the rate at which they emerge certainly is not. Reported grievance filing rates in nonunion firms also give us a useful way to determine how the union's presence affects the amount of grievance disputing. A recent study of grievance filing rates in five large nonunion firms with formal GPs found that these rates ranged from four to six grievances per 100 employees per year around an average of five.[54] If this finding is representative, a comparison with the above findings from union firms suggests that grievances in unionized firms are filed at two to three times the rate they are filed in nonunion firms with formal GPs. This indicates that grievance DR is a much more salient activity in union workplaces than in their nonunion counterparts.

Why are grievances filed? Recent reviews of research on grievance initiation discovered a hodgepodge of factors that had been found to influence the filing of grievances, including environmental, managerial, union, U-M interaction, and employee dimensions.[55] But the variation in research methods and sites makes it very difficult to distill an all-encompassing yet specific explanation for grievance filing behaviors from this research. For instance, there has been a great deal of research into the demographic characteristics of grievance filers compared to nonfilers. This large body of evidence does not appear to yield a consistent demographic portrait that describes grievance filers, except that younger employees appear more likely to grieve than older employees.[56]

There is evidence that the GP may be used as a battleground when U-M relations are confrontational. For instance, research has found that filing rates are higher when the labor relations climate at the site is poor,[57] and flooding the grievance procedure is a tactic used (sometimes as part of an in-plant strategy) to harass the employer where U-M relations are hostile. In addition, grievance filing rates often increase at contract negotiation time as a means of increasing the negotiating pressure on management.[58]

Similarly, other evidence indicates that the existence of a cooperative U-M relationship may have a salutary impact on grievance activity. For instance, one study found that employee participation in quality circles resulted in a decline in filing rates.[59] Another study found that higher levels of employee involvement in quality of work life (QWL) programs correlated with lower grievance filing rates across the plants of a large manufacturer.[60] Other research found lower rates at the third and fourth steps of the grievance procedure in participative work groups compared to adversarial groups in a large manufacturing plant.[61] In a paper mill that had a history of hostile labor relations, the conversion to a team-based production system that fostered greater cooperation saw the grievance filing rate plummet from 198 grievances per 100 employees per year to 4 within a two-year period.[62] Another study asked union and management participants about their perceptions of the impact of joint U-M programs on grievance filing rates in their plants, and half of them reported that rates were lower (about 20 per-cent reported that rates had increased).[63]

Taken together, this evidence indicates that grievance rates are likely to decline in the wake of cooperative/participative labor-management programs. In other words, this research suggests that the adoption of employee influence mechanisms that emphasize cooperation may reduce the use of such adversarial influence mechanisms as GPs. One study, however, suggested that union member belief in GP effectiveness may be a precondition for member acceptance of cooperative programs.[64]

B. Grievance Processing

Most GPs appear to operate in an efficient manner. Most grievances are resolved during the first two steps of the GP within two months of the filing date.[65] These resolutions usually are achieved without outside assistance, so for the typical grievance the processing costs are relatively low, especially if we ignore the cost of staff time spent on grievance handling.

Evidence also shows that only a small fraction of grievances are arbitrated. During the past fifteen years, several studies have shown that the arbitration rate in most workplaces is quite low. Arbitration rates appear to range from 1 to about 25 percent of all grievances filed, and the average appears to be under 10 percent.[66] Perhaps it is the time and expense associated with arbitration that causes unions and employers to use it sparingly. In 1994 the grievance arbitrator's average bill was about $2,300, and six months to a year was required to complete the arbitration step of the process.[67] Arbitration is a much more efficient method of grievance resolution than work stoppages or court-room litigation, but it is slow and expensive compared to negotiated resolution at the pre-arbitration steps of the GP.

An important factor that drives unions and employers to a pre-arbitration agreement with most of their grievances is their estimate of how an arbitrator is likely to rule. It is unlikely that unions and employers, with their opposing incentives about how the contract should be interpreted, would be able to resolve 90 percent or more of all grievances unless they held generally consistent views of how most grievances would be resolved if arbitrated. As a result, arbitration's influence upon grievance resolution extends well beyond the small fraction of all grievances that are arbitrated. Research confirms the feedback effect that arbitration has on pre-arbitration grievance resolution,[68] particularly the use of arbitration awards as precedents to guide future grievance processing.

The data in table 2 indicate that grievance arbitration has become firmly embedded in the union-management relation-ship. The table re-ports the annual number of arbitration awards issued via the FMCS and the American Arbitration Association (AAA), which are the two primary arbitrator referral agencies. If we assume that the FMCS and AAA awards reported in table 2 represent a constant fraction of all the awards issued in a year, these data suggest that the aggregate arbitration rate per 1,000,000 union members increased significantly from 1960 to the late 1970s and has remained fairly steady since then. Expressed another way, there has been no dramatic falloff in the use of arbitration during the 1980s as occurred with the use of the strike. Perhaps this is a reflection of the fact that taking grievance disputes to arbitration is a much safer way for unions to challenge management's judgment than going on strike.

Table 2.   Selected Labor Arbitration Awards in the U.S.

Year	Union Membership[1] (000s)	Awards Issued Via FMCS[2]	Awards Issued Via AAA[2]
1960	17,049	1,324	—
1965	17,299	1,887	—
1970	21,248	2,849	—
1975	22,361	4,484	6,784
1976	22,662	5,550	7,127
1977	22,456	6,935	7,195
1978	22,757	8,155	7,713
1979	—	7,025	7,525
1980	22,366	7,539	7,382
1981	—	6,967	7,256
1982	19,763	7,120	3,917
1983	17,717	6,096	6,956
1984	17,340	5,834	6,540
1985	16,996	4,406	6,563
1986	16,975	9,286	6,394
1987	16,913	4,145	
1988	17,002	5,447	
1989	16,960	3,769	
1990	16,740	5,288	
1991	16,568	5,451	
1992	16,390	5,558	
1993	16,598	5,276	
1994	16,748	4,949	
1995	16,360	4,835	

Notes:
1.   Union membership figures are from various publications of the U.S. Bureau of Labor Statistics, including the January issue of *Employment and Earnings* starting in 1983. Beginning in 1968, the BLS changed its definition from "unions" to "unions and employee associations similar to a union." This means the post-1968 membership figures are not directly comparable to the pre-1968 membership data. In addition, these membership figures exclude the approximately two million employees who work under a union contract but are not union members.
2.   The number of labor arbitration awards issued via the Federal Mediation and Conciliation Service are taken from the FMCS Annual Reports. The number of labor arbitration awards issued via the American Arbitration Association are taken from Feuille and LeRoy, 1990, p.41. The awards reported by both agencies include a small number of interest arbitration awards each year, but the vast majority are grievance arbitration awards. In addition, these figures exclude the many thousands of awards issued each year by arbitrators selected via other channels, including the National Railroad Adjustment Board, state agencies, and directly by the parties.

C. Grievance Outcomes

A review of research found that the proportion of employee-favorable grievance resolutions (defined as an outcome that fully or partly sustained the grievance) ranged from 22 percent to 70 percent across a variety of private and public workplaces.[69] In other words, employees frequently can expect to win something when they file a grievance. What is less clear is why employees are more likely to prevail in some grievances than in others. Research suggests that employees are more likely to prevail on some grieved issues than on others,[70] and that grievants with better work records and longer tenure are more likely to prevail.[71] But there is no general explanation for why some grievances are sustained and others denied.

At the arbitration step, AAA data for the 1983-93 period indicate that employers prevail in 51 percent of the awards (the grievance is denied), and that grievances are fully or partly sustained 49 percent of the time.[72] Assuming that these AAA data are representative of arbitration generally, this close approximation of a 50-50 split is not an accident in an alternative dispute resolution system where arbitrators usually are selected on an ad hoc basis (one case at a time, with no right to be selected again), and where the joint selection and compensation system means that arbitrators must maintain their acceptability with both sides.

There is little research that explains why unions or employers prevail at arbitration. Research has found that using an attorney to present one party's case, when the other party does not have an attorney, often increases the probability of prevailing.[73] This research helps explain why attorneys are so widely used in arbitration. One study found that a few arbitrators apparently "tilt" toward one side or the other in discipline cases and continue to be widely used.[74] Another study found that there is only a moderate level of consistency in how different arbitrators respond to the same set of hypothetical facts.[75] A series of studies found that female grievants in discipline arbitration cases were significantly more likely than male grievants to have their grievances fully or partly sustained by male arbitrators.[76] Other research has found that most demographic and professional characteristics of arbitrators are not significantly related to their decisions,[77] which means that arbitral rulings cannot be predicted with easily available data. Taken together, these findings suggest that there is sufficient variation in arbitrator rulings that employer and union expenditures on finding a sympathetic arbitrator are rational investments.

D. Alternatives to Arbitration

During the 1940s and 1950s arbitration became the terminal step of choice in American GPs. During this same period, there was a vigorous debate between the advocates of arbitration as an informal, problem-solving process that provided for some de facto mediation by the arbitrator, and the advocates who believed arbitration should be a formal process of contractual adjudication.[78] By the late 1950s, this contest had been decisively resolved in favor of the adjudicatory approach, which approach received a strong endorsement from the U.S. Supreme Court in the 1960 Steelworkers Trilogy decisions. The most visible result of the adjudicative form of arbitration is that courtroom features have become an integral part of the process, including the routine use of lawyers as advocates and arbitrators, court reporters and transcripts, subpoenas, post-hearing briefs, and written awards with lengthy opinions.

Accompanying this increased formalization has been a steady drumbeat of union and employer complaints about the cost, delay, and rigmarole associated with this "deluxe" version of arbitration. What is even more noticeable than this continuing stream of complaints, though, is that relatively little has been done to change the way that grievance arbitration operates. This multidecade stability is eloquent testimony to the fact that adjudicatory arbitration continues to be the mutually preferred method for the resolution of the most difficult grievances.[79] This continuing preference for formal arbitration, however, has not prevented unions and employers from experimenting with various DR alternatives.

Expedited Arbitration. Expedited arbitration is a method for producing faster and cheaper arbitrated decisions. It relies on techniques such as referring various grievances directly to arbitration and thereby bypassing some GP steps, prohibitions on lawyers/transcripts/briefs, faster hearings, tight time and writing limits for the award, and arbitral fee ceilings. During the past twenty-five or so years, expedited arbitration received much favorable publicity for its undisputed DR efficiency advantages.[80] Even more noteworthy, though, is the fact that this slimmed-down version of arbitration has not been widely adopted as the contractually required arbitral method, but the parties remain free to use it on an ad hoc basis whenever it suits their interests.

Grievance Mediation. During the 1980s, grievance mediation received a great deal of favorable attention in the wake of its successful use in the unionized areas of the coal industry.[81] This approach to resolving grievances relies upon the threat of arbitration to assist unions and employers in resolving grievances with the aid of a mediator. This kind of mediation operates as the penultimate step of the GP, with arbitration available if the grievance remains unresolved. This approach requires that the mediator, who is also an experienced arbitrator, hold an informal conference rather than a formal hearing with the parties to discuss the grievance. If this discussion does not produce a settlement, the mediator issues an oral advisory opinion, on the spot, that predicts how the grievance would be decided at arbitration. In short, this "peekaboo arbitration" process gives the disputants a low-cost and non-binding evaluation of their chances of prevailing in arbitration. This feature puts pressure upon the parties, especially the party who has been forecast as the loser, to re-evaluate the desirability of taking their dispute to arbitration.

This pressure is confirmed by reports that grievance mediation has successfully resolved more than 80 percent of the grievances which have been mediated, and it has done so in a much faster and cheaper manner than arbitration.[82] From a DR efficiency perspective, mediation has been a very successful grievance resolution technique for unions and employers with high arbitration rates. In spite of its widely reported successes, however, mediation still has not been widely adopted in union contracts.[83] Perhaps this limited adoption is the result of the fact that the vast majority of grievances are resolved without using arbitration, and thus most unions and employers do not appear convinced that they need this incremental DR refinement in their GPs.

E. The Impact of Grievance Filings

Much of the published commentary on union-management DR takes a benign view of most workplace conflict and the procedures established to resolve conflict episodes. This benign view is the result of the "pluralist" perspective held by most commentators. This perspective sees employers, employees, and unions as having legitimate and divergent interests, which can be succinctly summarized as the employers' efficiency interests competing with the employees' equity interests as advocated by the union with its own institutional interests. These divergent interests sometimes result in overt conflict, e.g., disciplinary actions, grievances, slowdowns, or strikes, over how the workplace should operate. Industrial relations scholars tend to have a benign view of this conflict, for it indicates that these legitimately divergent interests are being expressed and that neither party is overwhelming the other.[84] However, recent research has shown that the impact of some grievance filings can be difficult to reconcile with this "conflict is good" perspective.

Turnover. Proponents of the exit-voice perspective argue that the presence of the grievance procedure provides employees with a voice alternative to exit behaviors such as quitting. Thus, GPs contribute to lower quit rates and presumably lower turnover and retraining costs. Research has confirmed this proposition in school districts and hospitals.[85]

Productivity. Other research has examined the productivity results associated with the actual use of the GP, and these results are usually negative. Specifically, this research indicates that high levels of grievance filing are associated with reduced levels of productivity.[86] It is not possible to pinpoint the extent to which this diminished productivity is the result of the "displacement effect" (employee work time diverted from production tasks to grievance processing) or the "worker reaction effect" (reduced worker effort as a get-even reaction to the employer's perceived unfair administration of the contract). Whatever the specific causes of this relationship, this research indicates that high levels of grievance activity may exact a significant productivity tax. Another study of grievance filing in an aircraft manufacturing plant, however, found that increased managerial monitoring of workers resulted in increased grievance filing and higher productivity.[87] This study suggests that the relationship between grievance activity and productivity may be more complex than previously thought, and that a particular level of managerial monitoring may result in more grievances and increased output.

Grievant Consequences. Most GPs contain no-reprisal provisions. In the abstract, unions and employers agree that employees should not suffer retaliation for filing grievances. In practice, however, grievants may receive an unfriendly postresolution response. Recent research in four unionized organizations found that employees who filed grievances, compared to those who did not, were more likely to suffer such adverse consequences as lower performance ratings, lower promotion rates, and higher turnover in the period after they filed their grievances.[88] Moreover, this research also found that supervisors who had grievances filed against them, compared with other supervisors who did not generate grievances, suffered similar adverse consequences. Other research found comparable adverse results on grievants' performance appraisals, compared to the appraisals of nongrievants, in a public organization.[89] Similar results have been found in several nonunion settings.[90]

If this research can be generalized, it calls into question the usefulness of the conventional wisdom about how GPs and their use foster increased voice in preference to exit, which may result in such positive outcomes as reduced quit rates and turnover costs, and increased employee commitment.[91] Instead, this recent research on postgrievance resolution consequences suggests that an organizational reprisal perspective may be a more accurate lens through which to view the grievance process. This perspective suggests that some managers see grievances as negative events because they result in increased DR transaction costs, increased overt conflict, and reduced productivity, and they react accordingly.

F. Grievances and Public Policy

Arbitration. One of the federal government's key labor relations objectives has been to encourage the use of procedures to resolve workplace conflict. Accordingly, the federal courts have repeatedly supported the efforts of unions and employers to negotiate and use grievance procedures, and especially arbitration, to resolve their contract interpretation disputes. As noted earlier, the U.S. Supreme Court has said that, where unions and employers have promised to resolve grievances through arbitration and to accept the arbitrated decisions as final and binding, they must live up to these promises even if the results are not to their liking. The evidence shows that unions and employers do so the vast majority of the time, though the evidence also shows that during the past fifteen or

so years disgruntled employers have become more likely to appeal adverse arbitration awards by asking the courts to nullify some of these
decisions for one reason or another.[92] The courts reject most of these
appeals, so arbitration is in no danger of becoming merely a way station
on the path to the judicial resolution of difficult grievances.

There have been periodic predictions that the increasing government regulation of the workplace will result in the judicially determined
usurpation of grievance arbitration as a dispute resolution mechanism.
This concern erupted with a vengeance among arbitrators in the wake of
the U.S. Supreme Court's 1974 decision that the arbitration of an Afri-
can American employee's discharge did not prevent that same employee
from pursuing a discharge-based discrimination lawsuit in federal court
under Title VII of the 1964 Civil Rights Act.[93]

There is no evidence, however, that the increased number of laws
regulating the workplace has had any negative impact upon the use of
grievance arbitration in unionized workplaces. Further, the figures in
table 2 suggest that the demand for arbitrator services remained strong
during the 1980s and 1990s. The use of arbitration in the unionized
private sector may decline commensurately with the decline of union
coverage in that sector, but any such reduction is not the result of increased government regulation. Further, there is no persuasive evidence
that the federal courts have reduced their overall strong support for
grievance arbitration.

Arbitration in Nonunion Workplaces. In recent years, the public
policy spotlight on arbitration has shifted to the nonunion arena. In May
1991, the U.S. Supreme Court issued a controversial decision in which it
upheld the use of arbitration to resolve a termination dispute involving a
nonunion employee.[94] In this case, a fired stockbroker sued his employer
under the Age Discrimination in Employment Act (ADEA), and the employer sought to forestall the lawsuit and compel arbitration pursuant to
an arbitration clause in the securities registration agreement the employee signed when he was hired. By ruling for the employer, the Supreme Court sent a strong signal that arbitration may be the preferred
forum for resolving employer-employee disputes arising in nonunion
workplaces, including statutory-based discrimination suits. Since then,
federal judges usually have enforced mandatory arbitration provisions
in the face of employee efforts to pursue discrimination lawsuits in federal court.[95] Nevertheless, these employer-promulgated arbitration procedures continue to be controversial, and legal challenges against them
continue.

For decades employers were unwilling to provide grievance arbitration to their nonunion employees, but in recent years an increasing
number of employers have embraced arbitration as an alternative to litigation. At the same time, nonunion arbitration also has become quite
controversial, in part as a result of invidious comparisons with how it
functions in the union sector. In a nutshell, employee advocates worry
that arbitration will be used in a biased manner by nonunion employers

to avoid discrimination and wrongful discharge lawsuits and deny employees the opportunity for a fair resolution of their claims. These concerns are prompted, in part, by the fact that nonunion employees have no organization that can represent them during the steps of the arbitral process: establishment of the procedure, selection of the arbitrator, discovery and hearing preparation, hearing advocacy, payment of the costs, etc. These concerns are legitimate. The individual employee is usually at a substantial information and financial disadvantage, compared to the employer, when navigating through the arbitration process. At this point arbitration for nonunion employees is not yet widespread,[96] for most employers are not willing to voluntarily subject their managerial decisions to review and possible reversal by an outsider. Although it is too early to determine the extent to which arbitration will exist in nonunion employment relationships, the workplace arbitration spotlight clearly has shifted to the nonunion sector. At the same time, the manner in which arbitration operates in the union sector will remain one of the key benchmarks by which nonunion arbitration is assessed.

Duty of Fair Representation. An employee's legally enforceable right to be fairly represented by his/her union is a natural outgrowth of the inclusion of section 301 in the Taft-Hartley Act which allows unions and employers to be sued in federal court for violating contracts, the postwar growth in grievance and arbitration procedures, and the fact that the union typically has monopoly representation rights in a bargaining unit. A continuing stream of decisions by the U.S. Supreme Court and other federal appellate courts during the postwar period requires unions to be both diligent and fair in their representation of employee rights and interests.[97] This judicially created duty to fairly represent employees has resulted in thousands of duty of fair representation lawsuits filed against unions by disgruntled employees, with the vast majority resulting from employee disenchantment with the manner in which their union processed (or did not process) their grievance. Research indicates that the courts decide these lawsuits in the employees' favor about 5 percent of the time,[98] and there is nothing on the horizon to indicate that this modest employee success rate will change substantially. In other words, the courts will continue to grant unions wide latitude in their handling of grievances.

G. The Future of Grievance Resolution in the Unionized Workplace

During the 1940s and 1950s, the manner in which unions and employers resolved grievances changed considerably. Contract interpretation work stoppages became less likely and were replaced by the administrative processing of grievances through the grievance and arbitration procedures that unions and employers voluntarily negotiated. As union contracts became more complex and formalized, so the grievance adjustment process moved in the same direction. Most visibly, the arbitration step evolved from a less formal problem-solving procedure to a more formal contract adjudication forum.[99] Accompanying this increased formalization has been a continuing stream of complaints bemoaning the increased legalization, and its attendant costs, of the grievance resolution process.

Nevertheless, after the parties adopted these contractual grievance procedures and became accustomed to using them, there have been few significant efforts to find alternatives. In short, after the union-management grievance handling quid pro quo was worked out during the 1940s and 1950s, the key features of this accord have endured largely unchanged in the ensuing decades. This grievance processing longevity and stability is one of the great success stories of American collective bargaining.

Moreover, this grievance DR system seems to be maintaining itself relatively intact in spite of the unions' significantly declining share of the labor force and the unions' substantially diminished ability to conduct successful strikes. There does not appear to be any widespread effort by unionized employers to significantly alter the manner in which their grievance and arbitration processes operate. Instead, employer attempts to avoid union-imposed grievance and arbitration procedures (and other employee-favorable elements of the union contract) have taken the form of employer efforts to avoid unions altogether.[100]

VI. Conclusions and Implications for Future Research

The DR developments in this chapter highlight the shrinkage of collective bargaining as a labor market institution in the U.S. private sector. The eroding unionized share of the private labor force makes unions less influential as economic agents determining employment terms. Perhaps the most salient sign of this decline is that almost nobody labels collectively bargained wage increases as a cause of inflation any more. Politically, this erosion means that politicians are less likely to support reactive organizations representing one-sixth of the labor force compared to the days when unions were more proactive organizations representing one-third of a more homogeneous work force. Accordingly, we should expect that the contract negotiation balance of power will remain with employers and that the body of employer-favorable labor laws will continue. So will the increased employer willingness to operate during strikes, including an increased willingness to hire permanent striker replacements. Further, the strong position of unions in many public sector labor markets has had no apparent influence on the labor movement's declining fortunes in the private sector. The union voice in grievance resolution has remained quite strong, but unionized grievance processing systems apply to a smaller and smaller share of the labor force.

This survey of the U-M landscape and its most salient DR features indicates that unions in the 1990s, especially in the private sector, have been struggling against a DR ebb tide. In light of the factors that have resulted in this current state of DR affairs in unionized workplaces, what DR frontiers should we expect to see in unionized workplaces, and in related research, during the balance of the 1990s? The evidence supports four primary conclusions.

First, recent union and employer efforts to influence public labor relations policy will continue as ongoing traditional interest group efforts to obtain self-favorable laws that will enhance their ability to obtain favorable terms in the workplace. These political influence efforts resulted in union-favorable outcomes in the 1930s and early 1940s, but during the postwar period the political tide has run largely in the employers' favor, particularly during the 1980s and 1990s. In fact, the situation has progressed to the point that employers vigorously seek to protect the labor relations statutes that they condemned several decades ago, for they have learned how to effectively resist unions within the confines of the law. They also have learned that when they transgress the labor law's boundaries, the penalties are quite modest. Accordingly, the lobbying battle of the 1990's to statutorily prohibit strikers from being permanently replaced is simply one more legislative contest that resulted in the continuation of the employer-favorable status quo. Moreover, there is nothing on the horizon that will change this state of affairs, including the presence of a Democratic presidential administration or the 1994 recommendations from the Dunlop Commission. These public policy struggles will continue, but there is no persuasive reason to expect that the political tide is going to shift in the unions' direction.

Second, during the past fifteen or so years the frontier of private sector U-M disputing over new contract terms shifted noticeably in a management-favorable direction. This shift in the U-M balance of power has caused a corresponding shift in how unions represent their members' interests. The most obvious change has been the substantial reduction in strikes during the 1980s and 1990s compared to the preceding three decades, leading to the ironic result that during a time of considerable labor-management rhetorical friction the strike rate is unusually low. At the same time, we have seen the emergence of corporate campaigns and in-plant strategies as strike substitutes. We should expect to see a continuation of the high hostility quotient in labor relations rhetoric, a low strike rate, and an ongoing union search for effective pressure tactics to serve as strike substitutes. From a research perspective, future analyses will profitably examine the extent to which the historic positive association between strike rates and union-favorable contract terms has continued into the 1980s and 1990s' era of strike minimalism.[101] Similarly, research can usefully examine the extent to which strike substitutes such as corporate campaigns and in-plant strategies yield union-favorable outcomes.

Third, the public sector has been more receptive to the use of mediation, fact-finding, and interest arbitration, largely as a result of the continuing controversy surrounding strikes by public employees. On balance, these procedures contribute to dispute resolution without disruption, and interest arbitration helps unions achieve more favorable bargaining outcomes. To date, though, there has been no apparent carryover to the private sector, and there is no persuasive reason to expect that any such carryover will emerge in the near future. In the research arena, scholars will continue to usefully examine the extent to which public sector bargaining outcomes are shaped by various DR environments.

Fourth, U-M grievance disputing will continue along the same grievance DR path that was laid out in the 1940s and 1950s. Contract interpretation disputes are processed through the negotiated GP, and the vast majority of them are resolved directly by the parties, usually in a fast and inexpensive manner. A small portion of difficult grievances are referred to arbitration, which has become an attorney-dominated private judicial process in which arbitrators provide the parties with written explanations to serve as their grievance DR precedents. What is most noteworthy about this grievance system is that it functions today much as it did forty years ago. Its stability is testimony to its ability to serve both sides' interests in an acceptable manner. At the same time, there will continue to be union and employer experiments with other methods for handling day-to-day interactions. For instance, during the past fifteen or so years many unions and employers have become interested in adopting labor-management cooperation/participation methods, for these arrangements can have a more substantial impact on employee satisfaction and productivity, as opposed to tinkering with GPs. Although the evidence is mixed, in many workplaces the presence of these cooperative influence mechanisms results in increased satisfaction, improved productivity, and a reduction in the adversarial act of grievance filing.[102] The half-life of these cooperative mechanisms is unstable, however, and they are not designed to resolve rights-framed disputes over complex contract language. As a result, these cooperative programs will not displace formal grievance procedures, though they certainly may affect how frequently the grievance procedure is used as a DR arena.

The key research subject area for industrial relations scholars in the 1990s is the effects of employer-employee cooperation/participation programs in unionized workplaces. In particular, we need an improved understanding of how these cooperative programs can achieve long-run positive outcomes when they are administered by two organizations that traditionally have had an adversarial relationship. For instance, it is not clear how a productivity-enhancing cooperative program can operate effectively when the employer and the union are simultaneously disputing each other over the content of the next contract. How do union and management leaders fight each other over contract terms one week and then cooperate to implement more productive work methods the next week?

From an operational perspective, we will benefit considerably from research that examines the effects that cooperative programs have on the levels of disputing in a variety of U-M relationships, and vice versa. One of the keys to a successful American labor force in an increasingly competitive world economy is the extent to which U.S. employers and employees can cooperate to achieve world-class levels of productivity. It is not yet clear, though, how these productivity levels will be achieved in unionized workplaces if U.S. unions and employers continue to be locked in a wary embrace that has been described as "antagonistic cooperation" with more antagonism than cooperation.[103] As long as unions see themselves as agents of worker resistance to management's inequitable domination of the workplace, and as long as employers resist unions as expensive hindrances to productive employer-employee relationships, the union's "logic of equity" will be pitted against the employer's "logic of efficiency" and union-management disputes will be the natural order of things. The experiences of the past fifteen years indicate that the form in which these disagreements emerge will change over time, and each party's probability of prevailing likewise will change. But unfortunately we are in no imminent danger of having an epidemic of genuine union-management cooperation emerge and replace decades of antagonism.

Notes

1.   N. W. Chamberlain and D. E. Cullen, *The Labor Sector,* 2d ed. (New York: McGraw-Hill, 1971), chap. 12.

2.   R. E. Walton and R. B. McKersie, *A Behavioral Theory of Labor Negotiations* (New York: McGraw-Hill, 1965).

3.   D. Meyer and W. Cooke, "Economic and Political Factors in Formal Grievance Resolution," *Industrial Relations* 27 (1988): 318-35.

4.   J. J. Lawler, *Unionization and Deunionization* (Columbia: University of South Carolina Press, 1990).

5.   T. A. Kochan and H. C. Katz, *Collective Bargaining and Industrial Relations,* 2d ed. (Homewood, Ill.: Irwin, 1988); R. B. Freeman and J. L. Medoff, *What Do Unions Do?* (New York: Basic Books, 1984); B. E. Becker and C. A. Olson, "Unionization and Shareholder Interests," *Industrial and Labor Relations Review* 42 (1989): 246-61; S. G. Bronars, D. R. Deere, and J. S. Tracy, "The Effects of Unions on Firm Behavior: An Empirical Analysis Using Firm-Level Data," *Industrial Relations* 33 (1994): 426-51.

6.   This trichotomy borrows heavily from a similar classification in T. A. Kochan, H. C. Katz, and R. B. McKersie, *The Transformation of American Industrial Relations* (New York: Basic Books, 1986).

7. B.V.H. Schneider, "Public-Sector Labor Legislation—An Evolutionary Analysis," in *Public-Sector Bargaining*, 2d ed., eds. B. Aaron, J. M. Najita, and J. L. Stern (Washington, D.C.: Bureau of National Affairs, 1988).

8. G. M. Saltzman, "Bargaining Laws as a Cause and Consequence of the Growth of Teacher Unionism," *Industrial and Labor Relations Review* 38 (1985): 335-51.

9. U.S. National Labor Relations Board, *Annual Reports*, vols. 16 (1951), 56 (1991).

10. V. P. Floyd, "National Labor Relations Board Unfair Labor Practice Decision Making Bias: Analysis of the Reagan Board, 1981-1989," unpublished paper, University of Illinois, Institute of Labor and Industrial Relations, 1994.

11. C. B. Craver, *Can Unions Survive? The Rejuvenation of the American Labor Movement* (New York: New York University Press, 1993); P. C. Weiler, *Governing the Workplace: The Future of Labor and Employment Law* (Cambridge, Mass.: Harvard University Press, 1990). The Clinton administration has appointed more union-friendly appointees to the board, but it is not yet apparent how these appointments will alter the union-management balance of bargaining power.

12. Commission on the Future of Worker-Management Relations, *Fact-Finding Report*, May 1994, Exhibit IV-3, p. 134.

13. *United Steelworkers v. American Manufacturing Co.*, 363 U.S. 564 (1960), *United Steelworkers v. Warrior & Gulf Navigation Co.*, 363 U.S. 574 (1960), *United Steelworkers v. Enterprise Wheel & Car Corp.*, 363 U.S. 593 (1960) ("The Steelworkers Trilogy"); *United Paperworkers International Union v. Misco, Inc.*, 484 U.S. 29 (1987). See also the U.S. Supreme Court decisions favoring arbitration in *John Wiley and Sons, Inc. v. Livingston*, 376 U.S. 543 (1964); *Boys Market, Inc. v. Retail Clerks Local 770*, 398 U.S. 235 (1970); *Gateway Coal Co. v. United Mine Workers*, 414 U.S. 368 (1974); *Nolde Bros., Inc. v. Bakery & Confectionary Workers Local 358*, 430 U.S. 243 (1977); and *W.R. Grace and Co. v. Local 759, Rubber Workers*, 461 U.S. 757 (1983).

14. 304 U.S. 333 (1938).

15. P. Feuille and H. Wheeler, "Will the Real Industrial Conflict Please Stand Up?", in *U.S. Industrial Relations 1950-1980: A Critical*

Assessment, eds. J. Stieber, R. B. McKersie, and D. Q. Mills (Madison, Wis.: Industrial Relations Research Association, 1981), 255-95.

16. Sometime between the mid-1960s and the late 1970s, there occurred almost a complete reversal in the conventional wisdom about whose interests were favored by the government's regulation of the union-management relationship. For instance, in 1965, P. Ross authored *Government As A Source of Union Power: The Role of Public Policy in Collective Bargaining,* (Providence, R. I.: Brown University Press, 1965), and the title reflected the author's analysis of how the government's regulation of the negotiating process via the National Labor Relations Act (NLRA) assisted unions in their contract negotiating efforts. In contrast, the 1977-78 union lobbying efforts on behalf of the Labor Law Reform Act vividly demonstrated that by the late 1970s, American unions no longer perceived the content and application of the NLRA as favoring their interests.

17. The Dunlop Commission issued its *Fact-Finding Report* in May 1994, and in December 1994 it issued its labor law revision recommendations (Commission on the Future of Worker-Management Relations, Report and Recommendations, December 1994). These reports had almost no visible impact on policymakers inside the Beltway.

18. C. L. Gramm, "New Measures of the Propensity to Strike During Contract Negotiations, 1971-1980," *Industrial and Labor Relations Review* 40 (1987): 406-17; S. McConnell, "Cyclical Fluctuations in Strike Activity," *Industrial and Labor Relations Review* 44 (1990): 130-43; S. Vroman, "A Longitudinal Analysis of Strike Activity in U.S. Manufacturing: 1957-1984," *American Economic Review* 79 (1989): 816-26.

19. P. C. Cramton and J. S. Tracy, "Strikes and Holdouts in Wage Bargaining: Theory and Data," *American Economic Review* 82 (1992): 100-21. Cramton and Tracy's research, however, confirms that this decline in the strike rate does not mean that contract negotiating has become a less contentious process. They found that as strike rates declined, the "holdout" rate, or the share of negotiations that were not completed by the time the existing contract expired, increased from 39 percent during the 1970s to 53 percent during the 1980s in these large units. Similarly, a study of bargaining in small firms in Michigan found that 73 percent of negotiations during 1987-91 were not concluded by the time the existing contract expired; J. Cutcher-Gershenfeld, P. McHugh, and D. Power, "Collective Bargaining in Small Firms: Preliminary Evidence of Fundamental Change," unpublished paper, Michigan State University, School of Labor and Industrial Relations, November 1994.

20. Kochan and Katz, *Collective Bargaining and Industrial Relations,* 242.

21. These estimates are calculated from the negotiation notice and strike data presented in the Federal Mediation and Conciliation Service *Annual Reports* for 1976, 1977, 1991/1992, and 1993/1994. Another study uses FMCS data to report an overall strike rate during 1987-91 of 3 percent; Cutcher-Gershenfeld, McHugh, and Power, "Collective Bargaining in Small Firms," 14.

22. Unions and employers covered by the National Labor Relations Act are required to submit thirty-day dispute notices to the Federal Mediation and Conciliation Service if they have not reached agreement on a successor contract thirty days prior to the expiration of the existing contract. During 1976 the FMCS received 114,747 such notices, and during 1992 the service received 58,471 such notices (FMCS, Annual Reports, 1976, 1992). Assuming there has not been a substantial increase in average contract duration, and assuming that unions and employers have not learned how to reach agreement well in advance of the contract expiration date, this decline in the number of such notices is a strong indicator of the shrinkage in the unionized sector. This sector shrinkage also explains why strike levels (absolute numbers of strikes) have declined more than strike rates (strikes as a percentage of contract negotiations in the remaining bargaining units).

23. See Cramton and Tracy, "Strikes and Holdouts"; Gramm, "New Measures of the Propensity"; McConnell, "Cyclical Fluctuations"; Vroman, "A Longitudinal Analysis"; Clark Kerr and Abraham J. Siegel, "The Interindustry Propensity to Strike—An International Comparison," in Arthur Kornhauser, Robert Dubin, and Arthur Ross, eds., *Industrial Conflict* (New York: McGraw-Hill, 1954), 189-212; Arthur M. Ross and Paul T. Hartman, *Changing Patterns of Industrial Conflict* (New York: Wiley, 1960).

24. Cutcher-Gershenfeld, McHugh, and Power, "Collective Bargaining in Small Firms."

25. Ross and Hartman, *Changing Patterns,* chap. 5.

26. I. Bernstein, H. L. Enarson, and R.W. Fleming, eds., *Emergency Disputes and National Labor Policy* (New York: Harper, 1955); D. E. Cullen, *National Emergency Strikes,* ILR Paperback No. 7 (Ithaca, NY: Cornell University, 1968).

27. See the extremely informative memoir on this point in the Foreword by former Secretary of Labor/Secretary of State George P. Shultz in C. Kerr and P. D. Staudohar, eds., *Labor Economics and Industrial*

Relations: Markets and Institutions (Cambridge, Mass.: Harvard University Press, 1994), xiii-xiv.

28. C. M. Rehmus, "Emergency Strikes Revisited," *Industrial and Labor Relations Review*, 43 (1990): 175-90.

29. U.S. Government Accounting Office, *Strikes and the Use of Permanent Strike Replacements in the 1970s and 1980s*, GAO/HRD-91-2, January 1991; M. H. LeRoy, "Regulating Employer Use of Permanent Strike Replacements: Empirical Analysis of NLRA and RLA Strikes 1935-1991," *Berkeley Journal of Employment and Labor Law* 16 (1995): 169-208.

30. J. F. Schnell and C. L. Gramm, "The Empirical Relations Between Employers' Striker Replacement Strategies and Strike Duration," *Industrial and Labor Relations Review* 47 (1994): 189-206.

31. LeRoy, "Regulating Employer Use of Permanent Strike Replacements."

32. P. Jarley and C. Maranto, "Union Corporate Campaigns: An Assessment," *Industrial and Labor Relations Review* 43 (1990): 505-24; C. R. Perry, *Union Corporate Campaigns* (Philadelphia: Industrial Research Unit, Wharton School, University of Pennsylvania, 1987).

33. Jarley and Maranto, "Union Corporate Campaigns."

34. Ibid.

35. H. R. Northrup, "Union Corporate Campaigns and Inside Games as a Strike Form," *Employee Relations Law Journal* 19 (1994): 507-49; Arthur B. Shostak, *Robust Unionism: Innovations in the Labor Movement* (Ithaca, New York: ILR Press, 1991).

36. Northrup, "Union Corporate Campaigns," 526-27.

37. Ibid., 514-16.

38. Ibid.

39. There is also a more forceful form of mediation available in the railroad and airline industries via the Railway Labor Act. This statute requires the negotiating parties to participate in mediation as a condition of using economic weapons later, and the act gives the National Mediation Board (NMB) the authority to control the duration of the mediation process (during which time the status quo must be

maintained). The NMB, however, has no authority to impose a resolution.

40. B.V.H. Schneider, "Public-Sector Labor Legislation."

41. In that year the Nixon administration sent to Congress the Emergency Public Interest Protection Act, which sought to make final-offer arbitration an option the government could impose in negotiating disputes in the transportation industries. This bill was never reported out of committee.

42. An articulate summary of this view is found in O. W. Phelps, "Compulsory Arbitration: Some Perspectives," *Industrial and Labor Relations Review* 18 (1964): 82-91. Over the years Congress has imposed arbitration upon several intractable railroad negotiating disputes, but these were ad hoc laws strictly limited to the particular dispute at hand; see Rehmus, "Emergency Strikes Revisited."

43. Interestingly, the word "arbitration" appears nowhere in the title of this dispute resolution arrangement. This is a reflection of the internal union controversy generated by the ENA. See J. P. Hoerr, *And the Wolf Finally Came: The Decline of the American Steel Industry* (Pittsburgh: University of Pittsburgh Press, 1988), 112-15.

44. Hoerr, *And the Wolf Finally Came*, 120-29.

45. U.S. Bureau of Labor Statistics, *Arbitration Procedures*, Bulletin 1425-26, 1966.

46. R. A. Gorman, *Basic Text on Labor Law: Unionization and Collective Bargaining* (St. Paul, Minn.: West, 1976), 508.

47. C. Ichniowski, "Arbitration and Police Bargaining: Prescription for the Blue Flu," *Industrial Relations* 21 (1982): 149-66; C. A. Olson, "Strikes, Strike Penalties, and Arbitration in Six States," *Industrial and Labor Relations Review* 39 (1986): 539-51.

48. P. Feuille, "Selected Benefits and Costs of Compulsory Arbitration," *Industrial and Labor Relations Review*, 33 (1979): 64-76.

49. P. Feuille, J. T. Delaney, and W. Hendricks, "Police Bargaining, Arbitration, and Fringe Benefits," *Journal of Labor Research* 6 (1985): 1-20; P. Feuille, J.T. Delaney, and W. Hendricks, "Interest Arbitration and Police Contracts," *Industrial Relations* 24 (1985): 161-81; P. Feuille and J. T. Delaney, "Collective Bargaining, Interest Arbitration, and Police Salaries," *Industrial and Labor Relations Review* 39 (1986): 228-40; J. T. Delaney, "Strikes, Arbitration, and Teacher Salaries," *Industrial and*

Labor Relations Review 36 (1983): 431-46; J. T. Delaney, "Impasses and Teacher Contract Outcomes," *Industrial Relations* 25 (1986): 45-55; C. A. Olson, "The Impact of Arbitration on the Wages of Firefighters," *Industrial Relations* 19 (1980): 325-39.

50. Ichniowski, "Arbitration and Police Bargaining"; Olson, "Strikes, Strike Penalties, and Arbitration"; C. A. Olson, "Dispute Resolution in the Public Sector," in *Public-Sector Bargaining*, 2d ed., eds. B. Aaron, J. M. Najita, and J. L. Stern (Washington, D. C.: Bureau of National Affairs, 1988), 160-88; A. Ponak and H. N. Wheeler, "Choice of Procedures in Canada and the United States," *Industrial Relations* 19 (1980): 292-308.

51. Olson, "Dispute Resolution in the Public Sector."

52. D. Lewin and R. B. Peterson, *The Modern Grievance Procedure in the United States* (New York: Quorum Books, 1988), 87.

53. B. Bemmels, "The Determinants of Grievance Initiation," *Industrial and Labor Relations Review* 47 (1994): 285-301.

54. D. Lewin, "Grievance Procedures in Nonunion Workplaces: An Empirical Analysis of Usage, Dynamics, and Outcomes," *Chicago-Kent Law Review* 66 (1992): 823-44.

55. C. E. Labig, Jr. and C. R. Greer, "Grievance Initiation: A Literature Survey and Suggestions for Future Research," *Journal of Labor Research* 9 (1988): 1-27.

56. Labig and Greer, "Grievance Initiation"; R. E. Allen and T. J. Keaveny, "Factors Differentiating Grievants and Nongrievants," *Human Relations* 38 (1985): 519-34; M. E. Gordon and S. J. Miller, "Grievances: A Review of Research and Practice," *Personnel Psychology* 37 (spring 1984): 117-46.

57. J. Gandz and J. D. Whitehead, "The Relationship Between Industrial Relations Climate and Grievance Initiation and Resolution," in *Proceedings of the Thirty-Fourth Annual Meeting, Industrial Relations Research Association*, ed. B. D. Dennis (Madison, Wis.: IRRA, 1982), 320-28; H. C. Katz, T. A. Kochan, and K. Gobeille, "Industrial Relations Performance, Economic Performance, and the Effects of Quality of Working Life Efforts: An Interplant Analysis," *Industrial and Labor Relations Review* 37 (1983): 3-17.

58. Kochan, Katz, and McKersie, *The Transformation of American Industrial Relations*, 84-85; Lewin and Peterson, *The Modern Grievance Procedure*, 113-16.

59. K. Buch, "Quality Circles in a Unionized Setting: Their Effect on Grievance Rates," *Journal of Business and Psychology* 6 (1991): 147-54.

60. H. C. Katz, T. A. Kochan, and M. Weber, "Assessing the Effects of Industrial Relations and Quality of Working Life Efforts on Organizational Effectiveness," *Academy of Management Journal* 28 (1985): 509-27.

61. J. Cutcher-Gershenfeld, "The Impact on Economic Performance of a Transformation in Workplace Relations," *Industrial and Labor Relations Review* 44 (1991): 241-60.

62. C. Ichniowski, "Human Resource Practices and Productive Labor-Management Relations," in *Research Frontiers in Industrial Relations and Human Resources*, eds. D. Lewin, O. S. Mitchell, and P. D. Sherer (Madison, Wis.: Industrial Relations Research Association, 1992), 239-71.

63. W. N. Cooke, *Labor-Management Cooperation: New Partnerships or Going in Circles?* (Kalamazoo, Mich.: W.E. Upjohn Institute for Employment Research, 1990), 81-84.

64. A. E. Eaton, M. E. Gordon, and J. H. Keefe, "The Impact of Quality of Work Life Programs and Grievance System Effectiveness on Union Commitment," *Industrial and Labor Relations Review* 45 (1992): 591-604.

65. J. T. Delaney, D. Lewin, and C. Ichniowski, *Human Resource Policies and Practices in American Firms*, Bulletin No. 139 (Washington, D. C.: U.S. Department of Labor, Bureau of Labor-Management Relations and Cooperative Affairs, 1989); Gordon and Miller, "Grievances: A Review"; Lewin and Peterson, *The Modern Grievance Procedure*, 147-53.

66. R. P. Chaykowski, G. A. Slotsve, and J. S. Butler, "A Simultaneous Analysis of Grievance Activity and Outcome Decisions," *Industrial and Labor Relations Review* 45 (1992): 724-37; T. F. Gideon and R. B. Peterson, "A Comparison of Alternate Grievance Procedures," *Employee Relations Law Journal* 5 (1979): 222-33; C. Ichniowski, "The Effects of Grievance Activity on Productivity," *Industrial and Labor Relations Review* 40 (1986): 75-89; T. R. Knight, "Feedback and Grievance Resolution," *Industrial and Labor Relations Review* 39 (1986): 585-98; Lewin and Peterson, *The Modern Grievance Procedure*, 87; I. Ng and A. Dastmalchian, "Determinants of Grievance Outcomes," *Industrial and Labor Relations Review* 42 (1989): 393-403.

67. Federal Mediation and Conciliation Service, unpublished data supplied to arbitrators, April 1995.

68. Knight, "Feedback and Grievance Resolution."

69. Chaykowksi, Slotsve, and Butler, "A Simultaneous Analysis of Grievance Activity"; D. R. Dalton and W. D. Todor, "Composition of Dyads as a Factor in the Outcomes of Workplace Justice: Two Field Assessments," *Academy of Management Journal* 28 (1985): 704-12; Gideon and Peterson, "A Comparison of Alternate Grievance Procedures"; Lewin and Peterson, *The Modern Grievance Procedure*; Ng and Dastmalchian, "Determinants of Grievance Outcomes"; W. D. Todor and C. L. Owen, "Deriving Benefits from Conflict Resolution: A Macrojustice Assessment," *Employee Responsibilities and Rights Journal* 4 (1991): 37-49.

70. D. R. Dalton and W. D. Todor, "Win, Lose, Draw: The Grievance Process in Practice," *Personnel Administrator* 26 (May-June 1981): 25-29; Ng and Dastmalchian, "Determinants of Grievance Outcomes."

71. B. S. Klass, "Managerial Decision-Making About Employee Grievances: The Impact of the Grievant's Work History," *Personnel Psychology* 42 (1989a): 53-68.

72. American Arbitration Association, *Study Time* (a quarterly newsletter for labor arbitrators), no. 4, 1993.

73. R. N. Block and J. Stieber, "The Impact of Attorneys and Arbitrators on Arbitration Decisions," *Industrial and Labor Relations Review* 40 (1987): 543-55; S. M. Crow and J. W. Logan, "Arbitrators' Characteristics and Decision-Making Records, Gender of Arbitrators and Grievants, and the Presence of Legal Counsel as Predictors of Arbitral Outcomes," *Employee Responsibilities and Rights Journal* 7 (1994): 169-85.

74. Block and Stieber, "The Impact of Attorneys and Arbitrators."

75. R. J. Thornton and P. A. Zirkel, "The Consistency and Predictability of Grievance Arbitration Awards," *Industrial and Labor Relations Review* 43 (1990): 294-307.

76. Brian Bemmels, "The Effects of Grievants' Gender on Arbitrators' Decisions," *Industrial and Labor Relations Review* 41 (1988a): 251-62; Brian Bemmels, "Gender Effects in Discharge Arbitration," *Industrial and Labor Relations Review* 42 (1988b): 63-76; Brian Bemmels, "Attribution Theory and Discipline Arbitration," *Industrial and Labor Relations Review* 44 (1991): 548-62.

77. B. Bemmels, "Arbitrator Characteristics and Arbitrator Decisions," *Journal of Labor Research* 11 (1990): 181-92; Thornton and Zirkel, "The Consistency and Predictability."

78. D. R. Nolan and R. I. Abrams, "American Labor Arbitration: The Maturing Years," *University of Florida Law Review* 35 (1983): 557-632; R. Mittenthal, "Whither Arbitration? Major Changes in the Last Half Century," *Arbitration Journal* 46 (December 1991): 24-32.

79. Arbitration serves both sides' outcome interests by producing written (and lengthy) awards that provide the parties with a detailed explanation for the decision. Arbitration precedents and expenses also serve both sides' process interests by providing them an easily understood and non-threatening rationale for why most grievances must be resolved at the pre-arbitration steps.

80. N. Kauffman, "Expedited Arbitration Revisited," *Arbitration Journal* 46 (September 1991): 34-38.

81. J. M. Brett and S. B. Goldberg, "Grievance Mediation in the Coal Industry: A Field Experiment," *Industrial and Labor Relations Review* 37 (1983): 49-69; S. B. Goldberg, "The Mediation of Grievances Under a Collective Bargaining Agreement: An Alternative to Arbitration," *Northwestern University Law Review* 77 (1982): 270-315.

82. P. Feuille, "Why Does Grievance Mediation Resolve Grievances?" *Mediation Journal* 8 (1992): 131-46.

83. Bureau of National Affairs, *Collective Bargaining Negotiations and Contracts: Basic Patterns* (Washington, D.C.: BNA, 1989).

84. Feuille and Wheeler, "Will the Real Industrial Conflict Please Stand Up?"; Kochan and Katz, *Collective Bargaining and Industrial Relations*. These workplace conflicts also provide these scholars with research opportunities, and with moonlighting work opportunities as mediators and arbitrators.

85. D. I. Rees, "Grievance Procedure Strength and Teacher Quits," *Industrial and Labor Relations Review* 45 (1991): 31-43; D. G. Spencer, "Employee Voice and Employee Retention," *Academy of Management Journal* 29 (1986): 488-502.

86. C. Ichniowski, "The Effects of Grievance Activity on Productivity"; C. Ichniowski and D. Lewin, "Grievance Procedure and Firm Performance," in *Human Resources and the Performance of the Firm*, eds. M. M. Kleiner, R. N. Block, M. Roomkin, and S. W. Salsburg (Madison, Wis.: Industrial Relations Research Association, 1987), 159-

93; Katz, Kochan, and Gobeille, "Industrial Relations Performance, Economic Performance"; Katz, Kochan, and Weber, "Assessing the Effects of Industrial Relations"; and J. R. Norsworthy and C. A. Zabala, "Worker Attitudes, Worker Behavior, and Productivity in the U.S. Automobile Industry, 1959-76," *Industrial and Labor Relations Review* 38 (1985): 544-57.

87. M. M. Kleiner, G. Nickelsburg, and A. Pilarski, "Monitoring, Grievances, and Plant Performance," *Industrial Relations* 34 (1995): 169-89.

88. Lewin and Peterson, *The Modern Grievance Procedure.*

89. B. Klass and A. S. DeNisi, "Managerial Reactions to Employee Dissent: The Impact of Grievance Activity on Performance Ratings," *Academy of Management Journal* 32 (1989): 705-17.

90. P. J. Carnevale, J. B. Olson, and K. M. O'Connor, "Reciprocity and Informality in a Laboratory Grievance System," paper presented at the Fifth Conference of the International Association of Conflict Management, Minneapolis, Minn., June 1992; D. Lewin, "Dispute Resolution in the Nonunion Firm: A Theoretical and Empirical Analysis," *Journal of Conflict Resolution* 31 (1987): 465-502; Lewin, "Grievance Procedures in Nonunion Workplaces."

91. Freeman and Medoff, *What Do Unions Do?*

92. P. Feuille and M. LeRoy, "Grievance Arbitration Appeals in the Federal Courts: Facts and Figures," *Arbitration Journal* 45 (March 1990): 35-47; M. LeRoy and P. Feuille, "The Steelworkers Trilogy and Grievance Arbitration Appeals: How the Federal Courts Respond," *Industrial Relations Law Journal* 13 (1992): 78-120.

93. *Alexander v. Gardner-Denver Co.*, 415 U.S. 36 (1974).

94. *Gilmer v. Interstate/Johnson Lane Corp.*, 500 U.S. 20 (1991).

95. C. W. Sharpe, "The Law and Arbitration," *The Chronicle* (newsletter of the National Academy of Arbitrators), September 1994, pp. 6, 8.

96. P. Feuille and D. R. Chachere, "Looking Fair or Being Fair: Remedial Voice Procedures in Nonunion Workplaces," *Journal of Management* 21 (1995): 27-42. In this 1991 study 4 of 111 surveyed nonunion employers with formal GPs had arbitration. Similarly, a 1994 U.S. Government Accounting Office survey of about 1,500 private sector employers found that 10 percent had arbitration procedures for some of their nonunion employees; U.S. Government

Accounting Office, Employment Discrimination: Most Private-Sector Employers Use Alternative Dispute Resolution, GAO/HEHS-95-150, July 1995.

97. *Steele v. Louisville and Nashville Railroad,* 323 U.S. 192 (1944); *Vaca v. Sipes,* 386 U.S. 171 (1967); *Hines v. Anchor Motor Freight, Inc.,* 424 U.S. 554 (1976); *Bowen v. U.S. Postal Service,* 459 U.S. 212 (1983).

98. M. J. Goldberg, "The Duty of Fair Representation: What the Courts Do In Fact," *Buffalo Law Review* 34 (1985): 89-171.

99. Nolan and Abrams, "American Labor Arbitration."

100. Kochan, Katz, and McKersie, *The Transformation of American Industrial Relations*; Lawler, *Unionization and Deunionization.*

101. T. A. Kochan and R. N. Block, "An Interindustry Analysis of Bargaining Outcomes: Preliminary Evidence from Two-Digit Industries," *Quarterly Journal of Economics* 91 (1977): 431-52.

102. Cooke, *Labor-Management Cooperation.*

103. E. W. Bakke, *Mutual Survival: The Goal of Unions and Management,* 2d ed. (Hamden, Conn.: Archon Books, 1966).

3

CONFLICTIVE PARTNERSHIPS UNDER COLLECTIVE BARGAINING
A NEUTRAL'S PERSPECTIVE

Sylvia Skratek[1]

I. Introduction

One of the important and challenging frontiers in dispute resolution is the settlement of grievances in unionized work-places. In these workplaces the procedures and processes for managing grievances are defined in the language of the collective bargaining agreement. More than 96 percent of these agreements provide for arbitration. But many of the parties to the contracts are dissatisfied with the cost, the delays, and the outcome of arbitration as it has come to be practiced. This has resulted in a search for less costly, faster, and more satisfactory alternatives that will settle disputes in the stages of a conflict that precede arbitration. Two approaches have evolved as unions and management have developed "conflictive partnerships" to resolve disputes: grievance mediation and grievance prevention.

The purpose of this chapter is to review the evolution of this change in focus from antagonistic conflict to conflictive partnerships. The contributory roles played by the shift in emphasis in dispute resolution from power and rights to interests are explained. The history of the development of arbitration, grievance mediation, and grievance prevention is presented, illustrated by examples from several national industries and the state of Washington. The factors that influence the successful implementation of "conflictive partnerships" are discussed. Finally, the implications of this evolution for future research and practice are discussed.

II. Conflictive Partnerships

John Calhoun Wells, director of the Federal Mediation and Conciliation Service, remarked at the 1994 annual conference of the Montana Arbitrator's Association that labor-management relations in the United States have evolved to the stage of being "conflictive partnerships." Inherent in this term is the acceptance of disputes as commonplace occurrences within all organizational structures where people with different interests and backgrounds deal with each other on a regular basis. Where employee interests are advanced and protected by a labor organization, the nature of the relationship between management and labor will determine the focus brought to the resolution of workplace disputes. If conflict is properly managed, both parties will have the opportunity to maximize their joint productivity and performance. Furthermore, these conflictive partnerships recognize that both the union and management have a mutual interest in the survival of the employer. That survival depends on a partnership that accepts the power and rights embodied in the labor-management relationship while focusing on interests that will maximize the chances of survival.

Over the past two decades, conflictive partnerships have been developing in response to a variety of factors influencing the competitive environment. The changing dynamics at the workplace over the past two decades have fostered a climate of ongoing turmoil as organizations within both the public and private sectors have struggled to become more responsive to ever-growing demands. These demands are fostered by increased global competition, rapid technological change, government deregulation, and customer dissatisfaction with the status quo.

During the 1980s, organizations struggled with restructuring, realignments, mergers, acquisitions, and downsizings in an effort to cope with these competitive pressures. As a result, more than three million jobs were lost; 50 percent of the 1980 Fortune 500 companies were absent from the 1990 list. But these efforts created problems that the companies found to be as difficult as the initial change efforts. The best and brightest people, often with critical skills, left the organizations. In some cases, too many people left, resulting in rehiring costs that outweighed the savings of the restructuring effort. But most important, the negative impact on morale created a dysfunctional workplace.

In an attempt to refocus the workplace and mitigate the effects of the above efforts, cooperative programs were introduced in the 1980s that focused on participatory management. These programs had sporadic success with a failure rate as high as 70 percent. There were questions about the true motivation by management in the establishment of such programs: were the programs a path to survival and an enhanced role for employees? Or were they the road to co-optation and ultimate dominance of the workforce by management? A multitude of quality or "Q" combination acronyms developed during this time period: TQM, TQC, TQP, etc. Joint labor-management committees were established, and joint task groups tackled operational issues.

Unfortunately, failure rates remained high primarily because these efforts only tinkered at the margins, but they did lay the foundation for the emerging efforts aimed at the development of conflictive partnerships. These new approaches are based on an appropriate integration of the three basic labor management relationship variables: rights, power, and interests.

III. Power, Rights, and Interests

The movement toward mutual problem-solving negotiations and away from the more hostile, confrontational traditional negotiations can be explained through a review of the three approaches to resolving disputes: power, rights, and interests. While all three are linked and play a role in any negotiation, the shift to a strong emphasis on interests and away from power and rights has paved the way for the greater cooperation needed for conflictive partnerships.

Power is the ability to coerce someone to do something they would not otherwise do. The exercise of one's power means the imposition of costs on the other side or the threat to impose. In a labor strike, the union exercises its power by imposing economic costs on the employer. "The exercise of power takes two common forms: acts of aggression, such as sabotage or physical attack, and withholding the benefits that derive from a relationship, as when employees withhold their labor in a strike."[2] As discussed in chapter 2, a union may engage in corporate campaigns and in-plant strategies, while the employer may exercise its power by hiring, or threatening to hire, permanent replacement workers.

In labor-management relationships the question of who is more powerful is determined by who is less dependent on the other. If the employer needs the employees' work more than the employees need the employer's pay, then the company is more dependent and therefore less powerful. Conversely, if the employees need the pay, then the employees are more dependent and less powerful.

> How dependent one is turns on how satisfactory the alternatives are for satisfying one's interests. The better the alternative, the less dependent one is. If it is easier for the company to replace striking employees than it is for striking employees to find new jobs, the company is less dependent and therefore more powerful. . . . Determining who is the more powerful party without a decisive and potentially destructive power contest is difficult because power is ultimately a matter of perceptions. Despite objective indicators of power, such as financial resources, parties' perceptions of their own and each other's power often do not coincide. Moreover, each side's perception of the other's power may fail to take into account the possibility that the other will invest greater resources in the contest than expected out of fear that a change in the perceived distribution of power will affect the outcomes of future disputes.[3]

Rights are determined through an independent standard with perceived legitimacy or fairness. Rights in a labor-management relationship are represented in the collective bargaining agreement negotiated by the parties. Disputes that arise under the collective bargaining agreement are subjected to the grievance procedure specified in the agreement. If the parties fail to resolve the grievance internally, there is most often a binding arbitration step that provides for a neutral third party to adjudicate the matter. The parties present evidence and arguments to the third party who has the power to hand down a binding decision. That decision is based, in part, on the language in dispute, past practice between the parties, bargaining history, and the facts surrounding the dispute.

Interests are the actual needs of the parties, i.e., the things that are important to achieving a satisfactory resolution of a dispute. The determination of the parties' interests requires probing for deep-seated concerns, searching for solutions to those concerns, and making concessions where interests cannot be reconciled. Negotiation that focuses primarily on interests is referred to as "interest-based" bargaining or "problem solving" negotiation. The latter term clearly illustrates the goal of the process: to treat a dispute as a mutual problem to be solved by the parties.

Power, Rights, and *Interests* are all inextricably linked with each playing a role in the resolution of all disputes. It is the relative importance of that role that shifts. Parties who participate in interest-based bargaining are ever cognizant of the rights that are currently contained within the collective bargaining agreement. They also recognize both the power of their side and of the other side. Underlying their interests at the bargaining table are the levels of power and rights that are available to each of them respectively and their ability to invoke those powers and rights. It is not uncommon for the parties to shift their focus from interests to rights to power and back again. The key question becomes: which focus will yield the best result?

According to Ury, Brett and Goldberg,[4] the three different approaches to the resolution of disputes generate different costs and benefits. They use four criteria in comparing them: transaction costs, satisfaction with outcomes, effect on the relationship, and recurrence of disputes. *Transaction costs* include the "time, money, and emotional energy expended in disputing; the resources consumed and destroyed; and the opportunities lost." *Satisfaction with outcomes* is dependent upon how the resolution of the dispute fulfills the interests that led the parties to either make or reject a claim in the first place. Satisfaction may also hinge upon whether or not the parties believe that the resolution is fair and whether or not the parties believe that the process used to reach the resolution is fair. *Effect on the relationship* is determined by the long-term effect that the approach has on the ability of the parties to work together on a day-to-day basis. *Recurrence of disputes* measures "whether a particular approach produces durable resolutions." All four of the criteria are interrelated. Dissatisfaction with the resolution of a dispute may lead to recurrence of the dispute, which in turn will increase the transaction costs.

An interest-based approach can help the parties to uncover the underlying problems that may have led to a dispute. It can also help the parties to identify which issues are of greater concern to one party relative to the other. In the General Motors (GM) and United Automobile Workers (UAW) negotiations discussed below, it was to the mutual benefit of both parties to search for a way to keep the company economically sound while protecting the employees from loss of income. Only by focusing on those interests were the parties able to reach the unprecedented agreement that laid the foundation for ongoing cooperative relations. Reconciling interests in this manner leads to a higher level of mutual satisfaction with the outcome than does the use of power or the invocation of rights. Mutual satisfaction leads to improvements in the ongoing relationship which make the recurrence of the disputes less likely.

> In sum, focusing on interests, compared to focusing on rights or power, tends to produce higher satisfaction with outcomes, better working relationships and less recurrence, and may also incur lower transaction costs. As a rough generalization, then, an interests approach is less costly than a rights or power approach.[5]

IV. The Search for New Approaches to Dispute Resolution: The Historical Perspective

The fact that more than 96 percent of the collective bargaining agreements in the United States provide for the arbitration of grievances indicates that the process has been well accepted. The grievance procedure ending in binding arbitration provides a formal means of communication outside of the collective bargaining process and is consistent with the basic premise of voluntary agreement making.[6] "Underlying the momentum of popularity for arbitration are the very reasons which inspired its creation and development. Instead of strikes or some other form of economic force, the parties have substituted a private adjudicative process under the terms of a contract. Resort to the courts with their highly complex and technical dynamics is highly inappropriate for resolving grievances when the parties are committed to a continuing relationship."[7]

The "golden age of labor arbitration," according to David Feller, began with the U.S. Supreme Court decisions in the Steelworkers Trilogy cases of 1960.[8] Although *Textile Workers Union v. Lincoln Mills,* issued in 1957, had previously established that agreements to arbitrate were enforceable,[9] the Steelworkers Trilogy lent an air of special privilege to such agreements. The courts could, and would, defer disputes to arbitration provided that the party demanding arbitration was making a claim that "on its face is governed by the contract." Furthermore, an order to arbitrate a claim could not be denied "unless it may be said with positive assurance that the arbitration clause is not susceptible to an interpretation that covers the asserted dispute." Finally, an arbitrator's award is not subject to review by the courts if the award draws its "essence" from the agreement.[10]

The court's deference to arbitration illustrates the court's perception of the function of arbitration in labor relations. It is a function that is considerably different from other arenas where arbitration might be used as a substitute for litigation. Prasow describes labor arbitration as the "substitute for industrial strife" with the "agreement to arbitrate being the quid pro quo for the agreement not to strike."[11] He reviews the findings of the U.S. Supreme Court in the Steelworker Trilogy wherein the Court stated that the labor agreement itself is "more than a contract"; it is a "generalized code to govern a myriad of cases which the draftsmen cannot wholly anticipate," an "effort to erect a system of industrial self-government" with grievance machinery at its core and arbitration as a dynamic process, "part and parcel of the collective bargaining process itself."

Amidst all of this praise for the arbitration process arises the main criticism which has been well covered by a torrent of writers: "Briefly, the main criticism stems from the gap between what arbitration was supposed to be: cheap, simple, quick and informal; to what it has become: costly, complex, lengthy and formal."[12] The length of time from a request for arbitration to the issuance of the arbitrator's decision ranges from 60–120 days. The arbitrator's fees and expenses range from $500–$2,000 per party. It is becoming common practice for the parties to be represented by legal counsel and it is not uncommon to have one or both of the parties request an official transcript of the hearing, both of which add costs to the proceedings. Additional costs incurred by the parties may include hearing room rental, agency administrative fees, and payments to personnel who participate in the hearing.

Further underscoring these criticisms of arbitration are the remarks of Coulson[13] which focus upon what is happening "out there in the world of arbitration: tedious multiple steps in the grievance procedure; delays; unnecessary formality; briefs and transcripts which add to the cost; long-winded arguments by lawyers about arbitrability; attempts to keep out evidence; and adjournments, delays and postponements, for reasons that often relate more to the convenience of attorneys and company or union officials than to the merits of the case." Coulson does not suggest that arbitration is not a useful institution. He does suggest, however, that its usefulness has been somewhat mitigated by the fact that the parties have lost sight of the purpose of arbitration. He implies that arbitrators and attorneys have developed a "ho-hum" attitude toward grievance arbitration that has not only contributed to the time delays and cost increases, but also has contributed to the growing dissatisfaction by the employees and employers, the consumers of labor arbitration. Coulson views the union members of today as being mature, skeptical, experienced consumers who "expect a high degree of performance from their union" and "demand that management comply with each individual right contained in the contract." He believes that union members "expect arbitration to be a swift and rational avenue of justice" and they "become frustrated, alienated and bitter when they are faced with unexplained delays, when legal mumbo jumbo keeps them from telling their story, and when the resolution of their case becomes lost behind the opaque innuendoes of the lawyers."

None of the critics suggests the elimination of arbitration as a final step of the grievance procedure, but rather that the users of the process should do their part ". . . to cleanse arbitration of whatever unfairness or inefficiency or pettifogging may be creating complaints. . . ."[14] Over the past two decades there have been myriad recommendations provided by various authors and researchers regarding how the criticisms should be addressed. Suggested options include expedited arbitration, fact-finding prior to arbitration, and grievance mediation prior to arbitration. All three of these processes have the ability to resolve grievances more quickly and less expensively, but only the process of grievance mediation has led to more satisfactory resolutions of disputes.[15] Attention also has been given to the prevention of grievances so the need for any form of third party intervention is reduced.

Thus, two dispute resolution approaches have evolved within the parameters of the traditional labor-management relationship over the past decade. One approach focuses on the use of grievance mediation to resolve contractual disputes. The second approach focuses on the development of an ongoing means to address disputes that have not or will not become part of the grievance processing mechanism of the collective bargaining agreement between the parties. This latter is best characterized as grievance prevention.

V. Grievance Mediation

Grievance mediation is a step that is inserted in the grievance procedure of the collective bargaining agreement just prior to arbitration. After the parties have pursued all previous steps of the grievance procedure, they then have the option of referring the grievance to a mediator. The mediator assists the parties in their attempts to reach a mutually satisfactory settlement.

The process itself is not a new idea. Prior to World War II, mediation was the predominant method used to resolve grievances. The introduction of arbitration during World War II led to the displacement of mediation as the final step in the grievance procedure. After the war, there was little interest in abandoning arbitration, and as a result, grievance mediation remained dormant until the mid-1980s.

During the 1980s, two studies were conducted that documented the benefits of grievance mediation: one in the bituminous coal mining industry,[16] and the other in the K–12 public education industry.[17] The bituminous coal mining industry had been plagued by wildcat strikes, a heavy and expensive arbitration load, and considerable dissatisfaction with the grievance arbitration system on the part of both union and management.[18] Steve Goldberg and Jeanne Brett introduced mediation as a voluntary extension of step three of the parties' grievance procedure, thereby inserting mediation as a step prior to arbitration. Based upon the advice of the parties and subject to the consent of the parties, they selected six mediators who had substantial experience in arbitration in the coal industry and elsewhere. Four of the six mediators also had mediation experience. The mediators met prior to the first mediation conference to discuss the rules of mediation, mediation techniques and possible responses to anticipated problems. Subsequently, a mediator conducted training with the parties to acquaint them with the rules, procedures, and approaches of mediation.

Following is a general outline of the rules that governed the mediation of grievances:

- a request for mediation must be made within five days of the conclusion of step three;

- mediation conferences will be held at a convenient central location;

- the grievant shall have the right to be present;

- any written material provided at the conference shall be returned to the parties;

- proceedings shall be informal;

- an advisory opinion may be issued by the mediator;

- if the grievance does not settle, the mediator may not serve as the arbitrator and the parties may not raise the mediation discussion at the arbitration hearing.

During the first year, 153 grievances were taken to mediation. Of that number, 135 were resolved without resort to arbitration, a resolution rate of 89 percent. The time savings and cost-effectiveness of grievance mediation were considerable. Grievances were resolved three months faster than they would have been resolved through arbitration at one-third the cost of arbitration. Furthermore, the majority of the participants in the study were satisfied with all aspects of the mediation procedure and preferred mediation over arbitration. At the local level, company personnel preferred it six to one and union officers preferred it seven to one. The reasons given for their preference included the informality of the process, improved communications established through the process, more satisfactory outcomes achieved, and the absence of hard feelings that often accompany arbitration.[19]

Shortly after the results of the Goldberg and Brett study became known, several union advocates approached the Washington Education Association (WEA), the Washington state organization with which all local education unions are affiliated. They suggested that grievance mediation be considered for inclusion in negotiated grievance procedures. Subsequently, during the 1984–85 school year, grievance mediation was available on an experimental basis to all school districts and local unions that wanted to use the process.

Meetings and training sessions were held with advocates of both the WEA and its management counterpart, the Washington State School Directors' Association (WSSDA). Representatives of the WEA and WSSDA reviewed the names of established Northwest arbitrators and agreed upon several arbitrators to serve as mediators. Training in the conduct of mediation conferences was provided for the selected arbitrators by the Mediation Research and Education Project.[20] The advocates were provided with prototype contract language that paralleled the language in the coal mining industry, with the exception of the requirement for an advisory opinion. The advocates rejected such a requirement, choosing instead to make a determination on a case-by-case basis as to the desirability of an advisory opinion.

During the first year, fifteen grievances were referred to mediation. Of those fifteen grievances, thirteen were settled as a result of a mediation conference, a resolution rate of 86 percent. A follow-up study was conducted over a three-year period in which an additional thirty-two grievances were referred to mediation; thirty of those grievances were resolved as a result of a mediation conference. The average cost savings of mediation was $1,200 per case. All of the participants in the mediation conferences were satisfied with the procedural, substantive, and psychological aspects of the process.[21]

Since the conclusion of these studies, the process of grievance mediation has been introduced throughout the United States. Industries using the process today include coal, copper, iron ore, airline, telephone, manufacturing, mass transit, electric power, retail sales, municipal government, petroleum refining, and education. As of 1995, more than 2,600 grievances had been referred to grievance mediation with a settlement rate of 82 percent. The parties that have used the process have indicated that they do so for several reasons. First, the final decision remains with the parties. Second, the underlying problems are brought to the surface and addressed. Third, a "cooling off" period occurs. Fourth, communication skills are improved and ongoing labor relations are enhanced. Fifth, it is quicker and less adversarial than arbitration. Finally, mediation can provide an unbiased third-party opinion on a nonbinding basis if the parties request this.

VI. The Evolution toward Greater Cooperation

During the 1980s, increased emphasis was placed on cooperative forms of labor-management relationships, reinforcing grievance mediation. These forms of cooperation included problem-solving bargaining and quality of work life (QWL) programs. This, in turn, laid the foundation for increased efforts aimed at grievance prevention.

As any unionist knows, the 1980s was a time of trial for many labor unions. Concession bargaining threatened the economic gains unions had won over the years. Companies claimed that increased global competition was forcing them to retrench and to become more productive in order to meet the competition. One response on the part of some employers and unions was an attempt to foster a more collaborative labor relationship through increased worker involvement. . . . A second-wave response is the renewed attention grievance mediation has received from the government, neutrals, and unions/management.[22]

The interest in problem-solving bargaining as opposed to the traditional confrontational method of bargaining surfaced in 1982 in the education industry in the state of Washington. Economic factors were underlying the interest in greater cooperation and grievance mediation. Since 1980, the state of Washington has experienced severe financial setbacks that have directly affected all public employees within the state. As one response to these financial problems, a statutory provision entitled *Salaries and Compensation for Employees-Limitations-Exclusions-Rules* was passed by the Washington state legislature in 1981.[23] This statute restricted the amount of salary monies that could be provided to both certified and classified educational personnel. Salaries in several of the school districts were frozen and no provisions were forthcoming for salary increases for several years. As of the present date, there have been few significant salary increases allowed for educational personnel.

By 1983, several union and management advocates were actively participating in the problem solving method of bargaining. On an informal basis, several of the advocates stated that the shift in bargaining methods was caused by the legislative restrictions on salary increases. The knowledge that monies were not available caused the parties to approach bargaining in a less adversarial manner. The interest in grievance mediation also surfaced in 1983, and may be directly linked with the advocates' desires to resolve problems in a less adversarial manner. Hanami and Blanpain found that an economic crisis does lead, in most countries, to less open industrial strife: ". . . workers are less easily mobilized than before because of fear of losing jobs or of damaging the viability of the enterprise . . . workers seem to give up and accept the inevitable."[24]

The U.S. automobile industry provides an example of such lessening of industrial strife through problem-solving bargaining and QWL programs. In 1980, General Motors (GM) lost money for the first time since the Depression and "took the unprecedented step in 1981 of asking the UAW (United Auto Workers) to reopen the National Agreement early and to grant substantial economic concessions." The subsequent agreement reached by the parties provided GM the economic concessions it sought and provided the UAW the increased job security it needed. That agreement has been viewed as being "a wise and prudent step, benefiting not only the parties but also the nation's economy."

Concurrent with this unprecedented concessionary agreement was the maturation of the QWL programs which were exemplified by the Chevrolet (Livonia, Michigan) and the Fleetwood (Flint, Michigan) GM plants. The QWL programs were introduced in the late 1970s to provide employees an opportunity to participate in the decision making process. By 1980, it was evident that the programs had caused a decrease in the filing of formal grievances. In 1982, the majority of the grievances were being resolved informally. Representatives of GM and the UAW saw "a lessening of hostilities between them partly in response to the economic ills afflicting [the] auto industry."[25]

The economic crisis faced by the automobile and other industries in the 1980s led to an ongoing interest in improved performance and increased productivity. Both the public and the private sectors throughout the United States also were being challenged by the changes occurring in the world, the nation, and the economy. Those challenges will remain into the next century. How those challenges are met within the traditional labor-management relationship will determine the level of productivity and performance that can be achieved. In this context, grievance prevention became an increasingly important goal.

VII. Grievance Prevention

The evolution toward grievance prevention is illustrated by the experience of the Northwest Natural Gas Company (NNG) at its Portland, Oregon, facility. During one of the ongoing discussions regarding the grievances that had been processed, representatives of labor and management agreed to search for a better way to settle the issues that were being identified through the grievance process. This agreement reflected a marked departure from their traditionally structured labor-management relationship and the first step toward a new relationship reflecting the changes in the competitive environment.

NNG has been in business for 132 years and its employees have been represented by a union since the 1930s. Today, 72 percent of its 1,263 employees are represented by the Office and Professional Employees International Union, Local #11. The relationship between the union and management had historically been adversarial and the company's relationship with its employees had been paternalistic.

Deregulation of the industry in the mid-1980s forced the company to take a hard-line, confrontational stance in the 1986 negotiations. It was threatened with a strike and the subsequent hiring of replacement workers. After long and difficult negotiations, the union and management settled for a three-year agreement with no wage increases in the first two years and a modest 1.75 percent increase in the third year. The company had succeeded in reducing costs by $400,000 to $500,000 per year, but it did not take long for the company to realize that with the cost reductions came a productivity reduction. The workplace environment changed dramatically. Cooperation was drastically reduced and grievances soared. Morale was at an all-time low.

To address these problems, labor and management agreed to work with an organizational development consultant toward a more cooperative relationship. Representatives of labor and management were provided training in communication skills and conflict/dispute resolution. The most important skill was learning to understand the interests of the union and the employees that it represented. Emphasis was placed on determining the actual needs of the employees and finding ways to address those needs. Union officials and chief stewards learned that management could be responsive and did care about the employees.

The parties proceeded to focus upon mutual goals and shaped those goals into a mission statement:

> To make labor relations at Northwest Natural Gas Company a participative effort to oversee relationships between Union and Management personnel.

> To work toward the dissemination of information necessary to make decisions, manage change, and move decisions to the most effective level possible.

> [To] Develop a total commitment from each employee to improve the working environment and support the organization's efforts to prosper and grow.

The parties then tackled the grievance procedure and rewrote it into an issue resolution process. The process is intended to promote open communication and mutual respect and to resolve the issues in a manner that reflects the best interests of the employee and the company. It is a four-step process, the first of which involves the employee and the first-line supervisor. This initial step is intended to provide the parties who are closest to the problem with the opportunity to fully discuss the issue and resolve it in a manner that best reflects the interests of the disputants. Each of the following steps of the process retains the participants from the earlier steps so that when the parties reach step four the employee and the first-line supervisor are meeting with the union steward, chief steward, department manager, executive officer of the union, and the vice president of labor relations. If step four does not result in a resolution, the parties are free to proceed to grievance mediation and, if needed, arbitration.

Following early successes with this process, the parties obtained the commitment and support of their top-level personnel to proceed toward a new partnership in negotiations. Building upon the process they had previously established through the grievance procedure, the parties entered into an integrated negotiation process that focused upon the issues and interests of the parties. Through this negotiation process, a labor agreement entitled the "Joint Accord" was concluded within three months. It was ratified by more than 90 percent of the union membership.

The joint accord has been hailed as the beginning of a new era at NNG. Every employee in the company has attended a one-day issue resolution training program. Supervisors and stewards are paired together for the training and work on actual issues while learning the techniques of dispute resolution. The direct benefits include open communications, trust, mutual respect, patience, and understanding. Greater job security, financial rewards, and easier resolution of issues for all employees are the results of this joint accord.[26]

VIII. Implementing Change

The changes in the traditional labor-management relationship discussed above have not come easily, nor should they. To assume that the parties can simply move away from the adversarial nature that has historically permeated these relationships ignores the fact that today's relationships evolved over the decades based upon the needs of a given time in history. Indeed, many labor union activists will remind their members that none of their rights was won easily, and at times much blood was shed to obtain those rights. Feuille is correct when he states in chapter 2 that "Unions believe that these . . . are the desirable fruits of their valiant struggle with employers who are insufficiently attuned to the equity interests of employees, and thus . . . need to be protected and expanded." But to suggest that there is no room for change ignores the fact that today's workplace differs greatly from that of yesterday and that those differences may require an evolutionary approach. It must be emphasized that no one is suggesting that the hard-won rights be abandoned, but rather that they be integrated with the power and interests of the parties. By recognizing that change can occur without abandoning the historical perspective, the parties can move forward toward quicker, less adversarial, and less expensive resolution of their workplace disputes.

Successful implementation of the two changes highlighted in this chapter—grievance mediation and grievance prevention—hinges on four elements: initial preparation; developing the framework; training and persuasion; and evaluation of the process.

A. Initial Preparation for the New Process

As a new dispute resolution process is introduced to labor and management it is critical to establish a level of comfort that will encourage the parties to move beyond their traditional manner of doing things. They usually have a long history, whether it is fifty years of arbitrations or ten years of confrontational negotiations. The use of an outside person viewed by the parties as an objective expert in the process helps to lay the foundation for change.

The expert should be someone who has worked with parties in the labor-management relationship. This prior experience provides an understanding of the historical "beast" with which the parties are trying to work so the person can understand without much education the relationship that has existed between the parties in the given situation. The expert should be able to respond to glitches, intervene to design a correction, and address any hesitancies that the parties might have. The individual must have the ability to listen, respond, interact, and facilitate a group process; he or she must also have an understanding of problem-solving skills, and a belief in a value system that supports people solving their own disputes. The expert should focus on maintaining the conflictive partnership that has historically evolved between the parties while moving that partnership in a direction that will lead to less adversarial and more satisfactory resolutions of their disputes. Without such assistance, the parties too often dismiss a process as being useless when in fact they did not have the appropriate guidance to implement it in its early stages.

It is also critical to have initial meetings with key personnel on both sides. These meetings must determine which people are actually overseeing the disputes and which are ultimately responsible for the operations of the company and the union. Those responsible must support the process as an attempt to find less adversarial means of dispute resolution. Without that support, the process is subject to unfounded criticism and at times outright sabotage.

Early discussions with the parties should focus on an assessment of the organizational climate. Questions to be addressed include:

1. What are your goals for the process? (What is the mission?)
   A. What barriers do you foresee in the accomplishment of your goals?
   B. What opportunities do you foresee?
2. What are your interests/needs? i.e., what do you personally hope to accomplish?
   A. How do you hope to accomplish them?
3. What do you see as being the most critical issues for you to address through this process?
4. What do you see as being the most critical issues for the group to address through this process? (What do you see as being its scope of work?)
5. What is at stake for you personally? Why are you willing to participate in this process?
6. Whom do you represent?
   A. For whom are you negotiating?
   B. With whom are you negotiating?
   C. How will you communicate with them?
7. Are there other people who should be participating in this process?
8. Do you have decision making authority? (If not, who does?)

Are there limits to that decision making authority?
9. How would you define success?
10. What would cause failure of this process?
11. What do you see as being a "completed" process?
12. Have you participated in any previous discussions?
    Were any parts of the previous discussions successful?
    Why did they fail?
13. How would you describe the overall climate as it pertains to labor-management relations?
    A. What are the problems that exist today? Why?
    B. What good things are going on today? Why?
14. Is there anything else that I need to know?

All discussions are conducted individually and privately by the facilitator prior to convening the first meeting. While all responses are kept confidential as to who made a particular comment, the responses are used to build working documents for the parties to use as they develop the critical issues that they wish to address.

B. Developing the Framework

Prior to entering into any new dispute resolution process, the parties must reach agreement on the operating rules or framework of the process. This framework should cover a variety of issues, including the following:

1. How will the process work within their labor-management relationship?
2. What issues are appropriate for discussion? Are there any matters that cannot be discussed?
3. Who will participate?
4. Will outside assistance be needed?
   A. If so, how will other experts be selected?
   B. What will be the extent of their authority?
   C. At what point do the parties enter into the process?
   D. What will be the trigger mechanism?
5. Will all disputes be resolved in this manner or should there be mutual consent as to which disputes will be submitted to the process?
6. What will be the setting for the discussions?
7. What will be the duration of the process?

One option for the parties is to enter into an experimental period with a specific deadline after which the process expires. If the parties do not extend the deadline or negotiate to make the process ongoing, then the process simply disappears.

Experimental periods are advantageous because they allow the parties to move forward in a new direction with a relatively low level of risk. The parties can choose to discontinue the process once the experimental period ends. On the other hand, experimental periods limit the discussions to an artificial time period that may or may not reflect the dynamics of the ongoing relationship between the parties. The parties could conceivably abandon a process before it was actually given a chance to succeed. If an experimental period is the only framework under which the parties are willing to proceed, then it is certainly not to be dismissed. The preferred means would be to introduce the process with no artificial parameters, thereby giving the process adequate time to work. The parties always have the option of not invoking the process provided they have retained mutual consent language within the operating rules that have been drafted to govern the process.

C. Training and Persuasion

The actual participants in the process must receive training in the use of the dispute resolution process: What is it? Who is using it? How successful is it? Why use it? What is in it for us? Elements that are often missing in such training are the actual specifics of how a particular process works: What are the roles of the participants? What do I do in the process?

The emphasis should be placed upon the resolution of disputes and the interrelationship of power, rights, and interests in the achievement of that resolution. Many efforts of the past decade have focused solely on an interest-based approach with little or no attention given to the power and rights that have previously been established between the parties. Those efforts have led to frustration and failure due in part to unrealistic expectations that all disputes can and should be resolved with an interest-based approach. That is simply not so. The parties need to develop an understanding and appreciation of the costs and benefits of a given approach and the appropriateness of using an approach within a given situation. Only then will the parties approach a new process with realistic expectations that can be met.

The training should be joint with both labor and management in the room at the same time; this eliminates any questions as to what the other side might be hearing. It provides the opportunity for both sides to hear the concerns that one side or the other might have about the process. The participants must leave the training session ready to try the process and confident that they have the skills necessary to successfully participate.

D. Evaluation of the Process

Over the years, much research has been conducted about the effectiveness of grievance mediation and prevention. The parties often remain skeptical, however, as to whether a process will yield satisfactory results in their given set of circumstances. The parties can draw upon the research conducted to date[27] to develop evaluation systems that will help guide them through the determination of whether or not to continue with a process.

Briefly outlined, the evaluations conducted to date have included the collection of baseline data to monitor the process and determine the satisfaction achieved. Baseline data consist of the number and types of disputes that the parties have previously had; the cost of the disputes; the time expended in the resolution of those disputes; the satisfaction level of the parties after resolution; the effect of the resolutions on labor/management relations; and the recurrence of similar disputes. Monitoring the process entails tracking the number and types of disputes that are being referred to the process; the settlement rate of the disputes; and the cost-effectiveness and resource efficiency of the process. Satisfaction achieved is determined on three levels: procedural, substantive, and psychological. Procedural satisfaction is how satisfied the parties are with the specific resolution procedures that give order to the process during and after the resolution. Substantive satisfaction is how satisfied the parties are with the content or substance of the resolution. Psychological satisfaction is how the parties feel once the dispute has been resolved.

Participants in the process are surveyed using a variety of techniques, including telephone interviews, personal interviews, and mail questionnaires. The results of the evaluation are used to determine whether or not a process should be continued, modified, or eliminated. They provide the parties with information specific to their given set of circumstances and enable the parties to make the appropriate interventions to accomplish the desired changes in their particular relationship.

IX. Conclusions and Implications for Future Research and Practice

The evolutionary development of dispute resolution systems to address the work-place needs of today and tomorrow provides practitioners with an opportunity to work toward a conflictive partnership that will encourage the proper management of disputes. Workplace performance and productivity and employee morale are directly related to the successful management of disputes. Poorly managed disputes result in costs to the employer that range from a dissatisfied workforce to the loss of productivity and ultimately to the loss of optimal effectiveness. Properly managed disputes can be stimuli to growth and necessary prerequisites to constructive organizational change. Disputes can have positive consequences if the parties air their different interests, make difficult trade-offs, reach a settlement that satisfies the essential needs of each, and progress toward cooperation in other realms.

A common element emerging in dispute resolution processes is the ability to diagnose and resolve the underlying problems that led to a particular dispute. Grievance mediation and grievance prevention have both illustrated their ability to resolve those problems. The challenge for today's practitioner is to transform that ability into a systemic change throughout the workplace.

The high failure rate of labor-management cooperative efforts in the 1980s should encourage the parties to move in a new comprehensive direction. The total quality management and related initiatives that frequently focused on quality improvement in isolation had limited success. But the integration of the concepts contained within the quality phenomena with the elements of grievance mediation and prevention can lead the parties to the development of conflictive partnerships. The change will not be easily accomplished. It will require a slow, deliberate, chaotic, and often uncomfortable process. It is a continually forward looking movement that leads an organization from marginal work performance to high performance. The goal is to design and implement a process that enables an organization to perform more efficiently and at a higher level. The organizational characteristics to be achieved include: a sense of vision, a process driven by values, collaborative, caring and supportive, fast moving, and competitive. The airline industry has taken the lead in these efforts. It was forced by deregulation to undertake changes that would ensure survival. Granted, there have been problems (as discussed in chapter 2), but overall the airline industry is struggling to move forward toward conflictive partnerships that have as their goal the survival of the industry in the twenty-first century.

The AFL-CIO has developed *A Union Guide to Workplace Change,*[28] which has as its underlying premise the development of high-performing work organizations based on conflictive partnerships. As labor and management move toward conflictive partnerships, research opportunities become available to determine the effectiveness of such partnerships. Preliminary research should focus on the growth and establishment of partnerships. Questions to be addressed include: What factors need to be present to encourage the development of a partnership? What ongoing elements are needed to maintain a partnership? What causes a partnership to succeed or fail? What effect do such partnerships have on productivity, performance, and the ultimate survival of an organization? How do the previously established power and rights of the parties within a labor-management relationship interrelate with the interests of the parties?

The implications for the future are exciting. In contrast to my colleague Peter Feuille, who asserts in chapter 2 that we will see a continuation of great hostility in labor relations rhetoric and an ongoing union search for effective pressure tactics to serve as strike substitutes, I am hopeful that we are instead on the brink of a positive evolutionary change. This change is built on the power and rights previously established and exercised but has moved forward based upon the mutual interests of the parties as expressed in conflictive partnerships. Ongoing monitoring and evaluation of these efforts will determine which of us is correct.

Notes

1.   This chapter reflects my experiences over the past twenty-three years as a practitioner in the field of dispute resolution. My work has included several years as an advocate for both labor and management. I have conducted research in the implementation and use of a variety of dispute resolution processes; my early research took place in the state of Washington. The reader will find discussion of this research throughout the chapter. Currently I am working as a neutral party mediating and arbitrating labor disputes and facilitating joint labor-management efforts, including conflictive partnerships. This experience provides me with a unique perspective from "both sides of the table" on the changes that are occurring today in the labor-management relationship.

2.   W. L. Ury, J. M. Brett, and S. B. Goldberg, *Getting Disputes Resolved* (San Francisco: Jossey-Bass Inc., 1988), 7-8.

3.   Ibid.

4.   Ibid., 10–14.

5.   Ibid., 14.

6.   W. E. Simkin, *Mediation and the Dynamics of Collective Bargaining* (Washington, D.C.: BNA Books, 1971), 27.

7.   H. Cohen, "The Search for Innovative Procedures in Labor Arbitration," *The Arbitration Journal* 29 (June 1974): 104–5.

8.   D. Feller, "The Coming End of Arbitration's Golden Age," National Academy of Arbitrators, *Arbitration-1976, Proceedings of the 29th Annual Meeting* (Washington, D. C.: BNA Books, 1976), 97.

9.   *Textile Workers Union v. Lincoln Mills,* 353 U.S. 448, 40 LRRM 2113 (1957).

10.   Steelworker's Trilogy: *United Steelworkers v. American Manufacturing Co.,* 363 U.S. 564 (1960); *United Steelworkers v. Warrior & Gulf Navigation Co.,* 363 U.S. 574 (1960); *United Steelworkers v. Enterprise Wheel & Car Corp.,* 363 U.S. 593 (1960).

11.   P. Prasow and E. Peters, *Arbitration and Collective Bargaining: Conflict Resolution in Labor Relations,* 2d ed. (New York: McGraw-Hill Book Company, 1983), 415.

12.   Cohen, "The Search for Innovative Procedures," 106.

13. R. Coulson, "New Views of Arbitration," *Labor Law Journal* 30 (1980): 495–97.

14. Ibid., 497.

15. S. B. Goldberg, "The Mediation of Grievances Under a Collective Bargaining Contract: an Alternative to Arbitration," *Northwestern University Law Review* 77, no. 3 (1982): 270–315.

16. Ibid.

17. S. P. Skratek, "Grievance Mediation of Contractual Disputes in Washington State Public Education," *Labor Law Journal* 38, no. 6 (1987): 370–76.

18. J. M. Brett and S. B. Goldberg, "Wildcat Strikes in Bituminous Coal Mining," *Industrial and Labor Relations Review* 32 (1979): 467–83.

19. J. M. Brett and S. B. Goldberg, "Grievance Mediation: An Alternative to Arbitration," Industrial Relations Research Association *Proceedings of the Thirty-Fifth Annual Meeting December, 1982* (Wisconsin: IRRA, 1983), 258–59.

20. Mediation Research and Education Project, Inc., 357 East Chicago Avenue, Chicago, IL 60611 (312) 503-0090.

21. Skratek, "Grievance Mediation of Contractual Disputes," 372–73.

22. G. J. Gall, *Grievance Mediation: A Union Member's Guide* (University Park, Penn.: Pennsylvania State University Press, 1991),1–2.

23. *Salaries and Compensation for Employees-Limitations-Exclusions-Rules,* rev. Code of Washington 28A.58.095.

24. T. Hanami and R. Blanpain, eds., *Introduction to Industrial Conflict Resolution in Market Economics* (Netherlands: Kluwer Law and Taxation Publishers, 1984), 13.

25 T. J. St. Antoine, "Dispute Resolution between the General Motors Corporation and the United Auto Workers, 1970-1982," in *Industrial Conflict Resolution,* ed. Hanami and Blanpain, 300–14.

26. R. T. Oare and M. S. McCoy, "Labor Management Partnership: A Path to Alternate Dispute Resolution" (Unpublished paper, Oregon State Bar Association, 1994), 2–14.

27. Goldberg, "The Mediation of Grievances"; S. P. Skratek, "Grievance Mediation of Contractual Disputes in Washington State Public Education" (Ph.D. diss., University of Michigan, 1985), appendix C, 185–209.

28. R. Baugh, *Changing Work, A Union Guide to Workplace Change* (Washington, D.C.: AFL-CIO Human Resources Development Institute, 1994).

4

Dispute Resolution in the Non-Union Environment

An Evolution Toward Integrated Systems for Conflict Management?

Mary Rowe

I. Introduction

Dispute resolution within the nonunion workplace in the United States varies greatly from employer to employer. There are many small companies with no designated dispute resolution mechanisms. There are employers with dispute resolution procedures restricted to specialized situations such as harassment and discrimination, and some that will deal only with a formal grievance. Many employers are now experimenting with "appropriate dispute resolution" (ADR) mechanisms, such as mediation and arbitration, often using neutrals outside the workplace.[1] Much of the interest in these ADR mechanisms is oriented externally, toward those rare disputes that are particularly serious and will otherwise go outside the workplace to a government agency or to the courts. There is also an increasing number of employers with extensive internal systems—which include internal ADR options—designed to deal with all the different kinds of conflict in a workplace. These systems constitute a major change from a prior focus on one or another grievance channel.

There is no reliable estimate of the number of nonunion employers that have instituted internal dispute resolution procedures because the subject is poorly defined and observers discuss conflict management in different ways.[2] Even within a given firm, dispute resolution procedures are sometimes well described and understood and sometimes are not. What is clear is the fact that there has been a great deal of change over the past thirty years. One study[3] published in 1989 found that half or more of large employers had instituted some kind of grievance process for at least some nonunion employees, and that at least one-fifth of those used third-party arbitration as a last step in their formal procedure. The United States General Accounting Office reported in 1995 that "almost all employers with 100 or more employees use one or more ADR approaches" and in 1994, Organizational Resources Counselors reported that 53 percent of a survey of "ninety-six leading companies" used an ADR program to resolve employment-related issues.[4] My own consulting experience indicates that many organizations are now reviewing their dispute resolution structures and that many are moving toward a systems approach.

Some of these structures and systems appear to be working well, but in many small and large firms the mechanisms that exist are inadequate. For example, they may fail to cover one or another group of employees or fail to include managers and professionals. In some companies, the dispute resolution structures are treated cavalierly by management or are effectively unknown to the workforce they are supposed to serve.

Apparent shortcomings of nonunion dispute resolution have received a good deal of attention in the past fifteen years. Various observers have described a variety of problems as seen from the employee perspective. Perhaps the most common criticisms center on inadequate protection of employee rights,[5] including statutory, economic, and "enterprise" rights (those rights granted by a specific employer). Many criticisms center on the absence or inadequacy of formal grievance and appeal channels, focusing especially on the perceived absence of sufficient due process protection. In addition, rights-based formal procedures are believed not to work as well for women's complaints as they do for the complaints of men,[6] and the "gatekeepers" for complaint processes are found to be not as helpful for women and people of color as they are for white men.

Both men and women experience many problems in the process. Many people who use rights-based (formal) complaint procedures fear career damage—as do their supervisors. Fear of reprisal and conflict of interest are serious problems, especially where formal complaint and appeal procedures rise within a single line of supervision. The process of using complaint procedures is often difficult to understand. Nonunion grievants are seen to lack advocacy. Stakeholders are often left out of the process of building nonunion dispute resolution structures. Finally, providing only a single complaint procedure of any kind will shortchange employees and managers who do not like that particular kind of formal or informal procedure.[7]

Other common criticisms come from employers. Thousands of employers are reacting to the fact that the obvious tip of the iceberg of nonunion dispute resolution is handled slowly and expensively by government agencies and the courts. Some employers are also acutely conscious of a litany of other serious costs resulting from the lack of effective internal dispute resolution: damage to relationships in the workplace, loss of productivity, sabotage and theft, harassment and violence, and the like. Some employers are concerned with the particularly high costs that may ensue when managers and professionals feel unjustly treated. In short, many employers believe that the costs of employment disputes are far too high and that there must be a more cost-effective approach.

This chapter will review some innovations in nonunion dispute management and resolution. I first cite various explanations for the introduction of innovations among nonunion employers, and various opinions about dispute resolution procedures. I then turn to the concept of an effective integrated conflict management system. Since the success of a conflict management system depends for the most part on the needs and wishes of complainants, I discuss some characteristics of people who perceive a problem or want to complain in the workplace.[8] I then turn to the implications of the opinions of various critics, and of the characteristics of complainants, for setting the specifications for a good system and for providing the options needed in an effective complaint system. The experience of Brown & Root in developing an integrated conflict management system is briefly reviewed as an example of a contemporary systems design. I conclude with some suggestions for future research.

II. Why Has the Non-union Sector Been Innovating?

The reasons for nonunion innovations are varied and complex. To my knowledge there has been no satisfactory broad overview of this field or systematic description of the different innovations that are emerging all over North America. There is no comprehensive understanding about why these innovations are appearing or how well they are doing. Most authors have a particular focus, such as a special concern for employee rights, alternative dispute resolution centered on the interests of disputants, cost-control, or healthy organizational development. None seems to have a comprehensive perspective.[9] I will cite just a few of the varied studies about conflict management in the United States.

Ewing,[10] writing in 1989, pointed to erosion of reverence for the sacredness of management and management rights, with concomitant growth in concern for employee rights. He identified as causal factors the influence of education, mobility, and diversity in the workforce, rising expectations for fairness and happiness, a wish by management to create a sense of belonging and trust in participative management, a rise in decision making power by personnel departments, the proliferation of "conscientious objectors" or whistle-blowers, and a change in the legal climate toward thinking about jobs as "property." He also noted an increase in interest about procedural justice and substantive justice and indicated that the former cannot necessarily be delivered by line managers when there may be a perception of conflict of interest. Ewing noted, as do many others,[11] that employers realized that they needed to fill the void in conflict management left by the decline in unionization and therefore in union grievance procedures. He noted extensive changes in federal and state laws that restrict employment at will. In addition, some of these legal changes encourage and require employers to provide fair processes for complaints within their organizations.[12] Ewing also discussed the influence on thinking in the United States of worker rights and dispute resolution institutions in Europe (see Clarke's discussion in chapter 8).

The rise of individual rights and of corporate responses in the 1970s and 1980s also was chronicled by Westin and Feliu.[13] They stressed the importance of whistle-blowing, equal opportunity imperatives, and the rise of litigation. They noted the proliferation of corporate innovations in conflict management over a decade of major change. Bedman[14] has recently chronicled changes in how employment disputes are handled in the U.S. legal system; he took particular note of the expansion of tort law.

Ziegenfuss[15] discusses many of the same issues, emphasizing cost control where costs are broadly defined as including lost productivity. He wrote that conflict can be very expensive in a competitive environment, especially in a workplace that is subject to the dislocations of technological change. Cost control was also a central issue for Blake and Mouton[16] in their remarkable (and prescient) book on intragroup conflict within organizations. They looked at lost productivity in the aftermath of mergers, reductions in overhead, realignment of products, and many other situations where trust had been destroyed or was otherwise absent. They concluded that these costs could be lowered through a thoughtful, systematic approach to conflict management. McCabe[17] also focused on cost control, including the need to constrain the emotional costs of workplace conflict, ethical obligations increasingly felt by senior management, and the need for senior administrators to catch their mistakes so they can correct them.

Cost control, including, for example, the costs of wildcat strikes, also was the focus of Ury, Brett, and Goldberg.[18] This concern for cost-effectiveness contributed to the development of their brilliant theoretical analysis of providing mediation as part of a systems approach to conflict resolution in a unionized setting. They were among the first to popularize the notion of dispute resolution systems design. More recently they have extended their "alternative dispute resolution" orientation to dispute resolution in nonunionized settings and commercial disputes.[19]

In his 1993 overview of rights in the workplace, Edwards[20] wrote that the granting of nonstatutory rights in employee handbooks and the advent of innovative complaint mechanisms in the nonunion arena were motivated by four factors: the desire of employers to compete successfully for the best workers, a wish to avoid unionization, a wish to avoid costly lawsuits, and a belief that workers deserve rights. Lewin,[21] who has written extensively about dispute resolution, has suggested, in addition to other points cited above, that nonunion employers seek to improve work performance by providing dispute resolution structures. Edelman, Erlanger, and Lande[22] conclude that the chief impetus for employers to build internal dispute resolution structures is to smooth employment relations and get resolution to employee tension, as they put it, by appeasing employees.

In addition to studies that have concentrated on processes *internal* to the workplace, there has been a great deal of interest in the 1990s in *external* DR. External DR processes such as mediation and arbitration allow employers to deal with problems that would otherwise move from inside the workplace to external agencies such as the Equal Employment Opportunity Commission (EEOC) or to the courts for resolution. The driving forces behind the use of these processes are a concern for finding ways to reduce the workload of the courts, the control of legal and other costs of litigation and of settlements, particularly in jury trials and for statutory rights cases, as well as perhaps the search by lawyers for new areas of practice.[23]

Most of these external "ADR" devices are tightly focused mediation and/or arbitration steps at the end of or in addition to a grievance procedure. Most deal only with rare cases, though some are configured as part of a comprehensive systems approach to conflict management.[24] Some employers offer mediation and arbitration on a voluntary basis, some require agreement to noncourt dispute resolution involving employees who will benefit from stock options or who will receive other benefits, and some employers have made imposed arbitration a condition of employment.

Imposed arbitration as a condition of employment is very controversial. The National Labor Relations Board (NLRB) and the Equal Employment Opportunity Commission (EEOC) oppose imposed arbitration, particularly for civil rights cases. Some opposition also exists in the courts, although a few recent court decisions also support imposed arbitration. There is also both support and opposition in Congress. Many arbitrators have recently announced that they will not handle cases arising under an imposed arbitration program.

Criticisms of specific dispute resolution mechanisms have led many professionals besides Ury, Brett, and Goldberg to conclude that the best approach is to focus on a conflict management *system* that provides options. For example, taking an industry-based perspective, both Marcus and Slaikeu[25] have each recently discussed the need for conflict management systems in health care. Costantino and Merchant[26] have taken an organizational development approach to the subject, writing about the need for "productive and healthy organizations." According to them it is self-evident that disputes, internal competition, sabotage, inefficiency, low productivity, low morale, and withholding knowledge within an organization are symptoms that should lead to conflict management systems design.

In my own work at MIT on conflict management systems design,[27] I joined an effort focused on meeting the needs of a diversifying workforce and student body in a high-tech educational and research environment. As various issues emerged, increasing attention was given to meeting the "needs of the customer."[28] I found that people who wanted to raise a concern or complaint overwhelmingly wanted options, and preferred their own choice of options wherever this is appropriate.[29] Fortunately, the wish for a choice of options matched well with the MIT systems design tradition of providing "redundant" resources and structures for people with problems.[30]

My own employer has been evolving a systems approach to conflict management for about twenty-five years. Many other employers, including colleges and universities, government agencies, foundations, and corporations, have been designing their innovations in a similar way over recent years as they listen to requests and concerns within their own communities, to leadership from one or another innovative senior manager, to federal and state laws and agency requirements, to court decisions, to public demand (see, for example, the 1994 Dunlop Commission), and to outside consultants. Innovative companies in this area include Citibank, Federal Express,

McDonnell-Douglas, Motorola, Polaroid, United Technologies, Xerox, and more recently American Express and Brown & Root. Government examples include the departments of the Air Force, the Army, the Navy and Marine Corps, the Coast Guard, the U.S. Secret Service, the Federal Deposit Insurance Corporation, and many others. Innovative international institutions include the World Bank and the International Monetary Fund.

III. Designing an Effective Integrated Conflict Management System

There are several basic changes implicit in this evolution toward integrated dispute management systems. The first is the idea of a *system* which provides various options and various resource people for all persons in the workplace and all kinds of problems. This approach contrasts with the more traditional methods of providing a single grievance procedure that is only for workers grieving against management, or one designed for a limited list of disputes arising under a contract. A system provides "problem-solving" options based on the interests of the disputants, and "justice" options based on rights and on rights and power. The second major change is the broad idea of conflict management. This may, for example, include the idea of teaching peers, such as managers and teammates, how to negotiate their differences with each other, teaching a whole workplace to use constructive dissent for continuous improvement, and learning how to prevent some costly conflict. Conflict management is a more comprehensive idea than just a process for ending specific grievances. A third idea is that of integrating conflict management options and structures with each other, in the context of an overall human resource strategy.

A. System Development

My experience dealing with some hundreds of employers over twenty-five years suggests that most nonunion conflict management systems have developed structure by structure, in an ad hoc response to one or another concern, such as containing litigation costs, dealing fairly with diverse populations, or responding to a consent decree. Some employers, however, such as Federal Express, have taken from the beginning a relatively comprehensive "systems approach", and a few relatively complete systems are now emerging (such as that of Brown & Root discussed below). Whatever the history in a given workplace, I do not believe in ideal models. All the excellent systems that I know are evolving steadily and along somewhat different paths. Since different institutions have widely different missions, and operate within different legal environments and value systems, it seems reasonable to me that they have taken and will continue to follow different paths to systems that are custom-tailored.

B. Stakeholder Input

A major question with respect to systems design is how much input there should or will be from all the stakeholders of the given organization. Experts on labor relations and organizational development, observers concerned with the rights of respondents and those of complainants, and persons especially concerned with the rights of minority and women's groups, feel strongly about stakeholder input in the design phase. To build effectiveness and trust in a system, stakeholders should be asked first what they want and then be provided a structured means to give input into both design and continuous improvement. Design consultants offer structured plans for such input.[31]

It should be noted, however, that some important innovations in conflict management have occurred through the determined efforts of a CEO or other senior manager and even by what Walton, Cutcher-Gershenfeld, and McKersie might think of as "forcing" an innovation.[32] Paradoxically or not, some relatively thoughtful, integrated systems are being set up by using managerial power with relatively little input from employees and managers.

C. Begin with the Characteristics of Complainants

Whether a systems design comes from extensive stakeholder input, by fiat from above, or both, I believe, at a minimum, that certain characteristics of complainants, i.e., the initial "customers," must be considered in fashioning a system. This idea has not been sufficiently discussed in the literature, and it is not necessarily the same idea as "stakeholder input." Those who speak up about conflict management design are not necessarily those who will find themselves suddenly in need of a complaint system. This is especially true in a multicultural context. Many people who speak up about dispute resolution have thought mainly about the interests of employers, the rights of complainants or respondents, organizational development principles, or conflict resolution theory, all of which are important, and all of which contribute to the design of procedures people think complainants should want. But considering what complainants actually want, which is, if possible, to raise concerns *as they personally wish to raise them*, is critical to ensuring that a system is actually used.[33]

Probably the most common characteristic of people who have a concern or grievance is that they just wish their problem would go away—they "do not want any process." Many complainants are simultaneously uncomfortable about doing nothing, uncomfortable about taking any kind of action on their concerns, and angry if they feel they "either must do something or have to quit." In addition, most complainants disapprove of other options that easily come to mind, which employers also consider unconstructive, such as walking out, absenteeism, going slow, sabotage, agency complaints, legal suits, bitter gossip, anonymous attacks, and the like. In short, people with problems often feel that they have no options at all.

Why is constructive conflict difficult? One major reason is that most people in the United States still think first or only about formal grievance procedures although virtually every survey shows this option to be unwelcome to most people for most problems. There are, of course, some problems, such as criminal behavior, which require formal procedures. But there is a long list of reasons why most people do not wish to use formal grievance procedures for most kinds of complaints. People with concerns and complaints often fear loss of privacy and dignity with respect to family and relatives, supervisors, and coworkers. They may value the relationship they have with the person they see as the source of the problem, and other relationships they have inside and outside the workplace, and fear these relationships will be placed at risk if they file a grievance.[34] They often fear covert as well as overt reprisal from the employer, and dread criticism from family and from colleagues who may hear gossip about them. They fear being thought of as disloyal, lacking in humor, or a poor sport. "Token" professionals, including women, people of color, and anyone who is nontraditional in a traditional environment, may especially fear being seen as troublemakers rather than self-confident professionals. Many people also hate the idea of losing control over their concerns. (This issue appears especially true for professionals and managers.) Complainants may—rightly or wrongly—fear that they do not have enough evidence to prevail in an investigatory procedure. This fear is especially common regarding discrimination and other interpersonal problems. In addition, some people fear they will be criticized on free speech grounds if they complain in a formal grievance procedure about offensive communications.

Because most complainants "just want the problem to stop," they are often concerned that an adversarial option will result in punishment of the offender, rather than just fixing whatever is wrong. Complainants commonly fear that they do not have the skills to complain effectively. But many people dislike asking any third party for help, except maybe a friend, and many have very strong feelings about which third party they would or would not consider going to, if going to a third party is required by the employer. If the third party in a formal grievance process is not trusted, many complainants will not come forward at all. For all these reasons, a majority in the workplace will not choose and cannot be persuaded to file a formal grievance—even for such problems as civil rights violations which many people feel belong in a rights-based process.[35] If people with problems are to act in any constructive fashion, most of them must be provided with interest-based options designed with the wishes of complainants in mind.

On the other hand, a small number are satisfied only by a formal, rights-based, win-lose process. They typically wish to be able to move directly to file a grievance, and have it investigated, without prior, interest-based steps. They may not understand any option other than a formal grievance procedure, or they simply regard a rights-based option as the only just process. They may also have strong feelings about desirable elements in a rights-based procedure. Lewin has studied the wishes of complainants with respect to formal procedures. He identified their interest in an independent fact-finding procedure, in an impartial process, in obtaining feedback about grievance settlements, in protection from reprisal and from the disapproval of coworkers, in having several levels of appeal, and in having at least some outcomes favorable to those who file grievances.[36] If people oriented toward right and wrong are to be satisfied, they should be allowed in appropriate cases to move directly to a rights-based option designed with wishes of complainants in mind.

There are also a few people who present especially serious challenges for a fair dispute resolution system. They may deeply distrust other people, and may reject the idea of due process for people who are seen to be the source of problems. A few complainants want revenge. A few enjoy fights in and of themselves, and resist settling any dispute. Occasionally also a complainant brings a complaint for an ulterior reason, such as preventing a layoff or termination. In addition, a few people wish simply to disrupt the workplace. Rights- and power-based options are usually the most reasonable processes for these rare situations.

Many men and women who have a concern or grievance who say that they are unable to concentrate or think clearly, express fear that their work is deteriorating, and state that they do not know how to pursue a complaint. Systems should provide support for these complainants to find and use constructive options.

IV. Specifications for an Effective System

Building on many ideas raised in the literature, on my own experience, and the characteristics of complainants as I know them, I believe that an effective integrated conflict management system would include the following basic characteristics.

Values of the system: There is a general orientation toward conflict management that derives from the core values and human resource strategy of the organization. The orientation includes a commitment to fairness for everyone involved in a dispute and freedom from reprisal. The employer proscribes reprisal against any disputant, including supervisors who act in good faith, and including witnesses who speak up for any disputant. The strategies of fairness and freedom from reprisal are backed by top managers who hold themselves accountable, and are held accountable, for the success of the system. There is at least one powerful senior manager who embodies this commitment and understands the nature of conflict management. The employer presumes that the backbone of conflict management is not based primarily in staff offices such as human resources and the legal department, but is, rather, embedded in line management and team management. Preventing unnecessary problems through active listening and effective, respectful communications is seen as a major responsibility of line management and of members of teams. The importance of constructive questions and dissent is seen as a major part of "continuous improvement" of the organization and of teamwork.

Many options: A variety of interest-based and rights-based dispute resolution techniques are offered to employees and managers, and employed for the clients of the organization (e.g., visitors, students, patients, nursing home residents, vendors, policyholders, franchisees) as appropriate.[37] The interest-based options are usually available in parallel, rather than as sequential and required steps of a single procedure. With respect to the choice of options, the parties may in many cases agree to loop forward from an interest-based option to a rights-based option (or to a rights- and power-based option),[38] or loop back from a rights-based option to an interest-based option.[39] For most problems that are not of a criminal nature, these options are initially available to the complainant. This contrasts with previous approaches in which the complaint-handler chose how a problem would be handled in the nonunion environment, and with the single grievance procedure that was the usual option in a unionized environment. In the rights-based, formal grievance and appeal option there is an appeal mechanism that takes investigation or decision making, or both, out of the line of supervision. There are reasonable standards of conduct for formal investigations and decision making. Disputants have a right to be accompanied, though they may under ordinary circumstances be expected to represent themselves.

Multiple access points: People with concerns and problems can find access points of different ethnicity and gender, and varied technical backgrounds, to help them. These access points are people who have been trained to act as fair "gatekeepers" for the conflict management system. In a small company these might just be specially designated employees and managers. In a large firm, these would include professionals such as human resource managers, employee assistance providers, equal opportunity specialists, and occasionally religious counselors. They provide a degree of privacy and support for various options in the conflict management system. Access points also include specialized personnel in safety, security, environmental hazard, ethics, and audit departments. Some employers can provide 800 lines for people to talk, and seek advice, and provide information anonymously. All disputants may be accompanied, when using the system, by a colleague or coworker.

An organizational ombudsperson: There is, in addition, at least one ombudsperson, designated as a neutral, who is available to help informally with any workplace concern, and to provide formal mediation as appropriate.[40] In a small company one or several people may carry these responsibilities on a part-time basis. Ombudspeople report outside ordinary line and staff structures to the chief executive officer (CEO) or the chief operating officer (COO), or local plant manager. The ombudsperson maintains strict confidentiality, asserts a privilege to protect the confidentiality of his or her practice, and follows the Code of Ethics and Standards of Practice[41]of an ombudsman association.

Wide scope: The system is used by professionals and managers with concerns as well as by employees. The system takes virtually every kind of concern that is of interest to people in the organization. This includes, for example, disputes between coworkers and between fellow managers, teammates, and groups, as well as classic concerns about conditions of employment and termination. The system may also listen to recently fired employees, outsiders who feel badly treated by someone who works for the employer, anonymous complainants, and others as appropriate. The system can deal with multi-issue complaints.

Continuous improvement: An oversight committee is built into the system and meets regularly to improve the effectiveness of the system.

V. Options and Functions Needed in an Effective System

A. *Interest-based Options*

Interest-based options for "problem solving" attempt to address the real needs of the complainant, as distinguished from defining problems and their solutions solely in terms of legal rights. Options of this sort can provide several advantages to the complainant. For example, an effective, direct approach from a complainant to a respondent may lower the likelihood of reprisal, offer freedom for the complainant from the demands of evidence, and offer more control over, and greater comfort with, the process of problem resolution. Interest-based options can be prompt and swift. For example, some options can be pursued by the complainant or offered by line managers on the spot. Interest-based options also are particularly appropriate for dealing with offensive communication.

Listening: An important option that a person may choose is just to talk, and for the line manager, ombudsperson, or other resource person to listen, in an active and supportive fashion. The manager or resource person may affirm the feelings of the individual but should be impartial with respect to the facts of a situation unless or until the facts are known. In many cases, "being listened to" is what a person with a problem wants and needs. Listening and being gently questioned may help put a problem into perspective. It may help a person to deal with rage or grief or uncertainty or fear. It may help people deal with stress so they can take the time that they need to figure out what is happening to them or what the problem actually is. This option is probably the most cost-effective element of a conflict management system, both for people with concerns and for employers, although ironically it is the option most often overlooked. Still some employers such as the Internal Revenue Service, the Royal Canadian Mounted Police, and Brown & Root are attempting to teach listening skills to hundreds or thousands of supervisors.

Giving and receiving information: A person often needs information on a one-to-one basis. A manager, ombudsperson, or 800 line might provide a copy of a policy or obtain clarification of the meaning of a policy, so a person under stress does not need to search or read dozens of pages of a manual. The resource person usually can provide or find information that resolves a problem in one or two contacts. A manager, ombudsperson, or 800 line may also be *given* information about a problem in the workplace such as a safety issue, evidence about a theft, harassment or potential violence, or about equipment that needs repair. A team may be offered suggestions for improvement from a teammate who perceives a problem. These data may be offered anonymously, or surfaced in a quiet way, for fair handling by appropriate persons. Again, despite what I believe is the cost-effectiveness of this option, too many systems do not make explicit provision for giving and receiving information on a one-to-one basis.

Reframing issues and developing options: A manager, ombudsperson, or other resource person can often help a caller or complainant develop their own ideas about options they find acceptable for settling a conflict. As we have seen, many people believe they have no options or only bad ones. The supervisor or resource person may help frame or reframe the issues, identify or develop new and different perspectives, and describe additional, responsible and effective paths from which the caller or complainant may choose. This function is often especially useful to managers who have a problem and are seeking help. This option also is quite useful where complainants will ultimately choose to file a formal grievance but need time, information, and support to decide to do so. This option must be relatively private, so managers must be taught not to act precipitously when they hear of a problem that is not an emergency. Furthermore, for some people to be willing to use this option, it must be totally off the record, which means providing an ombudsperson.

Referral: Many disputants and complainants need more than one helping resource—in effect, a helping network. Some need the help of a person such as an employee assistance professional or a colleague who can accompany them in raising a concern. Every manager and resource person should know the other workplace resources available for people with problems, both to refer disputants and complainants to others, and to work effectively together with others on behalf of a person with a problem, when given permission to do so. The need for this function makes it imperative to integrate all the elements and resource persons in a conflict management system.

Helping people help themselves in a direct approach: An ombudsperson or other resource person, manager, or teammate may help someone with a problem to deal directly with the perceived source of a problem. Through discussion, support, and role-playing, a person with a concern may develop the skills and self-confidence to work on an issue without third-party intervention. When experts speak of "delegating disputes to the lowest possible level," this is the option on which they primarily should focus rather than on forms of third-party intervention. This is also an option to foster in the workplace for development of "individual accountability." In some cultures, however, the direct approach, or particular versions of the direct approach, may not be considered appropriate. Consequently, a sensitivity to cultural differences is important when discussing options.

This option includes A (the complainant) choosing to deal directly with B (the apparent offender or the perceived source of a problem) in any of several ways. A could choose to write a private note or letter to B, laying out the facts as A sees them, A's feelings about these facts, and the remedies proposed by A. Alternatively, A could choose to go talk directly with B, with or without presentation of a note or letter. A may decide to go back to B alone, or accompanied by a friend or colleague. It is possible that A will need to be taught or at least given some guidance on how to write a letter to or talk with B in the most effective way. If a manager or resource person knows that a direct approach is being chosen, he or she should typically follow up with A to find out if the situation is resolved and to check on any evidence of reprisal.

Shuttle diplomacy: A person with a concern may choose to ask a third party to be a shuttle diplomat, who will go back and forth between A and B or bring A and B together informally to resolve the problem. The third party could be a line supervisor, a human resource officer, an ombudsperson, or other staff member. Alternatively, a complainant might choose to ask a team-mate, uninvolved colleague, or other appropriate person to intervene. It is important in this approach that there should be no formal disciplinary action taken by a third party without a process that is fair to the alleged offender. For example, moving someone or reassigning duties[42] is not usually defined as disciplinary action where these are customary management responsibilities, but a formal letter of reprimand would be so defined. If possible, the person who was the go-between should follow up afterward, to see if the problem is resolved and to check about possible reprisal.

"Looking into" the problem informally: Most problems, especially if they are caught early, do not require a formal investigation. There are at least two kinds of informal data gathering that may be done by third parties, one by ombudspeople and another by line managers, administrative officers, human resource managers, and other appropriate staff. Assistance from an ombudsperson (except classic mediation as described below) is informal. Line managers, and staff people such as administrative officers and human resource managers, may look into a problem informally, but also may make management decisions as a result.

The role of an ombudsperson is different from that of a formal fact-finder (whose investigation becomes part of a case record and part of the decision making process for the employer), and from that of an arbitrator (whose decisions typically are binding on the parties to a grievance—see rights-based options below). Most U.S. organizational ombudspeople look into problems informally and typically keep no case records for the employer. They usually will report findings directly to the person that came to see them or, with permission, to a relevant manager, or the findings become part of the work of shuttle diplomacy by the ombudsperson. In many such cases the ombudsperson serves the purpose of providing informal neutral fact-finding and informal "early neutral evaluation" so the disputants can get an idea of what a peer review board or an outside arbitrator or judge might think if the problem went to formal grievance or to court. If the informal findings of an ombudsperson indicate the need for formal investigation, for example by line management, the audit department, ethics office, safety office, or security department, typically the ombudsperson will try hard to get permission to turn the matter over to the appropriate formal fact-finder.

A few organizational ombudspeople, especially in Canada, may agree to look into a problem on a fairly exhaustive basis and write a report including the ombudsperson's opinion of right and wrong. This action is typically at the request of someone in the organization other than the employer, and is typically not for disciplinary purposes.[43] The findings of an ombudsperson may be accepted in whole or in part, or ignored or rejected by the employer since the findings are not binding.

Classic formal mediation: Classic mediation is the only formal, interest-based option. This option is offered by employers in many organizations. In classic mediation, A and B are helped by an organizational ombudsperson, or another professional (neutral) mediator, to find their own settlement, in a process that is rather formal and has a well-defined structure. A and B may meet with each other and the mediator, or may deal with each other indirectly, with the mediator going back and forth between them. Classic mediation is purely voluntary for A and B and for the mediator. This option must therefore be chosen by both disputants, and agreed to by the mediator, if it is to occur. Settlements often are put into writing, and may be on or off the record as the parties may decide. Classic mediation, as offered by an inside neutral such as an ombudsperson, frequently results in off the record settlements and is therefore a private way to settle delicate issues when that is the wish of the parties. Classic mediation offered to the employer by outside neutrals may result in settlements kept by the employer if the employer is one of the parties, or as a condition of the settlement.

Formal mediation is still chosen infrequently, but is becoming somewhat more common. Some employers offer mediation only for certain issues such as termination, and a few only after termination has occurred. Some employers have ombudspeople or other specialists with training and expertise in intergroup and intragroup mediation and conflict management.[44] These specialists work with small or large groups, or may be called to advise managers who are interested in mediation techniques for managing dissent and disputes within and between groups. Some such specialists are called upon to train or support the work of self-managed teams.

Some employers are now offering a service called "mediation" by selected managers or in-house counsel who are not designated as neutrals or trained in the code of ethics and standards of practice of ombudspeople and mediators. This kind of dispute resolution can, at best, be likened to good shuttle diplomacy (see above). It should not be called mediation, or thought of as classic mediation by a neutral, and could not easily be shielded by a mediator's privilege if the dispute should go to court.

Generic approaches: A complainant may choose a generic approach aimed at changing a process in the workplace or alerting possible offenders to stop inappropriate behavior so the alleged specific problem disappears without the direct involvement of the complainant. For example, an ombudsperson might be given permission to approach a department head about a given problem without using any names. The department head might then choose to distribute and discuss copies of the appropriate employer policy, for instance to stop supervisors from requiring uncompensated overtime from nonexempt staff. Likewise, a department head might encourage safety training or harassment training, to stop and prevent the alleged inappropriate behavior. Generic approaches may be effective in stopping a specific offender and may prevent similar problems. The ombudsperson or other go-between should follow up to be sure that the complainant believes the specific problem has ended and that there have been no repercussions. Generic approaches offer the advantage that they typically do not affect the privacy or other rights of anyone in the organization.

Systems change: People with concerns often simply wish to suggest a change of policy, procedure, or structure in an organization, to recommend reorientation of a team project, or to start an orderly process of dealing with a policy, group, or a department seen to be a problem.[45] Such people may take a direct approach (as above) to try to change matters, may bring issues to relevant supervisors or complaint-handlers such as human resource officers or ombudspeople,[46] or they may make suggestions on anonymous employee surveys or on an 800 line. This is especially important for problems that are new to the organization. Those who supervise the complaint system should be on the lookout for new problems and for any pattern of problems that would suggest the need for a new policy, procedure, structure, or training program in the organization.

Training and prevention: The employer should, if possible, maintain ongoing training programs to teach the skills of teamwork, conflict management, and dispute resolution and to teach about specific topics such as diversity, ethics, safety, etc. The employer should ensure that supervisors know the principles of interest-based and rights-based dispute resolution. The employer should provide training that fosters individual responsibility and accountability at all levels. For most problems people should be encouraged to deal with problems directly and to help others to help themselves in a responsible and effective fashion.[47] A company with many teams might focus on management of conflict within self-managed teams. Many workplace disputes arise because of imperfect communication about rules and expectations, disagreements about performance, and interpersonal and diversity tensions. All supervisors should learn active listening, should know the policies and rules of the organization, and should know how to get authoritative advice when needed. Wherever possible, supervisors should be trained in setting performance standards and in performance evaluation, with explicit responsibility to recognize good performance and poor performance.

This training must also include issues of dissent and reprisal.[48] Preventing reprisal is, I think, the most important and most difficult issue for training. Retaliation stifles good communication and in many employment situations, including civil rights cases, retaliation is illegal. Differentiating constructive from unconstructive dissent is not easy. Those whose ideas are not accepted may feel in any workplace that they are meeting retaliation. Four different groups need training about raising questions, about disagreeing and about complaining: potential complainants, potential respondents, potential bystanders, and supervisors. The employer should specifically teach people how to raise a question or a complaint, what to do if one is the subject or recipient of a concern or complaint, and what to do if one is a bystander. The employer should train its supervisors and employees that it is not acceptable to punish someone who has raised or responded to a concern in good faith in an orderly manner. Complaint-handlers should be required to plan and take reasonable action to prevent reprisal and then follow up to see that they have been successful. The basic tasks for those who handle specific complaints are twofold: to deal fairly with the disputants, and to prevent reprisal for raising a complaint or concern in good faith.

Following through: Often a resource person or supervisor will undertake some action as requested by a person with a concern. In other cases a complainant will decide after consultation to act directly. Complaint-handlers can "follow through" on the problems brought to them in many different ways. For example, a manager might simply ask the complainant to call back, or follow up on administrative action to see that it was effective. A manager might listen for evidence of reprisal or might follow up months later with a complainant to see that all is well.

A custom approach: Where none of the options above seem exactly right, a person with a concern or complaint may ask for or need unusual help. A typical example would be action with a long or short time lag that is appropriate to the situation. If all options temporarily seem inappropriate, an ombudsperson or other resource person or manager can sometimes simply continue to look for a responsible approach that is tailor-made for a particular situation.

B. Rights-based Options

Disciplinary action and adverse administrative action against a respondent require a fair investigatory and decision making process. Definitions of appropriate process differ.[49] I think a fair internal process should include notice to the alleged offender, a reasonable opportunity for that person to respond to complaints and evidence against him or her, a chance to offer his or her own evidence, reasonable timeliness, impartiality of investigation and decision making and freedom from arbitrariness and capriciousness, the possibility of appeal, and the right of accompaniment by a colleague or coworker. The employer should have explicit rules about maintaining privacy in complaint handling. The employer should, if possible, provide for follow-up monitoring on each case settled formally, to check if the problem has been resolved and that there is no reprisal against any disputant or witness.

Investigation and adjudication and formal appeals: A supervisor, department head, personnel officer, formal fact-finder, or other appropriate staff person may investigate and/or adjudicate a concern in a formal fashion, or deal with an appeal in a formal grievance channel. Final appeal may be to a senior manager or to the CEO. Best practice in my opinion requires separation of fact finding from decision making in serious cases, and the possibility of appeal to a person or structure that is outside the relevant line of supervision. This avoids real and perceived conflicts of interest.

The best-known internal structures[50] include peer review, an off-line board of appeals that includes peers, or an off-line senior manager who makes a final decision. Peer or board review structures may act with power or, alternatively, result in a recommendation to a senior decision-maker, who typically honors the peer or board findings. I believe that complainants and respondents should be able to strike names, and/or choose the peers who will judge them from rosters maintained by the employer.

Other possibilities for formal action include inside and outside fact-finders. They may report to an internal decision maker or may offer an advisory opinion to the parties about how an arbitrator might decide the matter if it were to go to arbitration. Combinations of options also occur. For example, a peer review system may be coordinated by an ombudsperson who is empowered to offer mediation as a final step before the peer review panel meets. An outside neutral fact-finder might offer the results of investigation to the disputants, and then function, if asked, as a formal mediator between the parties.

Some employers are offering a rights-based option provided by outside neutrals as the last step in the employer's complaint procedure. Some employers require arbitration as the last step, as a condition of employment, for all complaints including statutory rights complaints. As noted earlier, many observers find this requirement to be wrong.[51] There is also much discussion about appropriate elements of due process for formal investigation and adjudication outside the workplace. Some observers[52] believe that the due process expectations for arbitration should include the right of counsel for the complainant, part or all of the costs of counsel,[53] and a chance to help choose the neutral.

Some organizations have their own security or sworn police force. This department may offer an option for emergencies based on both rights and power. A complainant who fears for her or his safety, for example, may approach a police or security officer at the workplace to ask that someone be called in—for discussion, for a warning, for investigation, or for other appropriate action. Some workplace police and security departments will support complainants in a request for a restraining order or for enforcement of a trespassing order. Except for emergency action, workplace security and police departments ordinarily coordinate with the employer's customary dispute resolution options.

C. Monitoring, Evaluation, and Oversight

The employer should provide for data collection and evaluation of the system. The statistical information provided should be used in a way that supports continuous improvement of the system and appropriately protects the privacy of individuals. Each organization needs to decide how to evaluate effectiveness; I will state a few of my own ideas. I believe that the most important element of evaluation is to ensure that the system is actually used by a wide cross section of men and women in all pay classifications and of roughly the demographic profile of the organization, since this is the best indicator that a program is trusted. The system should be used for all the problems that people in the organization think are important. It should be perceived as credible and fair by the various stakeholders. The system should produce demonstrable change and improvement in the organization, and it should save money.

In my opinion, the system should be overseen by a group rather than by one manager, except in very small organizations. In large firms there should be a specialized group in each major operating unit, including, for example, appropriate persons from senior line management, human resources, security, medical department, employee assistance, equal opportunity, religious counselors, ombudspeople, legal counselors, and those responsible for functions that generate much conflict, such as personnel transfers or housing. The oversight group should meet on a regular basis, at least monthly. It should talk regularly about difficult and dangerous cases and link the complaint system to other systems inside and outside the operating unit and to the local community as appropriate. In many organizations this will be the group that will receive comments from users, monitor, report on, and work to improve the system on a continuous basis.

VI. Overview of the Brown & Root Dispute Resolution Program

I know of no employer that has an integrated conflict management system with all the features that I have described in this chapter. There are, however, hundreds of employers adopting a subset of the innovations described here, and many that are evolving toward a comprehensive system. A well-known case in point is the dispute resolution program (DRP) of Brown & Root, a large, international, nonunion construction firm. The DRP began in June 1993 and covers only its domestic operations. The program began with focus group input from employees and managers of the company. It is, however, largely the brainchild of a creative associate general counsel, William Bedman,[54] and of an experienced consulting group, Chorda Conflict Management, of Austin, Texas.

The Brown & Root DRP is founded on principles of fairness and freedom from retaliation. It is overseen by committed and knowledgeable senior managers. It provides options both inside and outside the company. Internal options include listening, referral, discussion of options, informal fact-finding, shuttle diplomacy and mediation inside the company for any type of workplace problem. Four levels of options are presented in a clearly written booklet given to all employees. At level one there are parallel interest-based options. One is an open door policy within the line of supervision. Front-line supervisors are being trained in listening skills and conflict management, and the company plans to continue indefinitely to train supervisors in conflict management skills. Retaliation is forbidden (and at least one manager who was found to retaliate has been fired). A complainant may talk any time with the Personnel Office of the given business unit, or with Corporate Employee Relations or other specialized offices as appropriate. A complainant may also call off the record, either anonymously or with all the identifying details of a case, to an employee hotline staffed by advisers.

At level two, any unresolved problem may be brought to the DRP administrator who can arrange dispute resolution conferences. In the usual case, various options will be explored, including informal mediation by one of a number of trained, internal neutrals. In appropriate cases the DRP specifically allows for loops forward (for example, to arbitration) or loops back (for example, to in-house mediation), as complainants review their options. The lead professional in the DRP office is an experienced mediator who reports to a human resources manager but is designated as a neutral. She serves the program as an ombudsperson and practices as far as possible to the Standards of Practice of the Ombudsman Association.

At levels three and four, complaints about legally protected rights may be taken outside the company to mediation or arbitration at the request of the complainant. For legally protected rights, the administrator can arrange, if needed, for some reimbursement of legal consultation for the complainant. In the usual case the company pays most of the costs of legal consultation, up to $2,500. Imposed arbitration is a condition of employment for disputes that might otherwise go to court, although anyone at Brown & Root is free to consult with or appeal to any relevant government regulatory body. Arbitrators are empowered to provide any award that might be sought through the court system. They are assigned through private justice providers.

Statistics are not kept about use of the system at level one. The program advisers and administrators deal with about 500 cases a year, and 1 or 2 percent go to arbitration. (Brown & Root has lost and won cases—an out-come that I feel speaks well for the DRP.) A few employees have appealed to one or another government agency. Concerns that go to an adviser or administrator are monitored internally by the program office to be sure that they are addressed promptly; about 70 percent are resolved within one month. The program office also serves the company by keeping statistical data about problems brought to the advisers and program administrators. Program administrators may recommend systems change in the company and there have been a number of changes because of information brought forward to the DRP. The company reports that its legal expenses are sharply reduced. The company has commissioned several evaluations of the system.

I have some concerns about the design. I believe that an organizational ombudsperson should be designated as such and should report to the CEO or COO rather than to human resources; the position should stand apart from ordinary lines of supervision. I would have recommended much stronger emphasis at the program office level on helping people with problems help themselves. There should perhaps be more training for supervisors and employees on this option, and also further development within the program of the use of generic options. I might have recommended building in more capacity to deal with group conflict, and a stronger emphasis on serving managers with problems as well as employees. I prefer to see the possibility for disputants to have some input into the choice of an outside neutral. The usage rate is somewhat low, compared with other programs I have surveyed. I would like to see the program collect data on use of the system at level one, so the overall usage rate can be better assessed. I strongly recommend against requiring imposed arbitration as a condition of employment and hope that the DRP will change in this respect.

On the other hand, the DRP has great strengths. It reflects the interests of at least some stakeholders since management feels the DRP "fits" its environment. The DRP can be seen as a simple, easily understood, cost-effective program. It is a multiaccess, multioption system with an unusual degree of integration. In most respects it meets the specifications for a system discussed above. It is important that within the imposed arbitration structure there is affirmation for the rights of employees and managers to appeal to government regulatory bodies, for example on civil rights cases. It is also important that when people have in fact appealed outside the company, Brown & Root has cooperated with the agency involved and has sought to settle cases rather than push the issue of imposed arbitration. The program provides a high degree of flexibility both for people with problems and for management. The excellent emphasis on training of all supervisors provides a powerful scaffolding for the success of the program. Brown & Root has been open about its program, and has provided a great deal of information to many outsiders. The DRP is under constant scrutiny from inside and outside, which provides a strong basis for continuous improvement.

VII. Suggestions for Future Research

Workplace dispute resolution in the nonunion sector of North America is changing swiftly. There are many reasons for nonunion employers to be innovating in this area, and their innovations are varied. Some employers are experimenting with a systems approach to conflict management that goes far beyond a single grievance procedure. A systems focus represents an important, user-oriented improvement in conflict management that gives complainants greater flexibility and more options, particularly at the early stages of a conflict.

Research as to the effectiveness of specific innovations, and of a systems approach, is very much needed. For example, we need to know more about options people would choose under conditions of choice, and then how they would evaluate the choices they have made. We also need to know how respondents and supervisors and top management assess each option. This information would be most helpful if we had data for men and women, people of various ethnic backgrounds, managers as well as employees, people in teams and those working in hierarchies, those in small establishments and large, local establishments and multinational companies, organizations with a very strong culture and those that appear impersonal, stable establishments and those with high turnover, and for organizations with different workforce characteristics.[55] We know almost nothing about small informal systems in small companies and how people perceive them. We know little about the integration of internal systems with the external environment—for example, about the impact of different state laws.

It is not easy to address these questions. It would make sense to continue building a widely understood glossary of terms, and then continue to build a taxonomy of conflict management characteristics and functions, as I have tried to do here—of "specifications" for effective conflict management systems. Using such a taxonomy one may then see which structures appear in which kinds of organizations, describe them, and then evaluate them. Simultaneously we need to work on developing appropriate evaluation protocols. Case studies with respect to any of these questions will contribute greatly.

Notes

1.   Alternative—or appropriate—dispute resolution (ADR) means different things to different people. In the widest, technical sense I prefer to use the term to describe any kind of mechanism inside or outside a workplace that seeks to settle problems primarily on the basis of the *interests* of the disputants rather than on the basis of rights and power. In the United States in the 1990s, however, the word has largely been taken over by lawyers to describe narrowly based efforts to deal with commercial and employment disputes that are not being settled among the disputants and are otherwise on their way to the courts. I view this development as unfortunate since many people have come to understand ADR only in terms of specialized mechanisms at the edge of the workplace rather than as "appropriate dispute resolution"—the foundation of systems design that includes many kinds of options within a workplace.

2.   See for example an article by H. A. Simon and Y. Sochynsky, "In-House Mediation of Employment Disputes: ADR for the 1990's." *Employee Relations Law Journal* 21, no. 1 (summer 1995): 29–51, which used the title term "mediation" to refer to an extraordinary spectrum of informal and formal, interest-based and rights-based dispute resolution techniques inside and outside the workplace.

3.   J. Delaney, D. Lewin and C. Ichniowski, "Human Resource Policies and Practices in American Firms." *Bureau of Labor-Management Relations*, no. 137, 1989.

4.   U.S. General Accounting Office, *Employment Discrimination,* Report HEHS–95–150 (July 1995), 3; and Organizational Resources Counselors, Inc., "Preliminary Results of an ORC Survey on the use of ADR in Employment Related Disputes," Unpublished paper, November 1994.

5.   A good contemporary overview of these concerns may be found in R. Edwards, *Rights at Work* (New York: The Twentieth Century Fund, 1993). See also L. B. Edelman, H. S. Erlanger and J. Lande, "Internal Dispute Resolution: The Transformation of Civil Rights in the Workplace," *Law and Society Review* 27, no. 3 (1993): 497–534.

6.   D. H. Lach and P. A. Gwartney-Gibbs, "Sociological Perspectives on Sexual Harassment and Workplace Dispute Resolution," *Journal of Vocational Behavior* 42 (1993): 102–15; P. A. Gwartney-Gibbs and D. H. Lach, "Workplace Dispute Resolution and Gender Inequality," *Negotiation Journal* 7, no. 2 (April 1991): 187–200; and P. A. Gwartney-Gibbs and D. H. Lach, "Sociological Explanations for Failure to Seek Sexual Harassment Remedies," *Mediation Quarterly* 9, no. 4 (summer 1992): 365–73, for detailed discussion of the differential needs of women complainants. See also M. P. Rowe, "The Case of the Valuable Vendors, Subtle Discrimination as a Management Problem," *Harvard Business Review* 56, no. 5 (September - October 1978): 40–47,

and M. P. Rowe, "Dealing With Sexual Harassment," *Harvard Business Review* 59, no. 3 (May–June 1981): 42–47.

7.   M. P. Rowe, "People Who Feel Harassed Need a Complaint System with Both Formal and Informal Options," *Negotiation Journal* 6, no. 2 (April 1990): 161–72; and M. P. Rowe, "Options and Choice for Conflict Resolution in the Workplace," in *Negotiation: Strategies for Mutual Gain*, ed. L. Hall (Thousand Oaks, Calif.: Sage Publications, Inc., 1993), 105–19.

8.   I use the term complainant throughout this chapter to mean someone who perceives a problem, or who wishes to complain.

9.   I have been an organizational ombudsperson for twenty-five years and also teach negotiation and conflict management at the MIT Sloan School of Management. My own perspective is therefore that of a practitioner who has dealt with many thousands of persons involved in disputes, and from being a professor of negotiation.

10.   D. W. Ewing, *Justice on the Job* (Boston: Harvard Business School Press, 1989).

11.   See for example, D. M. McCabe and D. Lewin, "Employee Voice: A Human Resource Management Perspective," *California Management Review* (spring 1992): 112–23, who cite union avoidance as a major reason for the rise of nonunion grievance procedures.

12.   Many authors cite the statutory establishment of individual rights, such as laws which prohibit discrimination and harassment, regulate safety, pension plans, plant closings, and family and medical leaves, as major incentives toward the establishment of complaint systems. Courts have also expanded restrictions on wrongful dismissal, for example, discharge contrary to public policy, discharge which violates the concept of good faith and fair dealing or which is contrary to an implied contract such as an employee handbook. Some regulations, such as the Federal Sentencing Guidelines, also strongly encourage the establishment of complaint mechanisms. Some regulations which prohibit discrimination require complaint mechanisms.

13.   A. F. Westin and A. G. Feliu, "Resolving Employment Disputes Without Litigation" (Washington, D. C.: Bureau of National Affairs, 1988).

14.   W. L. Bedman, "From Litigation to ADR: Brown & Root's Experience," *Dispute Resolution Journal* 50, no. 4 (October–December 1995): 8–15. The other articles in this issue on employment ADR are also instructive.

15.   J. T. Ziegenfuss, *Organizational Troubleshooters* (San Francisco: Jossey-Bass, 1989).

16.   R. R. Blake and J. Srygley Mouton, *Solving Costly Organizational Conflicts* (San Francisco: Jossey-Bass, 1985).

17.   D. M. McCabe, *Corporate Non-union Complaint Procedures and Systems* (New York: Praeger Publishers, 1988).

18.   W. L. Ury, J. M. Brett, and S. B. Goldberg, *Getting Disputes Resolved* (San Francisco: Jossey-Bass, 1988). J. M. Brett, S. B. Goldberg, and W. L. Ury, "Resolving Disputes: The Strategy of Dispute Resolution Systems Design," *Business Week*, Executive Briefing Service 6 (New York: McGraw Hill, 1994).

19.   Brett, Goldberg, and Ury, "Resolving Disputes."

20.   Edwards, *Rights at Work.*

21.   See for example, D. Lewin, "Grievance Procedures in Nonunion Workplaces: An Empirical Analysis of Usage, Dynamics and Outcomes," *Chicago-Kent Law Review* 66, no. 817 (1990): 823–44, and D. M. McCabe, and D. Lewin, "Employee Voice: A Human Resource Management Perspective," *California Management Review* (spring 1992): 112–23.

22.   Edelman, Ehrlanger and Lande, "Internal Dispute Resolution: The Transformation of Civil Rights in the Workplace." Also see McCabe and Lewin, "Employee Voice." This article expresses extensive concern that in the process of meeting management interests such as peace in the workplace, appearing to conform to civil rights law and regulation, and avoiding lawsuits, the civil rights of employees are actually subsumed and are likely to be undermined.

23.   Significant differences in perspectives on ADR exist between some externally-oriented lawyers and some conflict managers internal to organizations. The concept of ADR, that is, *alternative* dispute resolution, prevalent among lawyers and arbitrators usually refers to processes that lie at the edge or outside the workplace, such as external mediation and arbitration. Some of these processes require the assistance of lawyers. The perspective of those who are generally unfamiliar with internal dispute resolution methods is in marked contrast with that of internal conflict management specialists. DR specialists *internal* to the workplace typically think of ADR as *appropriate* dispute resolution: a broad and varied set of options for dispute resolution that can be used both inside and outside the workplace.

24.   Note the Center for Public Resources Institute for Dispute Resolution, *Model ADR Procedures and Practices,* 1995. The final draft (July), recommends in section one that mediation and arbitration procedures might be added onto an internal system that provides a variety of internal mechanisms.

25.   See L. J. Marcus, *Renegotiating Health Care: Resolving Conflict to Build Collaboration* (San Francisco: Jossey-Bass, 1995), and K. A. Slaikeu, "Designing

Dispute Resolution Systems in the Health Care Industry," *Negotiation Journal* 5, no. 4 (October 1989): 395–400.

26. C. A. Costantino and C. Sickles Merchant, *Designing Conflict Management Systems* (San Francisco: Jossey Bass, 1996).

27. M. P. Rowe and M. Baker, "Are You Hearing Enough Employee Concerns?" *Harvard Business Review* 62, no. 3 (May–June 1984): 127–36; M. P. Rowe, "The Non-Union Complaint System at MIT: An Upward-Feedback Mediation Model," in *Resolving Employment Disputes Without Litigation,* eds. A. Westin and A. Feliu (Washington, D.C.: Bureau of National Affairs, 1988); M. P. Rowe, "Organizational Response to Assessed Risk: A Systems Approach to Complaints," in *Program Record of the 1988 Institute of Electrical and Electronics Engineers, Inc. Electro 1988 Conference, Risk Assessment and Response* (Boston, IEEE, Inc., 1988); M. P. Rowe, "The Post-Tailhook Navy Designs an Integrated Dispute Resolution System," *Negotiation Journal* 9, no. 3 (July 1993): 203–13.

28. In my first year at MIT, working together with others, I compiled a list of hundreds of concerns expressed by women, by people of color, and by white males. Many concerns affected white males, who in addition brought forward concerns of their own, but some problems appeared especially to affect the nontraditional members of the community. See also P. A. Gwartney-Gibbs and D. H. Lach, "Workplace Dispute Resolution and Gender Inequality," *Negotiation Journal* 7, no. 2 (April 1991): 187–200, and Lewin, "Grievance Procedures in Nonunion Workplaces." I found that some concerns of women and minorities, such as subtle discrimination, did not lend themselves to traditional formal grievance procedures. Furthermore, some people simply did not like formal grievance procedures. These findings led to consideration of new options for complainants. See M. P. Rowe, "Barriers to Equality: the Power of Subtle Discrimination to Maintain Unequal Opportunity," *Employee Responsibilities and Rights Journal* 3, no. 2 (1990): 153–63, and M. P. Rowe, "Helping People Help Themselves: an Option for Complaint Handlers" *Negotiation Journal* 6, no. 3 (July 1990): 239–48.

29. For most problems in the present day MIT, where having a choice of dispute resolution options is the norm for everyone (for problems that are not illegal in nature), most men and women want to discuss their options at length. Many complainants demonstrate in conversation that their choice of option depends on an assessment of the characteristics of the immediate problem and situation, the setting, the supervisor and the respon-dent, and their own personal preferences in dispute resolution.

30. The word redundancy has an unfortunate connotation in general speech but among engineers it is an important concept. If an engineering system is important, it needs backup, checks and balances, and devices for fail-safe op-

eration. By extension, if a person has a serious problem or complaint, there may be a need not just for one option but for several.

31. See for example, C. Moore, "Dispute Resolution Systems Design" (*Resource Manual*) (Boulder, Colo.: CDR Associates, 1995); the work of K. Slaikeu and R. Hasson of Chorda Associates in Austin, Texas; and Costantino and Merchant, *Designing Conflict Management Systems*.

32. See R. E. Walton, J. E. Cutcher-Gershenfeld, and R. B. McKersie, *Strategic Negotiations* (Boston: Harvard Business School Press, 1994).

33. Except as noted, this list comes from analysis of many hundreds of concerns a year over the past twenty-five years in my office as an ombudsperson. See Rowe, "People Who Feel Harassed."

34. The fear of loss of relationships might be, at an extreme, defined as a fear of reprisal. But this concern goes far beyond what is ordinarily meant by reprisal. It includes an interest in harmony, in team spirit, in humor, and fellow feeling in the workplace. It also includes a very common fear of disapproval from family and friends and colleagues outside the workplace. It is commonly thought that fear of loss of relationships is felt most strongly by men and women of certain ethnic backgrounds, and by white women. See for example, the remarkable article by S. Riger, "Gender Dilemmas in Sexual Harassment Policies and Procedures," *American Psychologist* 46 (1991): 497–505. However I frequently hear the same concern from white males, though sometimes cast in different terms.

35. See S. E. Gleason, "The Decision to File a Sex Discrimination Complaint in the Federal Government," *Proceedings of the 36th Annual Meeting of the Industrial Relations Research Association* (San Francisco, Industrial Relations Research Association 1983), 189–97, for a sensitive evaluation of the intangible as well as tangible costs to women for using a formal procedure.

36. Lewin, "Grievence Procedures in Nonunion Workplaces," 831.

37. Customers, vendors, and employers entering into partnering relationships are outside the scope of this paper, but it is of interest that the same kinds of innovations in conflict management have entered these relationships. See for example Brett, Goldberg, and Ury, "Resolving Disputes."

38. An example would be where someone has repeatedly asked a coworker to end offensive behavior, then despairs of classic mediation, and decides to make a formal complaint.

39. See Ury, Brett, and Goldberg, "Resolving Disputes," who originally proposed the term *loopback*, to refer to a shift from a rights-based to an interest-

based option. An example would be to shift from a formal, win-lose grievance procedure to formal mediation.

40. M. P. Rowe, "The Corporate Ombudsman: An Overview and Analysis," *Negotiation Journal* 3, no. 2 (April 1987): 127–40; M. P. Rowe, "The Ombudsman's Role in a Dispute Resolution System," *Negotiation Journal* 7, no. 4 (October 1991): 353–61; M. P. Rowe and J. T. Ziegenfuss, "Corporate Ombudsmen: Functions, Caseloads, Successes and Problems," *Journal of Health and Human Resources Administration* 15, no.3 (winter 1993): 261–80; M. P. Rowe and J. T. Ziegenfuss, G. Hall, A. Perneski, and M. Lux, "Perspectives on Costs and Cost Effectiveness of Ombudsman Programs in Four Fields," *Journal of Health and Human Resources Administration* 15, no. 3 (winter 1993): 281–312; M. P. Rowe, "An Overview of Client and Internal Ombudsmen," *Journal of Health and Human Resources Administration* 15, no. 3 (winter 1993): 259–60; M. P. Rowe, "Options, Functions and Skills: What an Organizational Ombudsperson Might Want to Know," *Negotiation Journal* 11, no. 2 (April 1995):103–14.

41. In many organizations, human resource managers and equal opportunity specialists work hard to maintain privacy. However, Human Resources and Equal Employment Opportunity managers are also compliance officers and therefore cannot offer a high degree of confidentiality to complainants. See, for example, the important concern expressed on this point by Edelman, Erlanger, and Lande, "Internal Dispute Resolution." In some organizations Employee Assistance Program and other health care practitioners may be also required to keep records and/or may be subpoenaed in cases that go outside the workplace. Ombudspeople, by contrast, typically keep no records for the employer. Contrary to the widespread misunderstanding of many writers, organizational ombudspeople are not adjudicators or formal investigators. They typically refuse to testify in any formal proceeding in or out of the workplace, for the employer or for anyone else. The several thousand organizational ombudspeople in North America are conflict management professionals, designated as neutrals, who have all the functions of any complaint handler except that of formal investigation and adjudication. They offer confidentiality under all but potentially catastrophic circumstances. See also C. L. Howard and M. A. Gulluni, *The Ombuds Confidentiality Privilege* (Dallas: The Ombudsman Association, 1996).

The survey by Organizational Resources Counselors, Inc., of New York City, *op. cit.*, found the most popular nonunion dispute resolution devices in a group of forty-five companies were an ombudsman office and a peer review system. Unpublished testimony submitted to the Commission of the Future of Worker-Management Relations, (Dunlop Commission), 1994.

42. Although job assignments are typically not considered disciplinary action, an employer should carefully consider the fairness of moving a complainant or respondent who does not want to be moved.

43.   A few organizational ombudspeople do occasionally act outside their ordinary role and agree to do formal investigations for the employer for the purpose of adjudication. Some ombudspeople have served as formal observers of
the fairness of an adversarial hearing process. On the basis of consultations
with several hundred practitioners, I believe that in such circumstances they
should write a memo to the file noting the exception from ordinary practice.
With respect to such exceptions they should not expect to be shielded from a
summons to testify in formal hearings inside or outside the organization, although they should attempt to preserve the privacy of anyone who has given
information.

44.   See Blake and Mouton, *Solving Costly Organizational Conflicts,* for an
example of an excellent model for intergroup facilitation and conflict management.

45.   See ibid. for an example of an excellent model for such action between
groups.

46.   My research indicates that about a third of the working time of organizational ombudspeople is spent on systems change.

47.   Rowe, "Helping People Help Themselves.".

48.   See R. L. Hutchins, *Reprisal, Retaliation and Redress,* (Dallas: The Ombudsman Association, 1996).

49.   Some lawyers wish that employers would adopt all the safeguards of due
process in law for internal workplace dispute resolution. Few employers agree.
My list of elements of fair process does however include many of the customary elements of due process.

50.   See Ewing, *Justice on the Job,* for a description of such structures.

51.   See J. W. Zinsser, "The Perceived Value of Considered Approaches to Internal Conflict Within Organizations," (Masters thesis, Antioch University,
1995) for evidence that imposed arbitration was seen within one firm as not
adding value to the dispute resolution process.

52.   See for example, Bureau of National Affairs, "A Due Process Protocol for
Mediation and Arbitration of Statutory Disputes Arising out of the Employment
Relationship," Employment Discrimination Report (May) (Washington, D.C.:
Bureau of National Affairs, 1995).

53.   The construction company Brown & Root offers to pay a substantial
amount of an employee's legal fees, for consultation about legally protected
rights and for accompaniment to arbitration, but most nonunion employers do
not pay such costs.

54. See Bedman, "From Litigation to ADR," and J. Zinsser, "Employment "Dispute Resolution Systems: Experience Grows but Some Questions Persist," *Negotiation Journal* 12, no. 2 (April 1996): 145–58, for longer presentations about the Brown & Root DRP.

55. Some of these questions may be answered by a 1997 survey conducted by David B. Lipsky and Ronald L. Seeber of the Cornell PERC Institute on Conflict Resolution. The survey is focused on dispute resolution techniques being used in the 1,000 largest corporations in the United States.

5

DISPUTE RESOLUTION AND TEAM-BASED WORK SYSTEMS

Joel Cutcher-Gershenfeld and Thomas A. Kochan

I. Introduction

Fundamental changes are taking place in the way work is organized. These changes are occurring in the private and public sectors in manufacturing, engineering design, and even service delivery operations. One of the most important changes, and certainly one of the most visible, is the increased use of teams as the basic unit for organizing work. In manufacturing, leading firms are increasingly establishing cross-trained work teams in which individuals are responsible for learning multiple skills and working together to coordinate production operations in their work area. In engineering, "integrated" or simultaneous design teams are becoming the world standard for new product design. These teams consist of groups of engineers who work together to integrate what has been in the past a fragmented, linear, sequential design process. In service operations, whether public or private sector, service delivery teams are being established in which groups of employees work together to ensure cross-functional or interagency coordination and response to customer requirements.

Too often it is assumed that the increased use of teams means that there will be an immediate and parallel increase in teamwork and cooperation. In fact, the initial experience of many organizations as they shift to greater reliance on a team-based structure is increased disorganization and the emergence of new forms of conflict. Over time, however, positive outcomes for individuals, teams, and the organization are possible, including higher levels of teamwork and cooperation.

This interconnection between team-based work systems and the management of workplace conflict is the focus of this chapter. We will be examining conflict by bringing together what is termed a systems perspective, an institutional approach, and continuous improvement principles. The systems perspective allows us to see a workplace as composed of a work system, a reward system, a training system, and many other systems. Each system has four elements: inputs, processes, outputs, and feedback for improvement. The institutional perspective allows us to see a workplace as composed of many stakeholder groups, with common and competing interests, as well as established patterns of interaction. The continuous improvement perspective allows us to identify the ways to address and improve the systems and institutional interactions associated with conflict in the workplace.

Specifically, we will be looking beyond the surface symptoms of conflict to identify the deeper root causes. We will see that conflicts in teams have root causes that reach beyond team boundaries to issues of organizational structure, strategy, and systems. Further, we will see that conflict, far from being pathological, should be an expected element of effective team operations. It can even be an indicator of healthy organizational change. This analysis points toward a reconceptualization of the very concept of dispute resolution in a team-based work system. Finally, the implications for future research building on this reconceptualization of conflict are explored.

II. Why Teams?

The dominant focus of the organization of work has changed over time. More than a century ago, work was primarily organized around individuals and their crafts. The rise of mass production and scientific management in the private sector and the bureaucratic/civil service form in the public sector elevated organizations and institutions as key units of analysis. The fields of organizational behavior, industrial relations, and industrial/organizational psychology which emerged in this century reflected these developments.[1] During these earlier periods there were always team-based work activities. Today, however, we may well be entering an era where the work group and clusters or networks of work groups rival individuals and hierarchies as the dominant method of organizing work.

The increased use of work groups or teams is emerging as a direct result of competitive market pressures, government deregulation, new information technologies, and the global diffusion of innovations in work practices. These forces are reflected in countless organizational change initiatives. Several common sources of change can be identified. The initiative may come from a visionary leader who encourages the use of teams based on an inner conviction that this is a better way to organize work. Sometimes the initiative is the product of a benchmarking study to identify the "best practice" or "world class" operations. Leading firms in manufacturing, product design, and service delivery are organizing work around teams and are being emulated by others who seek to replicate their success. In addition, the initiative may be in the form of re-engineering or process improvement in which the present work processes are "mapped" or traced sequentially, ideal processes or future visions are constructed, and improvement options are identified. Analysis of many work processes reveals the potential gains that are possible when the work is organized around groups, rather than individual jobs. Finally, some work has always been organized in groups on an informal basis, but now a decision is made to formalize these practices.

Groups and networks of interdependent groups will become especially important as organizational structures become more flexible and as organizational boundaries become more permeable.[2] Ultimately, organizational leaders will have to think not just in terms of individuals listed on an organizational chart, but of groups or networks of groups. Similarly, researchers will have to continue to expand the development of methods for studying groups and networks that permit the same degree of depth of analysis as the methods presently available for assessing individual and organizational patterns.

III. Conflict and Teams

Although teams are a common result of visionary leadership, re-engineering initiatives, quality analysis, or the formalization of informal patterns, the popular business literature on these subjects too often presents an overly simplistic picture of teams, especially with respect to workplace conflict.[3] Exhortations to all pull together and "optimize the whole, not the parts" are well intended, but incomplete as guidance for managing conflict in a team-based work system. Indeed, the emphasis on cooperation in the popular business literatures on quality and leadership directly or inadvertently implies that the emergence of conflict is somehow inappropriate or even pathological.

Too many managers move to team-based operations with the implicit assumption that it will automatically bring increased cooperation. Certainly such moves are made without sufficient preparation for the levels of conflict and contention that are subsequently experienced. Yet almost any plausible theory of social relations would predict that increased interdependency in an organization such as that created by teams will also involve an increased potential for conflict.

Workplace conflict is addressed in the literature on teams and group dynamics, but the focus is almost entirely on conflict within teams.[4] There is comparatively little attention in these books and articles to the conflicts between teams that can result from quality, re-engineering, or process improvement initiatives that represent the context for team-based operations. Yet many conflicts that arise in a team-based setting involve rivalries across shifts, tensions between internal customers and suppliers, and issues of organizational support. These systems-level problems are all intensified with the increased interdependencies when work is organized around teams. Thus, the approach presented here seeks to shift the focus to this broader systems perspective.

IV. The Analysis: Using a Process Improvement Model

In many workplaces, process improvement models provide a new way of thinking about work practices. Instead of viewing practices as discrete activities, the metaphor of a "work process" encourages people to see all the practices as part of a system with inputs, processes, outputs, and feedback for improvement based on experience. The goal then becomes more than just working harder on a given task; it becomes "working smarter" to improve the process. A standard process improvement framework will be used for the analysis in this chapter. Such frameworks typically employ the same basic steps. They begin by clarifying the *aim* or goal of the process. Then, they highlight the circumstances that represent what is actually happening, the present *reality*. This is followed by an analysis of the *root causes* of any gaps between the aim and the reality. Based on this analysis, *improvement options* are identified, a plan for *implementation* is developed, and criteria for *evaluation* are established.[5]

Using this framework, we begin with a statement of the aim with respect to dispute resolution in a team-based work system that has four elements. In the next step we examine the present reality of the typical experience in a team-based setting. This analysis is organized around the four core elements of the aim. Then, given the descriptions of the aim and reality, we trace root causes that help to determine why reality falls short of the aim relative to the four elements of the aim. We then identify improvement options to consider. Finally, issues of implementation and evaluation are addressed as part of the conclusion.

There are three assumptions guiding the analysis that must be clarified. These address social relations, workplace conflict, and the role of teams. First, we assume that social relations within and across work teams are inherently mixed-motive in nature. That is, all the stakeholders in a workplace will have a mixture of common and competing interests. For example, team members and middle managers will share many common interests on issues of quality or safety, but may have conflicting interests on how to allocate time freed up through their process improvement efforts. Building on this assumption, we anticipate that conflicting priorities will be inevitable in a team-based setting, but that there also will be a degree of cooperative potential in such settings.

In addition, we assume that most people in most workplaces encounter on a daily basis some aspect of their work experience or that of their coworkers that they experience as unfair or inappropriate. Thus, the potential range of issues for workplace conflict is vast. Of this vast array of potential sources of contention, we further assume that most of the issues cannot be dismissed as irrelevant to effective work operations. Many of the issues will involve conflicts around the substance of the work, such as disagreements on how to accomplish a task. Many will also involve interpersonal conflicts with direct implications for people's ability to be effective, such as feuds across shifts or between managers. Additionally, many conflicts will involve issues of ethics, respect, or basic decency that have implications for motivation and commitment. We also observe that most dispute resolution systems handle a relatively small subset of this vast array of potential workplace conflicts.

Finally, we assume that organizations do not adopt teams as an end in themselves. In this regard, we do not see teams as inherently good or bad. Rather, teams must be analyzed in their larger organizational context. They are a vehicle to achieve other organizational objectives which they may accomplish effectively or ineffectively. From this perspective, the standard to assess the effectiveness of a team-based work system is not the number of teams that have been established. Instead, we assume that success is reflected in the degree to which teams enable the organization to better accomplish its objectives.

The analysis will be largely inductive. We will be drawing on cases in the literature on teams, as well as our own personal experience conducting research or providing technical assistance in more than 100 team-based work settings. Our experience is in the public and private sectors and spans union-ized and nonunion operations in a wide range of industries. The analysis is not presented as definitive, but rather as one way to conceptualize conflict in a team-based work system.

V. The Aim

We suggest the following aim for managing workplace disputes in a team-based operation:

> The constructive surfacing and resolution of disputes within and across teams so that the organization and its stakeholders can better accomplish their respective goals.

There are four core elements to this aim:

1. Comfort in dealing with conflict.
2. Commitment to resolve disputes close to the source of the conflict.
3. Resolution of disputes based primarily on interests, rather then rights or power.
4. Organizational and individual capability to learn from experience with conflicts.

The first element is a level of comfort with conflict. People may not enjoy or look forward to conflict, but they cannot avoid dealing with conflict. This points toward the creation of organizations where people are not afraid to surface and address controversial issues that generate conflict.[6] It also is linked with the development and use of skills for effective communication and con-frontation.

For example, when we visited the General Motors truck assembly facility in Shreveport, Louisiana, a few years ago,[7] we observed what they termed "The Plant Creed and 20 Points," posted in many offices and meeting rooms. During interviews with a wide range of people, we asked which of the 20 points on the list was the most important, and consistently, people pointed to item #20 which was, "Be willing to confront and be confronted." In fact, during this visit and other work site visits we observed many instances where people would challenge one another or introduce controversial data. In each case the issues were addressed directly in a constructive manner that supported conflict resolution.

The second, related feature is a commitment to resolving conflicts close to the source of the conflict in both time and space.[8] This means addressing issues with minimal delay and not in distant offices. This part of the aim is to avoid festering disputes and to encourage resolution by the people directly involved. Usually this means resolution by the disputants in a given conflict, but it could also include other stakeholders, i.e., other people who have a stake in the way the dispute is resolved.

For example, in the mail sorting facility in Lansing, Michigan, the relations between the U.S. Postal Service and the American Postal Workers Union had deteriorated to the point that there was a back log of more than 2,000 unresolved grievances.[9] This occurred in a bargaining unit of less than 500 people. While the first steps in addressing this situation involved local union and management leadership, a key innovation involved the appointment of a joint labor-management team of grievance mediators for this facility. These individuals were closer to the sources of conflict and they had the authority to resolve backlogged grievances. For new grievances they also entered the four-step grievance process at step one-and-a-half, i.e., after the grievance was filed, but before it was appealed.

As the backlog was eliminated, the grievance mediators then suggested that training was needed even closer to the source for all supervisors and union stewards. In response to this recommendation, training was provided that focused on common interpretations for contract language on overtime and other issues that were frequently the subjects of grievances. While the training was helpful, even this was one step removed from the source of many conflicts. Subsequent to the training of supervisors and stewards, all of the employees from the shop floor were given peer mediation training. This focused on how any coworker could effectively assist in the resolution of workplace disputes. Everyone also participated in discussions that resulted in work-group agreements on "social contracts" that would govern their daily relations. These agreements include basic shared values, such as treating each other with decency and respect. They also cover specific understandings, such as how to proceed when someone is not treated respectfully. At this point the capacity for dispute resolution had moved closer to the source.

The third element involves the commitment to resolve disputes primarily on the basis of interests, rather than rights or power. Too often, disputes are framed around contrasting positions. This limits the scope of possible agreements to the range between the two positions. By contrast, a focus on underlying interests or concerns points to a much wider set of options that take into account the interests that are at play. This focus on interests has been widely disseminated through the book *Getting to YES,* by Fisher, Ury, and Patton, and further developed in *Getting Disputes Resolved,* by Ury, Brett, and Goldberg.[10]

For example, a dispute over the frequency of job rotation in a team could be resolved on the basis of power if the supervisor imposed a specific rotation scheme on the group. It could also be resolved on the basis of rights if the frequency of rotation was resolved through the application of contract or other policy language. The aim, however, would be a workplace where such issues are resolved by taking into account issues of ergonomics, safety, capability, skill development, employee preferences, and other factors important to the interests of both the employees and managers involved in the dispute.

Of course, there will always be disputes that are appropriately resolved based on legal or contractual rights. In fact, on issues involving precedent, a focus on rights may be the most appropriate. Similarly, some disputes may come to resolution only through the exercise of power. But as Ury, Brett, and Goldberg remind us in *Getting Disputes Resolved*, a system is unbalanced if the majority of issues are resolved on the basis of appeals to rights or imposition of power.

Finally, the aim should be to build the capacity to learn from experi-ence.[11] Individuals, teams, and even the overall organization should have the capacity to learn from conflicts that take place. It may not always be possible to prevent the recurrence of conflicts, but the capacity to learn minimizes the costs associated with disputes in the workplace. Sometimes lessons are learned from conflict that lead to improvements in work operations based on a deeper understanding of employee preferences, work processes, customer needs, or other matters.

For example, at NUMMI, the GM/Toyota joint venture in Freemont, California, the changeover in the production line for a new car model in the early 1990s became a source of conflict due to an increase in ergonomic inju-ries. Individual teams were unable to solve the problems because the root cause involved design changes between Toyota's Japanese assembly plant and its Japanese suppliers. Traditionally, this process is highly interactive with many design adjustments made on an informal basis in the Japanese operations. Consequently, not all changes were integrated into specifications with suppli-ers in the United States. This meant that some parts did not fit properly, so extra pushing and twisting by employees were required during the assembly process. Conflict around these ergonomics issues ultimately escalated to involve state of California safety and health authorities. During the next model change on the truck line, however, it was clear that the union and the employer learned from this experience. They established a number of preven-tive mechanisms to ensure that such conflicts would not again escalate.[12]

This is but one possible approach in analyzing the nature of dispute resolution in the context of new work systems. The advantage of the aim dis-cussed above is the way it integrates lessons from multidisciplinary literature on negotiations, dispute resolution, total quality, systems thinking, and group dynamics. It is broader in scope than traditional approaches to dispute resolu-tion in teams built only on group dynamics principles that are centered on disputes within the team.

While these core elements apply in any workplace, they are especially appropriate in a team context. Comfort dealing with conflict is essential since the increased interdependence associated with a team operation increases the potential sources of conflict. Resolving disputes as close to the source as possi-ble is not only useful, it is also consistent with the growing emphasis on em-ployee "empowerment" in conjunction with the movement toward team-based operations. Focusing on interests is critical since power solutions can be desta-bilizing and formal rights in contracts or organizational policies usually lag the day-to-day realities of a new work system. Finally, learning from experience is essential in the context of a workplace initiative such as teams that may take many years to fully implement.

VI. Reality

What is the typical reality when it comes to managing conflict in the context of team-based operations? How well does reality match the aim or future vision that we have presented? As we will see below, there are many gaps or "disconnects" between the aim and reality when it comes to dispute resolution in team-based operations.

A. Comfort with Conflict: The Reality

The first element of the aim is comfort dealing with conflict. This component of the aim is at least partly realized in many organizations with team-based work systems. Certain types of conflicts are usually anticipated and even sanctioned as legitimate. For example, most training materials on the implementation of work teams will highlight a four-stage developmental model of "forming," "storming," "norming," and "performing."[13] In the first stage, the team roles and regular operations are being formed. As people begin to interact in these roles, issues surface that drive the storming. Underlying the resolution of these conflicts are new emerging norms for group operations. While some teams may not move beyond the first two or three stages, those that do are then able to perform. Performance may be interrupted, however, if there is a change in membership, roles, technology, tasks, or other factors that cause the developmental process to start again. Unfortunately, prior experience with the team development process does not ensure that a team will adjust successfully to to such changes.

It is thus anticipated that all teams will go through a storming stage. The many within-team conflicts at this stage are not only predictable, but they may be essential to team development. Since many team-based training programs cover this four-stage developmental model, one part of reality is an awareness and even acceptance of the conflicts that occur at the storming stage.

There may be a measure of organizational comfort or at least acceptance of within-team conflict as a developmental stage. But there is far less recognition of, let alone acceptance or comfort with more permanent, institutionally driven forms of conflict that can arise at any stage in a team's development. This includes conflicts between teams and their leaders, conflicts among teams, and conflicts between teams and the larger organizational system. Conflicts between teams and their leaders, for example, are often like the proverbial elephant in the living room. Everyone sees it, but tries to carry on conversation and other activities as though it was not there. A dysfunctional team leader may continue to operate unchallenged in just this way, reflecting the reality that there is not always comfort in surfacing this sort of a conflict.

Another common conflict that can persist without being openly addressed arises in situations where teams are internal customers and suppliers for each other. A team that supplies partially completed subassemblies to other teams that are downstream in a production process, for example, can be thought of as a supplier to these teams. The same may be true in an office setting where teams are processing paperwork on a sequential basis. Such teams will always experience a level of tension as a result of their interdependency, but it is usually not anticipated that there will be ongoing conflict as a result of these relations, which creates discomfort.

Similarly, the creation of teams raises countless questions about existing organizational systems for sharing the information needed to do a job, rewards for work, and technical support. A focus just on conflicts within teams will result in pressure on teams to define problems in terms of task accomplishment or motivation, rather than surfacing the underlying issues of information, rewards, and technical support. When these larger conflicts involving changes in systems emerge, they are usually accompanied by high levels of discomfort in the organization.

For example, in one large manufacturing plant that is moving to a team-based work system, the teams have been criticized by some managers for not achieving sufficiently rapid gains in cost reduction, quality improvement, and on-time production schedules. Yet when the teams complain about not getting weekly or even monthly data on team-level performance measures of production, they trigger finger-pointing among senior managers. Supervisors and middle managers are blamed for not supporting their teams. The finance function is blamed for its "audit" mentality and for being unable to be customer-oriented. The central corporation is blamed for a finance system that is focused on labor and overhead costs rather than total costs. In all this finger-pointing, the same managers who are pressing the teams for performance lose sight of the simple reality that they are part of the problem.

A further, fairly subtle aspect of reality involves what some scholars refer to as boundary spanning conflicts.[14] These are the dilemmas that arise when an individual such as a team leader represents the team in an external forum, such as a weekly manager's meeting. If the team leader is not aggressive enough in advancing the interests of the team in this forum, there will be conflict between the leader and the team. If the team leader is too single-minded in advancing only team priorities, there will be conflict between the leader and other leaders or managers in the forum.

Thus, the reality in many team-based work systems includes some conflicts, mostly within team, that are expected and considered legitimate. But many more conflicts, mostly between the team and the larger system, do not have the same measure of legitimacy. The distinction is most evident in the training provided to most teams which centers on within group communications, decision making, leadership, and conflict resolution. Comparatively little training addresses conflicts between teams or conflicts involving deeper systems issues. In addition, individuals are not usually prepared for the dilemmas associated with representing a group externally and being expected to be loyal both to the group and to the external forum.

B. Resolution at the Source: The Reality

The second element of the aim involves a commitment to resolve disputes close to the source of the conflict. This notion of speedy resolution involving the direct participants is often implied or even explicitly supported via the language of empowerment that typically accompanies the introduction of team-based work systems. Yet the reality on many teams does not always match this rhetoric. Team members will bring with them values reflected in one of our least favorite bumper stickers: "I don't get mad, I get even." Consistent with this perspective, for example, perceived free riders in a team will be punished with poor assignments by the group without any open discussion of the performance problem.

For many within-team disputes, particularly those perceived as personality disputes among team members, the reality is one in which the resolution is more often close to the source than would probably be the case in a traditional organization. A traditional, hierarchical organization is a structure that supports mediation or arbitration by managers, but fosters mostly informal patterns of dispute resolution among coworkers. In contrast, the identification of team leaders, the existence of regular team meetings, the attention to group norms, and the training that team members typically receive all serve to legitimize and facilitate dispute resolution within the team. Of course, in some teams reality falls short of the aim in this regard when festering personality conflicts are not addressed. Still, the team structure does seem to facilitate the surfacing and addressing of these issues in comparison to traditional structures.

Even where many of the within-team conflicts are addressed close to the source, the reality in most team-based work settings is that other types of conflicts are driven far beyond the team context. For example, a conflict with racial overtones may not be addressed at the team level. This may happen because people are unwilling or unprepared to sort through the complexity of messy conflicts. It may often seem easier to bump the issue up to a higher level or to ignore the problem altogether.

It is true that some conflicts such as those involving organizational policies or contractual rights in a unionized setting will rarely get resolved at the team level. Indeed, the people with formal responsibility for these policies or contracts will typically insist, often appropriately, that resolution not take place at the team level. For example, a team conflict might have at its root a lack of regular feedback on performance, which requires resolution at the systems level through changes in the performance evaluation and measurement system. Thus, the reality is that some disputes are likely to be addressed close to the source, while others are not. Sometimes this is a problem and sometimes it is appropriate, depending on the nature of the conflict.

C. Focusing on Interests: The Reality

Most team-based organizations are established in conjunction with either total quality initiatives or fundamental re-engineering initiatives, and sometimes both at the same time. These two types of initiatives tend to make highly contrasting assumptions about interests. These assumptions, which are centered too much on either common interests or conflicting interests, make it more difficult for teams to be focused on both common and competing interests.

There is an implicit assumption in most quality initiatives that the interests of all stakeholders can be aligned toward a common goal, so the focus is almost entirely on common interests. This is usually expressed as something like "world class excellence" or "optimizing the whole." Teams in these settings will have extensive support for the use of problem solving and process improvement tools, but there will still be the assumption that team members primarily have common interests in the goals of top management. But this is not always an accurate assumption.

In the case of a re-engineering initiative, there is a reverse focus which is almost entirely on conflicting interests. It is usually assumed that people will resist incremental change. Instead, the imposition of radical restructuring is recommended. The advice of re-engineering author James Champy, for example, is, "if it's not broke, break it." This advice does not reinforce informal or formal efforts by people trying to identify and maximize common interests. Teams in these settings will have extensive support for developing ideas that involve the dramatic restructuring of work, but they will be seen as recalcitrant if they attempt to preserve aspects of the status quo, even if they find these aspects to be functional.

The teams that are established as a result of either a quality or a re-engineering effort are not likely to be trained in a negotiated approach to conflict resolution. Instead, they will reflect the dominant orientation toward common interests in the case of a quality initiative, or conflicting interests in the case of a re-engineering initiative. The results are predictable. In the case of the quality initiative, the appeal to shared interests rings hollow. In the case of the re-engineering, common interests are ignored or undercut. By contrast, a negotiated approach to conflict resolution would involve training teams to focus on interests, rather than positions, when faced with conflict.

There are, however, some team-based initiatives where these interest-based principles are built into the team training. This is true at the Ford Sterling plant, for example, where "negotiated change" is one of the four guiding principles as they implement a team-based work system. Reality, when it comes to interest-based bargaining, is mixed. The principles are used in some team contexts, but not in others.

D. Learning from Experience: The Reality

Finally, the typical reality when it comes to learning from conflict is that very few organizations have achieved the often-stated ideal of becoming learning organizations, especially with regard to conflict management. The ideal derives from popular business texts, such as Senge's *The Fifth Discipline*, where organizations are seen as systems that can only survive in a complex, global economy through processes of learning and feedback. Evidence of such learning involves the open sharing of information, viewing mistakes as data to be analyzed rather than occasions for blame, institutionalizing review and analysis following major initiatives, and valuing the employee knowledge that exists at the point of production or service delivery.

In some unionized settings there will be some systematic review of grievance activity patterns, but the majority of team-related disputes will not show up in such a review. Often there will be formal or informal mechanisms for team leaders, first-line supervision, or floor union leaders to communicate about challenging issues and common concerns. Festering conflicts will often be identified and addressed in these forums. But the reality is that time is rarely taken to identify lessons learned in ways that point toward broader organizational implications.

E. In Summary: Reality

This analysis of reality is highly stylized. General patterns are noted with illustrative examples. While the accuracy of the generalizations will need to be tested with more systematic data collection, the observations suggest that some parts of reality are disconnected from the aim.

Within-team conflicts are often addressed in ways that correlate with elements of the aim. In other words, there is a measure of comfort with these conflicts and they are often resolved close to the source. But conflicts across teams or between teams and the larger system are more likely to fall short of the aim. When it comes to resolution based on interests, the practice depends on the chance linkage with negotiations training. Finally, the establishment of a workplace environment or culture that truly learns from conflict seems to be the most elusive element of the aim. Given this analysis, the key question concerns why differences do or do not exist between the reality and the aim. This requires a root cause analysis.

VII. Root Causes

The concept of a root cause analysis arises out of the quality movement. It focuses on the importance of solving underlying problems rather than treating the symptoms of those problems. For each of the elements of the aim, it is important to identify potential root causes that would account for the gaps noted between the aim and reality. In each case, the causes identified can be presented as potential explanations which may or may not apply to any specific case.

A. Comfort with Conflict: Root Causes

There are several potential root causes of the discomfort with conflict that cut across teams or between teams and the larger systems. Certainly conflicts among teams and conflicts involving the larger system can be very complex. Some of the discomfort may lie in a reluctance to engage a difficult and complex issue, but this factor alone would not account for the incomplete attention to such conflicts. A more critical cause may well be the way that teams are conceptualized.

Many change initiatives involving teams have intellectual roots in the socio-technical systems framework that emerged in England and Scandinavia in the middle parts of this century. This framework emphasized the establishment of autonomous or self-managing teams. In many of today's workplaces, however, teams are being established as parts of work systems that involve high levels of interdependency. This is true in what are termed "lean" manufacturing methods as well as in the case of simultaneous engineering design processes. The concept of lean manufacturing involves just-in-time (JIT) delivery by suppliers, reduced buffers or in-process inventory in operations, and a process of continuous improvement targeted at eliminating wasted steps or motions in the work process.

In these contexts, there is increasing evidence of a direct trade-off. Increased interdependency among teams in the production system limits the amount of autonomy available within teams.[15] To the extent that there is such a trade-off, then some of the conflict across teams and conflict with the larger system may have its roots in training and team-member expectations centered on autonomy.

B. Resolution at the Source: Root Causes

What would account for some conflicts not being resolved close to the source? In some cases, the answer may lie with the lack of effective training and support for teams to enable them to resolve their own disputes. But the failure to resolve disputes close to the source can also be observed where such training is provided. Another factor may be the training and support provided to human resource/industrial relations officials and union leaders. Some of these individuals may not have the skills or knowledge required to manage the variation that can emerge from decentralized decision making. Further, some of these individuals may see the empowerment of teams as a threat to their authority and even their job security. In fact, this problem is less significant where there has been training and a redefinition of roles and rewards for these individuals.

Still, not all disputes are resolved close to the source even where these officials are given training and other forms of support. This suggests that some disputes should not be resolved at the team level. These would include disputes, for example, that require complicated contractual or policy interpretation or disputes that raise issues with systemwide implications. In these cases, resolution should be at higher levels.

Clearly, then, no one forum will be appropriate for the many types of issues that can emerge in a workplace. Where there are few available forums, disputes are shoehorned into the available definitions of what is a legitimate dispute. In this regard, the root cause is the dispute resolution system itself.

C. Focus on Interests: Root Causes

We noted earlier that there is a mixed reality around the use of interest-based dispute resolution in team-based settings. The absence of these interest-based principles almost certainly reflects the relatively small overlap between the literature on dispute resolution and writing on issues of teamwork, quality, and re-engineering. Furthermore, the professional associations in these arenas are also fairly distinct. But what about the team-based initiatives where interest-based principles can be found? In these cases, the practices can probably be traced back to the attendance of a key leader at a mutual gains negotiations training session. For example, the Ford Romeo engine plant in Romeo, Michigan, is a leading team-based facility in which workers are trained in interest-based principles. This topic was added to the training after the plant manager attended a "Getting to YES" seminar sponsored by the Program on Negotiations at the Harvard Law School. Hence, the root cause for teams resolving disputes on the basis of interests may well be the "accident" of a leader being exposed to the concepts.

D. Learning from Experience: Root Causes

The lack of a commitment to learning from experience is perhaps that hardest root cause to trace. In many cases, the cause seems clear: there are cultures that directly undercut attempts at learning. Here we find various manifestations of the adage, "take risks, but don't fail." Yet problems in this area arise even in companies that are explicitly attempting to support learning cultures. It is these cases that point toward deeper root causes, such as the approaches to learning that have traditionally dominated the U.S. school system and which emphasize demonstrations of accuracy, recall, and mastery of component parts rather than building the capability to explore, take risks, and creatively integrate ideas. Deeper still are issues of long- and short-term time orientations. Many Far Eastern cultures are characterized by their focus on long-term time horizons. They think in terms of decades and centuries. In contrast, the culture of the United States focuses on months and years. This short-term focus inevitably undercuts a learning orientation.

E. In Summary: Root Causes

This root cause analysis is only suggestive. It is far from complete, yet the issues highlighted identify a direct contradiction in the way conflict is often handled in team-based settings. While most approaches to dispute resolution for teams are focused on within-team conflict, we have seen that this is the area where dispute resolution capability is perhaps most advanced. At the same time, the reality is most troubling around other sources of conflict that are typically given the least attention. The root cause analysis helps to untangle the contradiction since the root causes of these other forms of conflict lie deep within the work system or society.

VIII. Improvement Options

Typically, dispute resolution systems that generate high volumes of disputes are addressed by efforts to reduce the number of complaints. Similarly, settings where few issues surface are seen favorably, with a stance of "if it's not broken, don't fix it." Our analysis points to a serious rethinking of both situations. A high volume of issues and discussion can be very favorable if the issues are being surfaced constructively and the capability to handle issues that generate conflict is being increased. At the same time, an absence of complaints may signify an unhealthy stifling of issues. The analysis of the aim, reality, and root causes presented above generates four recommendations for improvement discussed below.

A. Comfort with Conflict: Improvement Options

For leaders at all levels, we urge that the response to contention and conflict be constructive engagement in order to foster a climate where people are comfortable in public identifying and discussing difficult issues. Establishing such a climate is, of course, a long-term process. Initially leaders will have to tolerate issues surfaced in unconstructive or indirect ways; groups will be "testing the water" to see if deeds match words. Most critical and most difficult is a minimizing of the "paybacks," or retaliation for people who surface difficult issues.

Our root cause analysis suggests that merely calling for new attitudes from leaders will not be adequate for the task. Far more important is a more systematic analysis of aspects of the work system that drive conflict, such as competing demands on scarce resources, increased interdependencies, and incentives for parties to pursue narrow self-interests. Change will be more difficult in these areas, but is essential if we are going to truly foster increased comfort with conflict.

B. Resolution at the Source: Improvement Options

The aim of resolving disputes close to the source suggests anticipating increased variation in the way disputes are resolved. For example, when union stewards at Xerox's manufacturing operations began to work closely with work teams, supervisors, and labor relations representatives to support teams in their efforts to resolve more issues internally, the number of formal grievances declined dramatically. At the same time, the stewards had to establish regular weekly meetings to share information on the agreements and understandings being generated in different work areas. In some cases, understandings with implications for more than one area had to be reviewed in a more general discussion. In other cases, they discovered that some issues could be acceptably resolved in multiple ways. The key element, however, was establishing the mechanism to support and manage the variation as disputes were resolved closer to the source.

Beyond building the capacity to manage variation, our root cause analysis points to the critical importance of establishing multiple, redundant systems. Such systems must operate at various levels in an organization and be designed to accommodate a wide range of different types of disputes. As Mary Rowe points out in chapter 4 of this volume, no one system will be appropriate for all types of disputes.[16] Disputes can be resolved close to the source only to the degree that the process for surfacing and addressing the issue is well matched to it. Thus, issues that have legal implications need to move quickly into a forum where appropriate statutory and case law can be taken into account. Issues that involve delicate interpersonal relationships and power imbalances need to move quickly into a forum where there is a high degree of confidentiality and flexibility in crafting solutions.

C. Focusing on Interests: Improvement Options

Almost any major change initiative such as work redesign and re-engineering can be expected to generate conflict or controversy. Training in interest-based bargaining should be a key part of the implementation of the change in order to be most effective. This involves training and education focusing on interests and the related skills, such as active listening, constructive confrontations, brainstorming, and problem solving skills.

D. Learning from Experience: Improvement Options

Finally, the most critical aspect of the aim is also the most difficult for which recommendations might be generated: building the capability to learn from experience. As Peter Senge reminds us, most organizational systems have what can be thought of as serious learning disabilities. The organizational structure, rewards for work, and patterns of interaction are focused primarily on short-term results, rather than long-term development. Despite these learning limitations and short time horizons, some aspects of dispute resolution systems lend themselves well to periodic review and renewal. Even if aspects of individual cases may be confidential, it is usually possible to track the frequency of different types of cases, the form of resolution, and even some of the measurable costs of conflict.

In establishing or adjusting the operation of dispute resolution systems, we need to be mindful of the types of data about patterns of conflict that will be helpful guides to improvement. Some of these data are difficult to collect, such as the data on informal systems of dispute resolution. Nevertheless, it is only with feedback loops that there is any hope of constructing learning systems for the management of disputes. As we will see below, further research on dispute resolution in team-based work settings can play an integral role in facilitating movement toward the aim of learning from experience.

IX. Conclusions and Implications for Future Research

Workplace conflict is inevitable. In fact, given the many unfair and inappropriate circumstances that are part of the daily reality for most workers, it is perhaps most significant to remember that many if not most people respond with various forms of exit: they transfer to another work area, they quit, or they withdraw their effort and commitment. When issues are identified, they are rarely welcomed as opening stages in a constructive dialogue.

Hierarchical organizations conceal many of the costs associated with viewing conflict as evidence of dysfunction, rather than as a natural part of healthy interactions. As we move to team-based work systems, the potential costs of conflict become more readily apparent. Concurrently, the potential benefits from constructive dispute resolution also become more salient. Simply put, effective functioning teams become central to organizational effectiveness.

The overriding conclusion from this analysis is a classic lesson from the quality expert, Dr. W. Edwards Deming: don't blame the people; fix the system. Individuals involved in conflict may do many inappropriate things. These behaviors are understandable, although not necessarily excusable, as functional responses in a traditional system that is centered on individuals in a hierarchy. Instead, the focus should be on providing these individuals with the tools and capabilities to deal with their differences. Moreover, structural and systems causes can be seen as common underlying factors that require structural and systems solutions.

This suggests that the implementation of the ideas reviewed in this chapter is complex. The task involves establishing multiple redundant systems for dispute resolution and addressing root causes involving the structure and design of the entire work system. Any implementation process will have to involve multiple stakeholders and anticipate a series of negotiated interactions at every stage of the process. In this regard, teams are not only part of the problem because they add interdependency and complexity, but they are also part of the solution. The implementation and continuous improvement of a effective dispute resolution system can be driven with data and ideas generated at the team level.

The standard for evaluation is deceptively simple: Which conflicts in a team-based setting have been handled constructively in comparison to what would have happened in the absence of the above implementation efforts? While it is always hard to assess what has happened in comparison to what might have happened, it is at least possible to ask this question along the four dimensions outlined in this chapter: Are people comfortable with conflict? Are disputes being resolved close to the source? Are issues being addressed on the basis of interests? And, are people learning from their experiences?

Each of the above questions is an important issue for future research. Research on comfort with conflict in team settings might, for example, develop measures of the degree to which various types of conflict are anticipated and legitimized. Then it would be possible to go into organizations and assess the levels of anticipation and legitimacy of conflicts within the team in comparison to conflicts across teams or between teams and the larger organization.

Research around the resolution of disputes close to the source would also involve analysis in organizational settings. Here it would be important to track multiple channels and forums for dispute resolution and a mix of different types of issues that might be the subject of conflict. The interesting question would not be a simple classification of channels and forums and issues, but rather how these elements change over time. For example, it is not particularly interesting to learn that an issue such as sexual harassment in a team will tend to be resolved further from the source if it is handled through adjudication in a government agency in comparison to being handled by an organizational ombudsperson. Much more interesting, however, is whether and how government agencies are able to foster mediation and other interventions inside an organization prior to adjudication, thereby shifting the locus of dispute resolution. Similarly, it is more interesting to learn how an ombudsperson is able to address issues of precedent and other adjudicative concerns when taking an informal, off-the-record approach—so that lessons can be applied across many teams. It is even conceivable that different forms of dispute resolution might be simulated in laboratory settings. This also would allow us to examine the dynamics associated with those changes that shift resolution closer to the source.

In examining the issue of resolution based on interests, research can play a critical role in identifying and legitimizing the multiple interests at play in a team-based setting. At present, teams are often captive to some very limiting consensus-based assumptions about interests. More research is needed to help construct a model of teams that allows us to understand team dynamics as much more than unspecified individuals all working together to accomplish a job. Using this perspective, a given team member might simultaneously be seen not just as a team member, but as an employee, a union member, an expert on certain work operations, a parent, a child of aging parents, a concerned environmentalist, a deeply religious citizen, and as having numerous other roles. Teamwork can and often does emerge in a team-based work system, but it would not be seen as an inevitable outcome. Instead, it would be an important accomplishment worthy of close analysis.

Research on learning from experience presents a special opportunity for close collaboration between scholars and practitioners. Most organizations moving toward team-based work systems are overwhelmed with the scale and scope of the challenge, especially as they attempt to produce products and provide services at the same time. Learning and feedback may be valued in principle, but are rarely incorporated into the initiative in any systematic way. Scholars who are willing to adopt what Eric Trist referred to as an "action research" approach can study learning and provide ongoing feedback as organizations introduce teams, thereby improving our understanding of the dynamics of conflict. This creates the challenge of becoming part of the phenomena being studied in more than an incidental way, but it also provides the opportunity to learn through natural experiments.

In conclusion, effective resolution of conflicts in a team-based setting depends on anticipating the many types of disputes that can occur, rather than waiting for a crisis. Consider the comments of an hourly team leader in an auto parts manufacturing plant in the early stages of establishing team-based operations. This individual was one of a few people selected to meet with the plant's management operating committee and the union's bargaining committee to provide feedback on the progress of the team initiative. Prior to the session, he was reflecting on just what he might say that would make a difference with all of these top leaders. This is what he said:

> When things are going fine we don't hear from you. Yet, when we start missing schedule or having quality problems you are all over us. You come down and say, "work harder." What you have to understand is that we are having these problems because we are getting bad stock, the parts are not well designed, we are not being given the time to talk to each other or other reasons that have nothing to do with how hard we are working. In fact, at the times that we are missing the schedule or having quality problems we are usually working the hardest—because we are fighting against the system. Instead of coming down when there are problems and telling us to work harder, come down when things are going right and help us to improve.

Thus, to fully realize the aim of constructively surfacing and resolving disputes in a team-based setting, it is important to take a proactive approach to make dispute resolution a part of regular operational activities. As long as these disputes are seen as an adjunct to daily operations, dispute resolution systems will be constrained in their potential. Instead, the effective identification, management, and resolution of disputes must be integral to regular interactions. Only then is there the potential to truly develop cultures of continuous learning and improvement that build on, rather than attempt to minimize, the complex realities of life in a team-based work system.

Notes

1.   See, for example, Weber's analysis of the bureaucratic form and Michaels' analysis of oligarchy—both at the turn of the century. See M. Weber, *The Theory of Social and Economic Organization* (New York: The Free Press, 1964) and R. Michaels, *Political Parties* (New York: The Free Press, [1911] 1968).

2.   It may be more than a coincidence that organizational studies has become more fragmented in recent years and industrial relations more concerned about its future direction.

3.   See, for example, the analysis by M. Hammer and J. Champy in *Re-engineering the Corporation: A Manifesto for Business Revolution* (New York, Harper Business, 1993). There are notable exceptions, of course, such as B. Joiner et al., *The Team Handbook: How to Use Teams to Improve Quality* (Madison, Wis.: Joiner and Associates, 1988).

4.   Again, there are notable exceptions, such as D. Tsvold's book on *Team Organization: An Enduring Competitive Advantage* (Chichester, England: John Wiley & Sons, 1991).

5.   These six steps have been developed by Joel Cutcher-Gershenfeld and Kevin Ford in partnership with the Michigan Department of Natural Resources as part of the Continuous Quality Improvement efforts in that agency. The steps spell the acronym "ARRIVE"—Aim, Reality, Root Cause, Improvement Options, Value Added Implementation, Evaluations and Continuous Improvement.

6.   The core notion of comfort with conflict has roots in the writings of Mary Parker Follett, such as her essay "A Constructive Conflict" presented in 1925 and reprinted in P. Graham, ed., *Mary Parker Follett, Prophet of Management* (Boston: Harvard Business School Press, 1995).

7.   This visit was conducted as part of two separate research projects, one examining changing patterns in union leadership in UAW/GM locations and the other as part of MIT's International Motor Vehicle project.

8.   For a more complete treatment of issues around resolution close to the source, see J. Cutcher-Gershenfeld, "New Patterns in the Resolution of Shop Floor Disputes," *Bringing the Dispute Resolution Community Together*, 1985 Proceedings of the 13th International Conference of the Society of Professionals in Dispute Resolution, Cheryl Cutrona, ed. (Washington, D.C.: SPIDR, 1986).

9.   This case is presented in more detail in J. Cutcher-Gershenfeld and B. Barrett, "Transforming Workplace Dispute Resolution by Expanding the Scope of Grievance Mediation," *Beyond Borders*, 1991 Proceedings of the 19th Annual International Conference of the Society of Professionals in Dispute Resolution, Cheryl Cutrona, et al., eds. (Washington, D.C.: SPIDR, 1992).

10.   Ury, Brett, and Goldberg explicitly contrast systems of dispute resolution that rely primarily on power and rights with systems that rely primarily on interests. They point out, however, that all systems will place some reliance on all three ways to resolve disputes. See R. Fisher and W. Ury, with B. Patton, *Getting to YES: Negotiating Agreement Without Given In*, 2d ed. (New York: Penguin Books, 1991); W. Ury, J. Brett, and S. Goldberg, *Getting Disputes Resolved* (San Francisco: Jossey-Bass, 1987).

11.   As we will note below, this concept is central to the writing of P.M. Senge in *The Fifth Discipline* (Cambridge, Mass.: MIT Press, 1990).

12.   This case is addressed in a forthcoming book by Work Practices Diffusion Team (J. Cutcher-Gershenfeld, M. Nitta, B. Barrett, N. Belhedi, C. Coutchie, T. Inaba, I. Ishino, S. Lee, W. Lin, M.L. Moore, W. Mothersell, S. Rabine, S. Ramanand, M. Strolle, and A. Wheaton; with S. Chow, C. Coutchie, S. Lee, J.

Palthe and S. Rabine), tentatively entitled *Virtual Knowledge: Lessons from the Cross-Cultural Diffusion of U.S. and Japanese Work Practices* (New York: Oxford University Press). Also, a full analysis of this case is forthcoming in the *Industrial and Labor Relations Review.*

13.   The model is presented in B. Tuchman's classic article "Development Sequences in Small Groups," *Psychological Bulletin* 63 (1965): 384–99.

14.   See the analysis in D.G. Ancona and D. F. Caldwell "Briding the Boundary: External Activities and Performance in Organizations," *Administrative Science Quarterly* 37 (1992): 634–65.

15.   See J. Cutcher-Gershenfeld, M. Nitta, B. Barrett, N. Belhedi, C. Coutchie, T. Inaba, I. Ishino, S. Lee, W. Lin, W. Mothersell, J. Mulder, S. Rabine, S. Rammanand, and A. Wheaton, "Japanese Team-Based Work Systems in the United States: Explaining the Diversity" *California Management Review* 37, no. 1 (fall 1994): 42–64.

16.   See M. Rowe and M. Baker, "Are You Hearing Enough Employee's Complaints?," *Harvard Business Review* 62 (1984): 127–36.

6

LESSONS FROM WORKERS' COMPENSATION
PERCEPTIONS OF FAIRNESS IN DISPUTES

Sandra E. Gleason and Karen Roberts

I. Introduction

Historically, procedural justice, or the fairness of processes and procedures used to decide outcomes, has been a critical component of such formal dispute resolution techniques in labor relations as grievance procedures. The language of collective bargaining agreements indicates the specific steps to be followed and the rights and privileges of the labor and management parties as they participate in the process and provide "voice" input about that process.[1] In recent years, however, the focus of procedural justice at the work site has been broadened to include a wide array of activities affecting employees in both union and nonunion settings.[2] For example, the fairness of treatment by a union has been used as the basis for union members to evaluate their satisfaction with their union.[3] Attention has been given to nonunion methods of handling complaints about various forms of discrimination. The fairness of procedures that generally do not include participation by the employee, such as the determination of pay raises, is increasingly being examined.[4] Finally, employees' perceptions of the fairness of the handling of their workers' compensation claims is one of the most recent topics of exploration. What these studies have in common is showing "that a concern about fairness on the job is one of the most prevalent life values noted among a wide variety of workers."[5]

The purpose of this chapter is to present an overview of the concepts and dimensions of procedural justice and use them to explore the perceptions of injured workers in Michigan who received or tried to receive workers' compensation benefits.[6] An overview of the theoretical model of the dimensions of procedural justice is presented. The unique features of workers' compensation conflicts are identified. The major findings from our research about the important determinants of procedural justice for injured employees are reviewed. Implications of this research for the creation of "fair organizations" with effective dispute management systems and issues for future research are discussed.

II. Procedural Justice: An Overview

In the Western world "psychological contracts," or unwritten expectations about the workplace relationship of employees and employers, include an expectation of fair treatment of employees. When that contract is violated by an employer, trust is undermined and a damaged relationship is not easily restored.[7] The "victim" experiences anger, resentment, a sense of injustice, and wrongful harm. The intensity of the reaction is directly attributable not only to unmet expectations of specific rewards or benefits, but also to more general beliefs about respect for persons, codes of conduct, and other patterns of behavior associated with relationships involving trust.[8]

The increasing awareness in recent years of the importance of fairness to employees has focused the attention of employers on organizational justice, or the role of fairness in the workplace. This typically has resulted in the consideration of the two components of organizational justice: distributive justice and procedural justice. Distributive justice, the allocation of resources between the personnel in an organization and how the personnel react to this allocation, has the longest history and therefore is the most studied of the two components. During the 1980s, however, more attention was given to procedural justice. This became an important perspective as researchers began to understand that perceptions about the fairness of outcomes were based on the processes and procedures used to decide those outcomes.[9]

Scholars agree that individuals use multiple criteria to evaluate fairness since fairness is a complex and multifaceted concept. In a seminal paper, Leventhal, Karuza, and Fry[10] suggest the following six criteria as important dimensions of procedural justice: representation/control, consistency, ethical appropriateness, bias suppression, decision accuracy, and correctability.[11] Although other scholars have identified sets of criteria that differ in varying degrees from these six, there is substantial agreement about the basic dimensions specified.

Representation/control emphasizes the nature of the individual's participation in how the decision is made, e.g., the degree of direct control over the decision, whether one has the opportunity to present one's views, and whether these views are adequately considered by decision makers. The evaluation of the consistency of treatment is made by comparing the treatment received in a specific situation to that received by yourself or others in similar circumstances in the present or over time, or compared with your expectations. Dimensions of interpersonal interactions, such as courtesy or rudeness, honesty or deceit, are reflected in ethical appropriateness. Appropriate treatment respects the rights, dignity, and self-worth of the individual by adhering to commonly agreed upon moral standards. Bias suppression by an authority figure such as a decision maker is the effort by that person to be impartial, honest, and fair in the decision making process by suppressing their own self-interest and prejudices.[12] Decision accuracy reflects whether the authority figure has sufficient and accurate information to judge a case on its merits. Finally, correctability refers to the availability of opportunities to modify, reverse, or rebut what is perceived to be a bad decision. Such corrections may be made through an appeal mechanism or appeal to a person or organization that will intervene.

If a process is judged fair by these criteria, then procedural due process is thought to exist. As a result, employees will be encouraged to file what they believe are legitimate complaints with no fear of retribution, and the procedures to evaluate their complaints will treat all parties fairly. If this occurs, the likelihood of substantive due process increases: the individual or group that must make the decision has all of the necessary information and can rule on the merits of the case. When procedural and substantive due process coexist, the former to protect employee rights and the latter to protect employee interests, then employees perceive the existence of organizational due process.[13]

A critical and largely unanswered question is: Which dimensions of procedural justice are the most important and under which circumstances? Lind and Tyler[14] argue that in a short-term relationship in which a dispute occurs, individuals are more likely to focus on outcomes and thus value the control dimensions of procedural justice such as representation/control, decision accuracy, and correctability. In a long-term relationship, however, improving the present or future position of the group also becomes an important objective. Thus, those dimensions of procedural justice that enhance the group position, such as ethical appropriateness and consistency, become relatively more important. Other research indicates that the importance of procedural justice concerns depends on the nature of the outcome.[15] But we do not understand how the stage of a complaint or the specific actors or people involved influence the relative importance of the different dimensions of procedural fairness.

The issue of the presence or absence of these six dimensions of procedural justice in the workers' compensation claim filing system as perceived by an injured employee has been investigated only in our research. While one earlier survey of injured workers in the state of Washington identified many costs and problems experienced by injured workers,[16] these were not analyzed using the procedural justice framework. Thus, since no other work exists now to corroborate the findings presented below on the dimensions of procedural justice, it is important to stress that while these findings offer useful insights, they also are exploratory.

III. Workers' Compensation: The Experience of the Injured Worker in Michigan

The perspectives of injured employees on procedural justice in the workers' compensation system were investigated using a sample of workers in Michigan who filed a workers' compensation claim with a data of injury between 1 April, 1984 and 15 March, 1985. The research proceeded in two stages. First, due to the lack of information about the experience of injury from the employee perspective, focus groups were conducted. These helped clarify the critical components of the claims filing process and identify the major problems and issues faced by injured employees. They also provided the language used by injured employees to describe their experiences for subsequent use in the survey. In the second stage a questionnaire was developed to collect information from injured employees on the six dimensions of procedural justice as applied to the workers' compensation claims process. The questionnaire was mailed to 634 randomly selected injured employees. A final sample of 182, a 28.7 percent response rate, was achieved.[17] The survey respondents were similar to all Michigan workers' compensation claimants in gender: approximately 2/3 were male. But they were slightly older, more concentrated in the service sector, more heavily employed in the occupational category "craftsmen and kindred," and a higher proportion had experienced a sprain or strain.

The experiences of our sample showed that the process of filing a workers' compensation claim was far more complicated than it appears on the surface. A flowchart of the process would include the following seemingly clear steps. When an injury occurs and medical care is sought, the employer is informed of the injury so that claim processing can begin. The employer informs its insurance company. The insurance company assigns a claims examiner to investigate the claims, monitor the disability, pay the wage and medical bills, and approve medical, physical therapy, and rehabilitation treatments. Claims examiners choose physicians and schedule the medical examinations with the evaluating physicians used to decide whether the employee is ready to return to work. If an employer contests a claim, e.g., by arguing that an injury is not work-related, the employee requests a hearing by the State of Michigan Workers' Compensation Board of Magistrates.

In reality, the process for a sizable minority of injured employees is much more complicated. This reflects the uniqueness of the experience for most employees, their lack of information about the process and their rights and responsibilities in it, and the interactions of multiple actors at different steps.[18] These actors include the employers' human resource personnel who are handling claims, the claims examiner of the insurance company, the treating and evaluating physicians, personnel involved with rehabilitation, and employees of the state of Michigan's workers' compensation system. All of these factors and multiple actors interact to generate the potential for many conflicts throughout the process. These conflicts result in delays and frustrations for the injured employee. For example, in Michigan approximately 20 percent of lost time cases involve a formal dispute that goes to the Board of Magistrates.[19] This final stage of dispute resolution can last between sixteen and twenty-one months.[20]

Several types of conflicts may interfere with the workers' compensation claims process. First, an employer may argue that the injury did not happen on the job and therefore the employer is not liable. Second, there is often much ambiguity about the nature and degree of disability and the degree of recovery. This reflects the limitations of current medical diagnostic techniques and understanding of many disabilities. The injured employee in Michigan is expected to return to work as soon as possible upon recovery, so an employer can stop paying benefits if an employee refuses an offer of reasonable employment. It is often difficult, however, to separate legitimate refusals by employees who believe they have not recovered adequately due to continued pain or other symptoms from what employers perceive as "faking it" to avoid work. Third, conflict may arise over the appropriate medical care and rehabilitation. Thus, the injured employee has the potential for conflict with the multiple actors involved in making decisions about health, employment, and financial welfare.[21]

The experience of being injured is highly individual and is often a first-time experience for an employee. In addition, these individuals may not know anyone who has been injured, and thus have little understanding of what to expect. Injured employees report being frustrated by several factors, including their lack of information, feeling isolated from coworkers and sometimes family and friends, being worried about their job security and economic welfare, and being in pain, while coping with a complex system that is not "user friendly" and seems to "blame the victim."[22]

IV. Empirical Findings about the Dimensions of Procedural Justice

Three sets of research findings that explore the perceptions of injured workers in Michigan are summarized below. First, the major findings from the focus group discussions are presented. Second, the findings of two analyses based on all the respondents to the mail survey are reviewed. A comparison of the perspectives of union and nonunion respondents on the fairness of the process is presented. In addition, the data for the entire sample were combined with administrative data and analyzed to determine the influence of procedural justice concerns on the decision to formally contest the outcome of a workers' compensation claim.

A. Focus Group Results

Most of the focus group participants felt they had been treated unfairly at one or more stages of their claim and/or by one or more actors in their case.[23] Since focus group participation was voluntary, however, it is possible that there was substantial self-selection of participants with a bias toward those who felt most strongly that they had been treated unfairly. The most important dimensions of procedural justice for the focus group participants were representation/control, ethical appropriateness, and outcome correctability. The less important dimensions were consistency, bias suppression, and decision accuracy.

The participants expressed strong resentment regarding their lack of representation/control over the process that generated the decisions, or the decisions actually made. Even those workers who were relatively satisfied with the final outcome of their claim felt out of control. A major factor contributing to this feeling of lack of control was the lack of readily available, reliable information or clarity about information sources. One consequence was a lack of understanding of the specific entitlements provided under Michigan law. The frustration experienced by these employees made it easier for them to ascribe negative intentions toward them by the various actors in the process. Resentment was particularly strong toward the claims examiners of the insurance carriers who appeared to delay processes unnecessarily and physicians whose evaluations were used to return employees to work in pain before they were fully recovered.

A strong sense of ethically inappropriate behavior emerged. While this occasionally reflected the belief that an actor had lied deliberately, it more often reflected a perceived indifference to their concerns and rights as injured workers, and their dignity as people. For example, employers were reluctant to provide the light-duty jobs required by the medical restrictions resulting from their injury. This treatment seemed inconsistent with the respect the injured workers felt they deserved as valued employees who had been injured in the service of their employer. These employees saw themselves as ordinary people who happened to be injured while trying to do their job well.

In general, participants expressed frustration about the apparent lack of accountability of employers, insurers, and medical professionals. Without such accountability, outcome correctability was difficult. This difficulty was further aggravated by the bureaucratic structure and delays that had to be endured to contest a claim from mediation though an Appeal Board hearing.

In contrast to the three dimensions discussed above, consistency, bias suppression, and decision accuracy were relatively less important. Consistency seemed less important because most participants had no basis for comparison since they did not know others who had gone through the process. This lack of exposure to the experiences of others also resulted in a sense of isolation since there was no support network. In addition, friends, families, and coworkers seemed to "blame the victim" for being injured. Despite the lack of a reference group, injured workers expected to be treated with dignity and respect, but found this expectation was seldom met. They thought the system worked better for cases in which the injury was unambiguous, such as a broken leg. Conflicts were more likely to emerge when injuries were more difficult to diagnose and/or link to a job, such as carpal tunnel syndrome or back sprains.

Despite the differences in race, gender, and age in the focus groups, bias suppression was relatively unimportant. The main form of discrimination reported against injured workers was by physicians who did not want to treat workers' compensation claimants. This reluctance by some physicians reflected the paperwork, payment delays, and potential for time-consuming depositions that result from the structure of the workers' compensation system in Michigan.

In general, decision accuracy did not contribute to a sense of unfair treatment, but two concerns were expressed about incomplete, if not inaccurate, information being used for decisions. First, participants noted that cursory medical examinations were used to make decisions about their readiness for employment. Second, there was a feeling that workplace injuries were ignored, misunderstood, and possibly suppressed by employers.

B. Survey-Based Results

The results of the focus groups clearly suggest important issues of procedural justice are not satisfactorily being addressed when judged from the perspective of an injured employee in Michigan. But since the focus group findings employ qualitative data, two quantitative analyses were completed using the data collected from the survey respondents. These analyses explored the relative importance of procedural justice concerns in two different contexts: the evaluation by union and nonunion employees of the fairness of the process, and the decision to contest the outcome of a claim.

For the first analysis the sample was broken into union and nonunion groups to detect whether there were differences between the two groups in their perceptions of procedural justice.[24] The dimensions of procedural justice were grouped using a Likert scale. MANOVAs were run subsequently to test whether there were significant differences between the two groups.

The major conclusion is that union membership has little impact on the perceived fairness of the claim process: 42 percent of both groups believed that overall they had not been treated fairly. There was little difference between the two groups in their evaluation of the fairness of treatment by the individual actors in the process. The two groups were similar in their views of consistency and decision accuracy, but they did differ in some aspects of representation/control, bias suppression, and ethical appropriateness. Where there were differences, the union members tended to report having less control and facing more discrimination due to their disability; there were often difficulties with returning to work on light-duty jobs. Thus, membership in a union that is expected to provide "voice" does not significantly alter the perceived overall fairness of the workers' compensation claim process.

The data also were analyzed to examine how injured workers weight the various dimensions of fairness when evaluating the outcome of the claims process and whether to contest the outcome of that claim. Factor analysis was used to create scales for the four exogenous variables: dimensions of the quality of interaction, i.e., the assessment of the ethicality and professionalism of the actors in the process; consistency, decision control, and information accuracy. In addition, an endogenous variable used as a global or summary measure of procedural justice was developed that reflected all four exogenous variables. These variables were analyzed using a recursive path model.[25] In the first stage the analysis examined the extent to which the individual dimensions of procedural justice contributed to a global evaluation of fairness. In the second stage, process outcomes also were considered. This allowed the examination of the questions about the relative importance of perceptions of fairness and actual outcomes in determining the decision to formally enter a dispute about a claim.

Although all four dimensions of procedural justice made statistically significant contributions to the overall perception of fairness, the dimensions are not equally important. The quality of interaction was by far the most important determinant of the global fairness impression. Consistency also was important, but not as important as decision control. These results suggest that individuals form an overall impression of the fairness of a process based on multiple and different dimensions of procedural justice. In contrast to the global evaluation of fairness, the results of the analysis suggest that only information accuracy affects the decision to formally contest the outcome of a claim.

V. Conclusions

Much attention has been devoted in the past to the organizational structure of dispute processing, but not enough attention has been given to how the process actually works from the viewpoint of the person who must use it. Thus, the focus in the research reported here on employee-user perceptions of procedural justice in the workers' compensation complaint system begins to rectify this imbalance in perspectives. The use of responses from actual claimants in focus groups and from a mail survey provided a richness of understanding of an actual process that a laboratory study cannot generate. It clearly shows that the procedural justice paradigm is useful in understanding how injured workers feel about their experience as they go through the process and after it is completed. This suggests that the same methodology can be applied to the study of a variety of other workplace dispute resolution mechanisms to evaluate their effectiveness and make recommendations for improvements in dispute management systems.

This research suggests that a major challenge in the future for employers and personnel in labor relations and human resources is to use information from studies such as these that focus on the employee perspective to create "fair" organizations. Creating such organizations means more than designing complaint systems which management expects to operate fairly. It means checking with the users of the systems, the employees, to see whether the goal of fairness actually has been achieved since procedural justice has an important social aspect or "interactional justice" feature.[26] Furthermore, "if differential organizational perspectives offer different views of morally, ethically, and socially appropriate behaviors . . . it may be in the best interests of effective management to sensitize oneself to others' perspectives on fairness."[27]

Issues of procedural justice at the work site will remain important in the future due to two major considerations: the decline of unionization in the United States and the growing involvement of American companies in the global economy. A dramatic decline in the rate of unionization in the American economy has occurred since the 1950s. As the relative importance of non-union employment has grown, some employers have sought to prevent unionization. Major tools used for this purpose are the provision of dispute resolution systems that mirror those embedded in union contracts, as well as the development of "fair organizations" which emphasize procedural justice for employees.[28]

Our increasingly competitive global economy encourages a concern for procedural justice from at least two perspectives. First, this highly competitive environment forces management to pursue multiple areas of cost savings and to ensure the maximum productivity of their workforce. These internal management-generated pressures to ensure competitiveness can generate employee complaints of many types. Ewing[29] argues that where corporate due process works effectively, the majority of workplace complaints can be handled successfully through informal procedures. This saves the employer a wide range of expenses, including litigation expenses, while simultaneously building trust and morale within the organization. In addition, the reduction of dissatisfaction and frustration can be expected to reduce employee turnover and the passive response of working less intensively.[30] Furthermore, such desirable employee behavior as "good corporate citizenship" is promoted, including improved teamwork.[31] This citizenship behavior is seen in those employees who "go the extra mile" on their jobs to do work that promotes the effective operation of the organization even though it is neither part of their job description nor subject to the reward structure.[32] Moorman[33] and Tansky[34] found that such organizational citizenship behavior was positively linked to perceptions of procedural justice.[35]

The second impact of the global economy is the expansion of operations abroad by an increasing number of Western companies. Locating in another country requires these companies to develop and/or adapt their human resource management practices to a wide variety of local cultures.[36] This includes paying attention to procedural justice issues and expectations of appropriate employee treatment that may be quite different from those of the Western world. Conflicts between ideas about a "fair organization" and procedural justice are particularly likely in those cultures where the group is relatively more important than the individual. [37]

VI. Implications for Future Research

Two major directions for future research can be identified. First, a recent survey of employees has documented that members of the workforce at all levels have higher expectations about due process at the work site than in the past.[38] While a well-designed dispute management system should ensure procedural justice, employees need to be asked whether it does so. More research in a variety of specific situations at the workplace must be undertaken to investigate from the perspective of the employee whether procedural justice prevails.[39] This research should explore two issues: the perspectives used by individuals to evaluate conflict situations and the relative importance of the dimensions of fairness at various stages of a dispute. Second, more work is needed on procedural justice as perceived in other countries, particularly non-Western nations.

Recently researchers have begun to focus on the perspectives or "conflict frames" through which disputants view and evaluate conflict situations. These lenses are used to explain why the orientation of a given individual leads them to focus on some features of a conflict situation while ignoring others.[40] More specifically, individuals appear to vary in the degree to which they focus on the following: (a) ongoing relationships with the other parties or the material aspects of the dispute; (b) the emotions associated with the dispute or the actions and behaviors that result; and (c) cooperation in settling a dispute or trying to maximize one's own gain. This focus on the orientation of the individual also raises the question of the degree to which racial, ethnic, and educational differences influence the evaluation of procedural justice and whether this evaluation will change over time as the labor force becomes increasingly diverse and better educated. It is not clear to what degree these differences in conflict frames are related to the dimensions of procedural justice, but it seems likely that a link does exist. For example, the emotions associated with a dispute might be linked to the procedural justice dimensions of ethical appropriateness, the degree of representation/control over decisions, and bias suppression.

Our exploratory research suggests that the relative importance of the dimensions of fairness varies with the different actors in a dispute[41] and at different stages of a dispute, particularly for those disputes that include multiple actors and extend over a substantial time period.[42] If substantiated by research in other conflict situations, this might generate better techniques for solving disputes at an earlier stage. If we can identify those dimensions of fairness that are the most critical at the early stages of a dispute, we can design systems to resolve disputes earlier, thereby reducing the costs of workplace disputes.

Finally, we need studies in different nations to find out to what extent the determinants of procedural justice in the United States also apply in other cultures. Since the expected standards of treatment and expectations of what is fair treatment of employees vary by culture and by country, there is good reason to expect that the dimensions of procedural justice used to evaluate fairness also will vary. Thus, when viewed from a global perspective, fairness becomes an open-ended social construct.

Notes

1.   E. A. Lind and T. R. Tyler, *The Social Psychology of Procedural Justice* (New York: Plenum, 1988).

2.   For example, see the discussion by Mary Rowe in Chapter 4 of procedural justice concerns in handling employment disputes in nonunion workplaces.

3.   P. Jarley, S. Kuruvilla and D. Castell, "Member-Union Relations and Union Satisfaction," *Industrial Relations* 29 (1990): 128–34.

4.   J. Dulebohn and J. J. Martocchio, "Employees' Procedural Justice Perceptions of Pay Raise Decisions" from *Proceedings of the 47th Annual Meting of the Industrial Relations Research Association* (Washington D. C., January 6–8, 1995), 21–29.

5.   J. Greenberg, *The Quest for Justice on the Job: Essays and Experiments* (Thousand Oaks, Calif.: Sage Publications, 1996), 120.

6.   This research was supported by the Fund for Research on Dispute Resolution. The opinions expressed herein do not necessarily reflect the position of the fund. The authors also gratefully acknowledge the support of

the Institute for Public Policy and Social Research of Michigan State University.

7.   G. S. Spindler, "Psychological Contracts in the Workplace—A Lawyer's View," *Human Resources Management* 33 (1994): 325–33.

8.   D. M. Rousseau, "Psychological and Implied Contracts in Organizations," *Employee Responsibilities and Rights Journal* 2 (1993): 121–39.

9.   R. Folger and J. Greenberg, "Procedural Justice: An Interpretive Analysis of Personnel Systems," *Research in Personnel and Human Resources Management* 3 (1985): 141–83; J. Greenberg, "Organizational Justice: Yesterday, Today, and Tomorrow," *Journal of Management* 16 (1990): 399-432.

10.   G. Levanthal, J. Karuza, and W. Fry, "Beyond Fairness: A Theory of Allocation Preferences," in *Justice and Social Interaction*, ed. G. Mikula (New York, N. Y.: Springer-Verlag, 1980), 167–218.

11.   Subsequent scholars have developed these concepts in more detail. For examples see the following: Folger and Greenberg, 1985, *op. cit.*; Lind and Tyler, 1988, *op. cit.*; T. R. Tyler, "What is Procedural Justice? Criteria Used by Citizens to Assess the Fairness of Legal Procedures," *Law and Society Review* 22 (1988): 103-35.

12.   The issue of self-interest versus fairness is discussed in depth by Diekmann et al. in chapter 9.

13.   R. B. Peterson, "Due Process in the Work Place—Towards a Better Model," *Bulletin of Comparative Labor Relations* 28 (1994): 89–100.

14.   Lind and Tyler, *op. cit.*

15.   R. Folger and M. Konovsky, "Effects of Procedural Justice and Distributive Justice on Reactions to Pay Raise Decisions," *Academy of Management Journal* 32 (1989): 115–30; E. A. Lind, R. Kanfer and P. C. Earley, "Voice, Control, and Procedural Justice: Instrumental and Noninstrumental Concerns in Fairness Judgements," *Journal of Personality and Social Psychology* 59 (1990): 952–59.

16.   M. Ray, *Work Related Injury: Workers' Assessment of its Consequences for Work, Family, Mental and Physical Health* (Pullman, Wash.: Injured Workers' Project, Washington State University, 1986).

17.   For a more detailed discussion of the methodology and sample characteristics, see the following references: S. E. Gleason and K. Roberts, "Worker Perceptions of Procedural Justice in Workers' Compensation: Do Unions Make a Difference?" *Journal of Labor Research* 14 (1993): 45-58; K. Roberts, "Predicting Disputes in Workers' Compensation," *Journal of Risk and Insurance* 59 (1992): 252-61; K. Roberts, "Perceptions of Fairness and the

Decision to Dispute in Workers' Compensation," *John Burton's Workers' Compensation Monitor* 8 (1995): 4-16; K. Roberts and S. E. Gleason, "Procedural Justice in the Workers' Compensation Process," *Bulletin of Comparative Labor Relations* 28 (1994): 77-88.

18. For a more detailed discussion of the workers' compensation claims process in Michigan, see the following references: Roberts, 1992 and 1995, *op. cit.*; Roberts and Gleason, 1994, *op. cit.*; K. Roberts and S. E. Gleason, "Dispute Resolution Within the Michigan Workers' Compensation System: The Workers' Perspective," Final Report to the Fund for Research on Dispute Resolution (Washington, D. C.: 1991, unpublished).

19. In Michigan, workers who expect to miss work due to an injury must file a lost-time claim to receive income to replace earnings lost while not working. Income benefits can be received after a one week waiting period. K. Roberts, 1995, *op. cit.*, p. 4

20. E. M. Welch, "Trial Delays," *On Workers' Compensation* 2 (1992): 71.

21. In chapter 10 Greenhalgh and Chapman discuss the issues involved in the relationships between disputants. They point out that the relationship between the parties is a relatively unexplored aspect of negotiation.

22. K. Roberts and S. E. Gleason, "What Employees Want From Workers' Compensation," *HR Magazine* 36 (1991): 49–54.

23. K. Roberts and S. E. Gleason, 1994, *op. cit.*

24. S. E. Gleason and K. Roberts, 1993, *op. cit.*

25. K. Roberts, "Perceptions of Fairness," 4-16.

26. D. E. Eskew, "The Role of Organizational Justice in Organizational Citizenship Behavior," *Employee Responsibilities and Rights Journal* 6 (1993): 185–94.

27. J. Greenberg, "Looking Fair vs. Being Fair: Managing Impressions of Organizational Justice," *Research in Organizational Behavior* 12 (1990): 116.

28. D. W. Ewing, *Justice on the Job: Resolving Grievances in the Nonunion Workplace* (Boston: Harvard Business School Press, 1989).

29. Ibid.

30. S. L. Robinson and D. M. Rousseau, "Violating the Psychological Contract: Not the Exception, but the Norm," *Journal of Organizational Behavior* 15 (1994): 245–59.

31. A. M. Korsgaard, D. M. Schweiger, and H. J. Sapienza, "Building Commitment, Attachment, and Trust in Strategic Decision making Teams: The Role of Procedural Justice," *Academy of Management Journal* 38 (1995): 60–84.

32. K. Aquino, "Relationships Among Pay Inequity, Perceptions of Procedural Justice, and Organizational Citizenship," *Employee Rights and Responsibilities Journal* 8 (1995): 21–33; D. W. Organ, *Organizational Citizenship Behavior: The Good Soldier Syndrome* (Lexington, Mass., Lexington Books, 1988); S. L. Robinson and E. W. Morrison, "Psychological Contracts and the OCB: The Effect of Unfulfilled Obligations on Civic Virtue Behavior," *Journal of Organizational Behavior* 16 (1995): 289–98.

33. R. H. Moorman, "Relationships Between Organizational Justice and Organizational Citizenship Behaviors: Do Fairness Perceptions Influence Employee Citizenship?" *Journal of Applied Psychology* 76 (1991): 845–55.

34. J. W. Tansky, "Justice and Organizational Citizenship Behavior: What is the Relationship?" *Employee Responsibilities and Rights Journal* 6 (1993): 195–207.

35. The multiple dimensions of organizational citizenship behavior were explored in a series of articles in 1993 in the *Employee Responsibilities and Rights Journal* (vol. 6, no. 3).

36. C. Pavett and T. Morris, "Management Styles Within a Multinational Corporation: A Five Country Comparative Study," *Human Relations* 48 (1995): 1171–91.

37. Discussions in a doctoral seminar with participants from five countries plus the United States revealed that non-Western participants had difficulty understanding the Western notion of procedural justice and its importance as a workplace issue.

38. D. M. McCabe, "Non-union Grievance Procedures: A Strategic Analysis of Organizational Due Process," *Bulletin of Comparative Labor Relations* 28 (1994): 101–13.

39. J. Greenberg, 1996, *op. cit.*

40. R. L. Pinkley and G. B. Northcraft, "Conflict Frames of Reference: Implications for Dispute Processes and Outcomes," *Academy of Management Journal* 37 (1994): 193–205.

41. A logit analysis was conducted to explore how injured workers use procedural justice concerns to evaluate their treatment by four actors in the claims process: the employer, the claims examiner, the evaluating physician, and the

treating physician. Four logit models were estimated to test the applicability of procedural justice theory. The dependent variable in each model was a dummy variable coded one if the actor was perceived as treating the injured worker fairly and zero otherwise. Several statistically significant results emerged from this analysis, but their reliability is debatable due to the small sample size. Consequently, although these results have not been published, they are presented here to illustrate possible issues to pursue in future research (see Roberts and Gleason, 1991, "Dispute Resolution within the Michigan Workers' Compensation System," *op. cit.*, for a more detailed discussion).

First, the coefficients for the ethical appropriateness variables were highly significant for the employer, but not for the other actors. This suggests that ethically inappropriate behavior most violates one's sense of fairness when it is from an actor whom one knows well, perhaps of whom one had high expectations, and/or when some well established relationship norms are violated.

Second, the possession of complete information is only important for those actors whom one might view as adversaries, in this case, the claims examiner or the evaluating physician. This suggests that decision accuracy is an important dimension of fairness only when the actor may be predisposed against the individual. However, it is less important either when the actor has other sources of information about you, such as your employer, or is not making direct decisions about your case, such as the treating physician.

Third, honesty is very important for the treating physician, approaching significance for the claims examiner, and not important at all for the evaluating physician. One explanation for its importance for the treating physician is that most workers always expect the treating physician to be honest with them. Thus, when this is not the case, it may be seen as an especially egregious violation of fairness. The claims examiner was likely to be the most knowledgeable actor about the workers' compensation system in general. Perhaps workers expected honesty from the claims examiner in this role and perceived a lack of it to be unfair. The evaluating physician may be seen as an adversary and not expected to be honest.

Finally, consistency was important only in the evaluation of the claims examiner. This may be because workers had prior experience with other types of insurance and therefore had a basis for comparison that they lacked for evaluating their workers' compensation claim relative to other workers. Most people, however, have had prior medical care, but apparently lower quality medical care did not affect perceptions of fairness.

42. K. Roberts, 1995, *op. cit.*

Part Two

Perspectives From Japan
and Western Europe

7

DISPUTE RESOLUTION AND PREVENTION IN U.S.-JAPANESE STEEL JOINT VENTURES

TWO CASE STUDIES

Michio Nitta

I. Introduction

This chapter focuses on the types of disputes and dispute management mechanisms that arise over conflicts of interest of a collective nature at the levels of plants and workplaces. Traditionally, this type of dispute resolution has been a major area of interest for scholars in industrial relations, so much research has been done on this topic. But major changes have been occurring in the basic characteristics of industrial relations in the United States because of efforts directed at increasing cooperation between labor and management.[1] This changing context for dispute resolution requires a reexamination of our understanding of how industrial relations systems now operate.

The two case studies discussed here provide insights into the types of industrial relations innovations occurring in the United States by reviewing the developments in two unionized U.S.-Japanese steel industry joint ventures established in the 1980s and located in the U.S.: National Steel, Great Lakes Division, and L-S Electrogalvanizing (LSE). The sites discussed are significant model cases not only for the Japanese-affiliated firms in the U. S. steel industry but also for innovation-minded manufacturing firms in other industries in the United States. National Steel is a model case of a systemic reform of work and labor relations systems in a large existing "brownfield" site with previously established employment relations practices. The experiment at National Steel subsequently served as a catalyst in the development of the new participative model of union-management relations established in the contract negotiations in 1993 and 1994 with the major integrated steel producers (Inland, USX, Bethlehem, and LTV). LSE, the joint venture between LTV and Sumitomo, is a model case of systemic innovation relying on the socio-technical systems (STS) approach that stresses fitting together social and technical systems when developing a team system.[2] It employs joint committees in an entirely new facility or "greenfield" plant. Information about these cases was obtained through interviews with managers and union representatives as well as document review.

Since the reforms of the U.S. industrial relations system discussed in these two cases have drawn heavily on the experience in Japan and Germany, a brief overview of the critical features of the systems in these two countries is provided. These systems emphasize features that focus on the proactive prevention of disputes, rather than waiting to resolve disputes after they emerge.[3] The systemic changes toward more preventive modes of dispute resolution in the United States will be traced and reviewed with specific reference to each of the two joint-venture steel companies. Finally, the implications of this analysis for future research are discussed.

II. Types and Changes in Voice Mechanisms at the Plant Level

In the traditional industrial relations system in the United States (known as the "New Deal System"), the mechanism for the expression of worker concerns or "voice" [4] in unionized organizations consists of three key processes embedded in the collective bargaining agreement: negotiating detailed rules regarding the terms and conditions of employment through collective bargaining which typically occurs every two to three years; interpreting and applying the negotiated rules through a formalized grievance system; and the use of third-party arbitration as a final means of resolving a dispute in those cases where labor and management do not reach agreement. In contrast, the German and Japanese systems employ a mechanism specifically designed to provide workers with a voice in company operations that is separate from collective bargaining. The development of these mechanisms reflects fundamental differences in the philosophy of labor-management relations and the need for flexibility in a competitive global economy.

The German system has two components. Collective bargaining, usually at the industry-regional level, decides the wages and conditions of work. This is combined with codetermination, a joint decision making process that involves both employer and worker representatives. Plant-level issues of labor and management relations are handled through codetermination. A central element of this process is a worker organization, separate from the union, known as a works council. The works council is limited in its range and degree of voice by the law. For instance, in issues concerning discipline, hours worked each day, and the method of payment, management is required to obtain agreement from the works council (codetermination rights). On employment issues, the works council can veto decisions made on hiring and transfer (veto rights). The works council also has the right to obtain information (information rights) and to express opinions (expression of opinion rights) regarding the business condition of a company and strategic decision making on important business issues. When no agreement can be reached on the issues covered by the codetermination rights and veto rights, disputes are mediated or arbitrated by a third party or the issue is brought to the labor court. No strike action is allowed.[5]

The mechanism for worker voice in a Japanese workplace also has two components: collective bargaining and a Joint Labor-Management Committee

(JLMC). The parties involved are the management of a firm or plant and the enterprise-based unions. The activities of the JLMC are usually translated as "joint consultation" in English, but this interpretation is misleading. Joint consultation is a system in which managers provide information to a representative(s) of workers, and discuss the business plan with them, but the final decision is made by managers with sole responsibility.[6] In contrast, the Japanese JLMC system is one of prior consultation and joint decision making between firm-based and plant-based unions and management at a level that is equivalent to the one on which most daily industrial relations issues are negotiated. Practically, it is difficult to differentiate the JLMC from collective bargaining conducted between the same parties.

Under the Japanese system, contractual obligations to maintain labor peace are generally weak. The line between collective bargaining, typically adversarial, and the JLMC, typically focused on peaceful consultation, is not clear. It is not unusual for the issues discussed at the table by the JLMC to be discussed later in collective bargaining if either the management or labor side wants to do so. In addition, some important issues discussed only in the JLMC, such as the transfer of employees, can become the target of a strike during the term of an effective labor contract.

Consequently, as a practical matter, almost any issue in industrial relations can lead to strike action during the term of a labor contract. The Japanese system thus lacks the structural means to ensure industrial peace in daily labor-management relations. The development of a peaceful and co-operative relationship between labor and management in the private sector in Japan depends not on the structured means of industrial peace found in the U.S. and German systems, but instead relies on two factors. First, there is a mutual choice by both parties to use collaborative labor relations strategies based on the "lifetime employment" concept. Second, a societal framework supports this mutual commitment by the parties, such as the structures of corporate governance. [7]

Although the Japanese system has some unique characteristics, there are aspects of the Japanese and German systems that are more similar as compared with the American system. In particular, there are differences in the process used to express worker voice and the subsequent decision making on workplace issues. The traditional American grievance and arbitration system is characterized by the expression, "Management acts, the union reacts," which illustrates the ex post facto nature of approach to conflict resolution. In contrast, the Japanese and German systems emphasize prior consultation and joint decision making to prevent disputes. Since the 1980s, however, the industrial relations climate in the United States has been changing, and the mechanisms for worker voice and decision making at the plant level have been evolving away from the traditional solutions that focus on solving disputes after they arise. They are moving toward mechanisms that employ more prior consultation and joint decision making similar to the Japanese and German models. This evolution reflects a change in both philosophy and the competitive environment.

The attempt to move toward a dispute prevention and management system based on prior consultation and joint decision making must be accompanied by a change in the ideological underpinnings of the employment relationship, specifically, from one based on a market transaction view to an organizational membership view. For industrial relations institutions to become established as a system, ideological consistency is required. [8]

In comparing the fundamental philosophies on which the traditional American dispute resolution system has been based with the systems in Germany and Japan, we find that the American perspectives on employment relationships are strongly oriented by what can be called "market culture." This American perspective sees the employment relationship as primarily a transaction in the labor market, so the principles controlling the market mechanisms also dominate employment relations. While it is true that an employment relationship has the characteristics of market transactions in which market mechanisms decide levels of wages and employment, research in organizational behavior and sociology has identified complicated organizational processes that are also affecting the relationship. It seems, however, that such views did not have a strong influence when employment and industrial relations practices were established in the United States. The institutionalists themselves accepted the ideas of the Webbs. [9] They invented the idea of "collective bargaining" and tried to legitimatize collective worker voice systems as systems of bargaining collectively rather than individual bargaining efforts.

In contrast, the ideological basis for industrial relations in German and Japanese workplaces in which prior consultation and joint decision making are dominant is the view that an employment relationship represents membership in an organization rather than just a transaction in the market. [10] If an employment relationship is based on the assumption of membership in an organization or "community," an organization will allow repre-sentatives of employees to speak out about important issues concerning their work life and encourage managers and workers to jointly solve problems and execute jointly made decisions. When this type of employment relations view is shared, it is easier for management to develop the expectation that if prior consultation is done appropriately and the mechanisms for worker voice are functioning properly, workers' representatives behave within an acceptable range. In these cases, the trust relationship is nurtured so shared information is neither used opportunistically as a bargaining tool nor distributed outside the organization. In other words, without the develop-ment of a relationship based on cooperation and trust, a dispute resolution system based on prior consultation and joint decision making will not work well.

Even if mechanisms for prior consultation and joint decision making are established, we must pay close attention to how they function in those situations in which the interests and opinions of labor and management are in conflict. It is typical in industrial relations for shared interests to be inseparably connected with interests over which there is conflict; this may be called a mixed motive situation. The establishment of a perspective based on organizational membership does not mean that these deeply rooted structural differences in interests that exist among members of an organization will disappear. Rather, such a perspective is maintained or re-created as long as the industrial relations system effectively resolves such conflicts of interest. Thus where innovations in industrial relations discussed above are observed, dispute resolution is carried out in a different but effective manner.

The evolution toward more consultation and joint decision making also reflects a response to increased competition in the global economy. In the steel industry, for example, several factors have made changes in production and work systems a prerequisite for survival. First, global competition has intensi- fied between industrialized countries; second, the newly industrialized economies (NIES) added competition beginning in the 1980s; and third, competition from mini-mills added pressure to once powerful integrated producers. These changes in the economic environment, combined with rapid technological innovation, require flexibility in the organization of work and the commitment of workers to improve both productivity and quality simultaneously.[11] To accomplish this task, it is critical to review and adjust existing employment systems and work rules in unionized workplaces to create more flexible systems such as those that are team-based.[12] This requires the cooperation of labor and management in new work environments that protect employees' voice, since the traditional tactics of establishing and enforcing clearly codified rules such as seniority systems will hinder this flexibility.

III. Cooperative Partnership and Continuous Negotiation at National Steel, Great Lakes Division

National Steel became a "brownfield" joint venture between National Intergroup Incorporated (NII) and NKK in 1984: 50 percent was owned by NII and 50 percent by NKK. In 1990, NII sold two-fifths of its stake to NKK. National Steel is now 70 percent owned by NKK, one of the Big Five steel- makers in Japan. It specializes in the production of flat products, particularly for the auto and appliance industries. The Great Lakes Division is the largest integrated operation of the company. There are about 5,000 employees, of whom 70 percent are production-related workers.

This joint venture negotiated an agreement in 1986 with the United Steel Workers of America (USWA) called the "Cooperative Partnership." The com- ponent parts of this partnership agreement have received much attention, particularly the employment security and the Trade and Craft Combination Agreements discussed extensively elsewhere. [13] Less well known, however, is the fact that innovative practices in dispute prevention and resolution have played a key role in the success of this partnership through the operation of the Joint Labor Management Cooperation Committee (JLMCC). The discussion here is limited to the Great Lakes Division of the company due to its use of a unique innovative feature, the off-site meeting.

The formal mechanism used for the expression of worker voice and communication in the cooperative partnership at National Steel is the JLMCC.

It is a structure of regular committees operating at each of five levels: headquarters, division (plant), process area, department/unit, and working groups. These committees and work groups usually meet once a month.

The most important function realized by JLMCC is the sharing of information on business plans, production, and work. The top-down nature of this process is apparent from the schedule of regular monthly meetings that starts at the top of the organization and flows to the bottom, and from the plant level to the working groups level. Enormous energy and time are required for 240 working groups and teams to meet and thoroughly share information. This is done because such extensive information sharing with all employees is necessary to enhance their sense of participation. Additional effort is needed to promote cooperation, avoid unnecessary friction, and overcome the strong mutual distrust that existed between management and the workers in the past.

The purpose of the cooperative partnership is not limited, however, to information sharing and smooth labor/management relations. It also aims to improve business performance by exploring the abilities of employees and encouraging their participation in daily management and work. The working groups are regarded as the primary units to achieve these goals. In fact, there are some reported cases of working groups that have improved their workplaces.[14] For example, at a cold rolling mill, a work group came up with ideas to reduce scrap and to decrease downtime by adding a new guide and other revisions to the line. In another case, a maintenance crew at the steelmaking plant proposed changes in the parts used and work procedures to reduce workload and increase efficiency. Such examples are model cases, however, and should not be considered the norm.

The contract language of the cooperative partnership and JLMCC does not refer to the procedures to deal with issues upon which both parties disagree, but focuses instead on integrative issues that basically do not involve conflict. Thus, distributive issues are left to the traditional collective bargaining, grievance, and arbitration systems.

The achievement of the goals of the cooperative partnership—improving the business performance and competitiveness of the company without worsening working conditions or creating massive layoffs—cannot be accomplished solely by the activities of the working groups. Other measures to improve productivity and other features of firm performance, such as job combination and flexibility in seniority systems, are necessary. As a matter of general principle, the union agrees with this. The 1986 agreement on employment security allowed such a productivity improvement plan as a tradeoff for the employment security provided by the management. This is a departure from the traditional job-control unionism in the U.S. steel industry. The employment security clause does not assume that the union will accept specific rationalization plans. Such an issue will become a topic for negotiation at the plant level.

A unique mechanism called the off-site meeting plays an important role in negotiation processes. It is intended to promote new relationships between the USWA District 29 and the Great Lakes Division under the cooperative partnership agreement. Under this mechanism the Labor Relations Department of the division, USWA district representatives, and local union representatives meet outside the plant for two days each month. They discuss issues of mutual interest. It is agreed that even if they find the issues insolvable, a strike or lockout will not result and the issues will not be taken to a higher level for resolution.

The off-site meetings deal with various issues that could become the subject of disputes, such as employee transfers arising from a plant closing, the range and application of incentives, the incentive structure of the newly built galvanizing plant, internal training of safety personnel requested by the union, a training plan for employees, and combining jobs. For example, at the closing of the Slab Mill required by the building of the No. 2 Continuous Caster in 1987, the discussions in two off-site meetings focused on how the resulting staffing issue could be managed while respecting the commitment for employment security established by the 1986 collective bargaining agreement. Before 1986, there would have been no such prior negotiations on plant closings. In these meetings, the possibilities of early retirement and transfer to other departments were discussed based on the list of all employees at the mill. The result was that all employees knew where they would go before the actual closing of the mill.

Not all issues in labor-management relations have been resolved by the off-site meetings. Although the number of grievances has dramatically decreased, grievances related to the interpretation of the agreement are continuously filed and processed through the formal procedures. The new channel, the off-site meeting, functions side by side with the traditional system of dispute resolution. Only the important issues identified by the parties will become the topics of the off-site meeting. The decision to bring an issue to the off-site meeting is made by mutual agreement. Theoretically, the issues upon which no agreement can be reached could be brought to the formal dispute resolution procedure, but this has not been necessary to date. Thus, the off-site meeting has been functioning as the channel for the resolution of the most important issues that have the potential to become sources of conflict between management and labor at the plant level.

In a case where the parties do not agree on the issues discussed in the off-site meeting, one option is to postpone the decisions and actions. This will naturally make the whole process last longer, and hard decisions may be delayed or avoided. This is a risk associated with this type of continuous negotiation. It has been pointed out, however, that the formal dispute resolution process also can take a long time and be very expensive, particularly if the grievance goes to arbitration. In addition, since the arbitration decision may create a precedent to be followed in future cases, it will reduce the flexibility needed to reach practical compromises on a case-by-case basis. From this point of view, resolving disputes through the off-site meeting at the Great Lakes Division can be evaluated as a successful innovation in industrial relations.

The cooperative partnership has realized its purpose: continuous negotiation is working and disputes are being successfully prevented or resolved without the use of more formal mechanisms. What is critical to this success is not just the creation of an institutionalized system, but a mutual commitment by management and labor to nurture these new processes to resolve disputes in a proactive, preventive mode.

IV. Participative Management and Dispute Resolution at LSE

L-S Electrogalvanizing (LSE) is a "greenfield" joint venture between LTV and Sumitomo Metal, one of the Big Five major steelmakers in Japan. The ownership arrangement is LTV 60 percent and Sumitomo 40 percent. It specializes in the production of galvanized steel. There are 97 employees, 70 of whom are production-related workers and members of USWA. Since beginning its operation in 1986, it has used innovative production and work systems, such as autonomous work teams (AWT) and a Pay for Skill system. AWTs are composed of union members who work without a formally designated team leader. Members of the team direct themselves in specified areas of work in daily operations. A pay for skills system bases higher pay on the achievement of greater skills rather than just seniority.

Certainly the most outstanding innovation implemented at LSE is the use of various participative committees. This is a direct participation system in which workers join a committee to discuss and make decisions about issues related to their work and work life. The LSE work and production systems rely heavily on problem solving through the consensus that occurs in these committees. This participative committee structure consists of ten separate committees such as the pay and progression committee which handles the pay for skill system, the scheduling committee, and the hiring committee.

The participative committees can be considered joint committees. Their "jointness" reflects the membership that includes both workers and managements. Agreement from management, or the union in some cases, is required for a decision made in these committees to become final. For example, the skill scale established by the pay and progression committee must be approved by top management. To date there have been no reports that management has rejected any decision made by these committees. Management's acceptance of the decisions of the committees stems from three broad conditions. First, the decisions reflect a consideration of not only the needs of workers but also of the business. Second, a persistent effort is made to reach a consensus even in cases of disagreement and conflict. Finally, regulations established or decisions reached at higher levels by management and the union present a framework on such distributive issues as pay systems and wage levels.

There still may be some cases in which the processes employed by the participative committees do not function smoothly, especially regarding those issues that reflect the conflicting interests of workers and management. Some problems, such as wage levels or standards of working conditions, are resolved through regularly scheduled contract negotiations, but this type of negotiation is not effective for issues related to daily company business. During contract negotiations in 1989, the union took the initiative to establish a new dispute resolution procedure. Under this system, when a participative committee cannot resolve a case, the management and union can appoint a mutually acceptable arbitrator within sixty days and solicit the judgment of that arbitrator.

There has been only one case in which the procedure was considered; it has never been used.

At issue in this dispute were education and training opportunities. The opportunity to receive appropriate education and training is critical for workers at LSE because of the pay for skill system. Generally, LSE management has paid substantial attention to the value of employee skill development. Much energy has been devoted to training. As a result, the qualification levels of employees have steadily improved and the pay for skill system has been an important incentive to gain employee support for the participative system as a whole. Training, however, can disrupt work schedules because of employee absence during training. In a unionized setting, this can become an industrial relations issue. Generally, it has been handled smoothly through the channels of the training and scheduling committees.

A problem arose, however, in training for fully qualified advanced technicians. These employees work as maintenance technicians based on a high level of knowledge and experience. The qualifications of fully qualified advanced technician were specified by the agreement in 1989. The candidates for the highest qualification are the core members of a work team and essential for the practice of preventive maintenance needed for uninterrupted production. Managers in charge of production and maintenance were concerned about the performance of the mill while those people were absent for training. As a result, the training for fully qualified advanced technicians was not provided on some occasions despite requests from the employees and the union.

The union became frustrated with the situation that kept some of its members from receiving the training they needed. Referring to the newly established dispute resolution procedure, the union finally expressed willingness to have an arbitrator rule on the issue. The management ultimately changed its approach and the issue was resolved before an arbitrator was appointed. Thus, it can be said that this is a case in which the dispute resolution procedure formalized by the 1989 contract agreement functioned effectively.

To understand the role of the dispute resolution procedure at LSE, however, we also should note that the workers and the union do not rely on this procedure easily and frequently. They consider this the final option since dependency on this type of procedure will undermine the principles of the LSE system manifest in the willingness to solve problems with mutual agreement. If this happens, the joint discussions of the participative committees will become merely a pre-negotiation process headed for third-party arbitration. The functionality and future evolution of this system is supported by institutional mechanisms such as autonomous work teams, pay for skill, and employment security, all of which function to prevent disputes. Ultimately, however, success depends on how strongly managers, employees, and labor unions commit to the self-direction and participative management systems, as well as how flexible they continue to be in solving problems and preventing disputes arising from the daily operation of the systems.

V. Conclusions and Implications for Future Research

The case studies discussed present two innovative approaches to work systems in unionized joint-venture steel companies located in the United States. This review illustrates four important features of these innovations. First, the trend in mechanisms for worker voice and decision making at the plant level is to move from the traditional focus on resolving disputes after they develop toward more prior consultation and joint decision making to prevent disputes or resolve them in the early stages of a conflict. This trend is observed in the JLMCC and the off-site meetings at National Steel/Great Lakes Division and participative committees at LSE.

Second, the changes toward prior consultation and joint decision making are accompanied by a change in the ideological underpinnings of the employment relationship that views participants as members of an organization or community. This is observed in the cooperative partnership, employment security, and productivity agreements at National Steel. At LSE, the changes in employment relations philosophy are reflected in the principles of participative decision making, the salary system for all employees including production-related workers, and employment security. These changes in philosophical underpinings are not complete, however: it takes time for any deep change in ideology and values to reach all the workers and managers.

Third, global competition in the steel industry imposes the need for a dispute resolution mechanism that provides flexibility while also encouraging the maximum contribution of each employee. But these innovative dispute resolution mechanisms cannot succeed if the parties neglect their commitment to solve problems in advance and in the spirit of collaboration and mutual trust.

Finally, the structural features employed for these innovations suggest some inspiration from the systems employed in Germany and Japan. Particularly, some leading members of the management and labor at those sites have visited Japan and had an opportunity to investigate the structure and function of JLMC at the sites of the Japanese partners. But the Japanese connection should not be emphasized too much in understanding these innovative systems. The driving forces behind the innovation were primarily American managers and union leaders who had been searching for better, workable systems that accommodate both worker welfare and the economic success of the company. [15] The "Japan model" was just one of the many sources of inspiration for them. [16] More influential were the experiences of innovative work systems, such as team systems, in other manufacturing sites inspired by the STS approach.

Several implications for future research emerge from this study. Our understanding of the operations and impact of the dispute resolution innovations discussed here is based on case studies focused on two unionized companies. First, past studies of innovative work systems suggest that it is important to monitor the course of events in these two companies to see how their systems evolve. We have seen how well-functioning models can slide into difficulties or even fail because of changes in their internal and external environments. Second, more case studies of industry experiences with innovations in participative management are needed to determine to what degree the experiences reported here can be generalized by identifying those internal and external factors that contribute to the creation and operation of successful dispute man-agement. Third, expanded case analyses can serve as the foundation for the development of guidelines for successful implementation of these innovations in a variety of other organizations. Finally, to examine the potential for the diffusion of these innovative work systems to other work sites, we need to ex-plore how the ideological underpinnings of employment relations that support these new systems can become more widely accepted and supported by the social structures surrounding employment relations.

Notes

1.   T. A. Kochan, H. C. Katz, and R. B. McKersie, *Collective Bargaining and Industrial Relations*, 2d ed. (Homewood, Ill.: Irwin, 1986); G. Strauss, D. G. Gallagher and J. Fiorito, eds., *The State of Unions*, (Madison, Wis.: Industrial Relations Research Association, 1991); R. E. Walton, J. Cutcher-Gershenfeld, and R. B. McKersie, *Strategic Negotiations* (Boston: Harvard Business School Press, 1994).

2.   J. Cutcher-Gershenfeld,'M. Nitta, B. Barrett, N. Belhedi, J. Bullard, C. Coutchie, T. Inaba, I. Ishino, S. Lee, W. Lin, W. Mothersell, S. Rabine, S. Ramanand, M. Strolle, and A. Wheaton, "Japanese Team-Based Work Systems in North America: Explaining the Diversity," *California Management Review* 37, no.1 (fall 1994): 42–64.

3.   See A. Verma and J. Cutcher-Gershenfeld, "Joint Governance in the Workplace: Beyond Union-Management Cooperation and Worker Participa-tion," in *Employee Representaion: Alternatives and Future Directions*, ed. B. E. Kaufman and M. M. Kleiner (Madison, Wis.: IRRA, 1993), 229 for a clearly stated discussion of this topic.

4.   A. O. Hirschman, *Exit, Loyalty and Voice* (Cambridge, Mass.: Harvard University Press, 1970).

5.   T. Hanami and R. Blanpain, eds. *Industrial Conflict Resolution in Market Economies—A Study of Australia, The Federal Republic of Germany, Italy, Japan and the USA* (Deventer, Netherlands: Kluwer, 1989).

6.   H. A. Clegg, *The System of Industrial Relations in Great Britain* (London: Basil Blackwell, 1972).

7.   M. Aoki, *Information, Incentives, and Bargaining in the Japanese Econ-omy* (Cambridge, UK: Cambridge University Press,1988); K. Nakamura and M. Nitta, "Developments in Industrial Relations and Human Resource Practices in Japan," in *Employment Relations in a Changing World Economy*, ed. R. Locke, T. Kochan, and M. Piore (Cambridge, Mass.: MIT Press, 1995), 325–58; M.

Nitta, "Joint Labor-Management Committees in Japan," in *Managing Together: Consultation and Participation in the Workplace*, ed. E. Davis and R. Lansbury (South Melborne, Australia: Longman Cheshire, 1996).

8.   J. T. Dunlop, *Industrial Relations Systems* (New York: Holt, Rinehart and Winston, 1958).

9.   S. Webbs and B. Webbs, *Industrial Democracy* (London, UK: Longmans, 1897).

10.   This contrast resembles the comparison between "market principle" and "organization principle" used by R. Dore in *British Factory-Japanese Factory* (London, UK: George Allen and Unwin, 1973) to describe the difference between Japanese and British labor relations. Pointing out similarities between employment relations in Japan and Germany does not suggest that these systems are identical. While the membership of intrafirm occupational groups plays an important role side by side that of the firm and plant in Germany, a stronger sense of membership and homogeneity among regular employees is observed in Japan.

11.   For the most clearly exemplified case study in the United States, see S. Rubinstein, M. Bennett and T. Kochan, "The Saturn Partnership: Co-Management and the Reinvention of the Local Union," in *Employee Representation: Alternatives and Future Directions*, ed. B. E. Kaufman and M. M. Kleiner (Madison, Wis.: IRRA, 1993), 339–70. This describes the "joint management" used at Saturn by the Ford Motor Company and the United Automobile Workers (UAW).

12.   P. Cappelli and R. B.McKersie, "Management Strategy and the Design of Workrules," *Journal of Management Studies* 24, no. 5 (September 1987): 441–62.

13.   J. P. Hoerr, *And the Wolf Finally Came: The Decline of the American Steel Industry* (Pittsburgh: University of Pittsburgh Press, 1988); T. Kochan and H. C. Katz, *Collective Bargaining and Industrial Relations*, 2d ed. (Homewood, Ill.: Irwin, 1988); U.S. Department of Labor, Bureau of Labor-Management Relations and Cooperative Programs, *Cooperative Partnership: A New Beginning for National Steel Corporations and the United Steelworkers of America* (BLMR 114, 1987).

14.   For example, see Hoerr, *op. cit.*, 619, and Japan Institute of Labor, *Amerika Tekko Snagyo no Saikin no Rosikankei no Tenkai ni kansuru Kenkyu (Recent Developments in Industrial Relations in the American Steel Industry)* (Research Report, Tokyo: Japan Institute of Labor, 1995).

15.   For example see U.S. Department of Labor, 1987, *op. cit.*

16.   This does not mean all the innovations in production and work systems at those sites were solely initiated by American managers and union leaders. For example, the Trade and Craft Combination at the Great Lakes Division of National Steel is closely associated with the organizational restructuring of maintenance systems promoted under the leadership of a Japanese engineer (Japan Institute of Labor, *op. cit.*).

8

DISPUTE PROCEDURES IN
WESTERN EUROPE

R. Oliver Clarke

I. Introduction

The purpose of this chapter is to review a variety of dispute resolution procedures in Western Europe. This introduction will discuss two distinctions made in many European countries. It will indicate the comparative experience of work stoppages and look at the relevant international standards. The means of resolving disputes then will be examined with reference to four European countries which exhibit substantially different procedures: Britain, France, Germany, and Sweden. The examination will cover both arrangements for mediating disputes made by the parties themselves and the arrangements offered by the state. The final section of the chapter will draw conclusions from the experience of the four countries examined, noting trends and points of comparison with the procedures used in the United States. It will also compare experience in the particular case of "emergency" disputes, that is, disputes that have an important impact on the national interest.

Two distinctions are important for an understanding of European industrial disputes—or more particularly for continental Europe, for they do not have equal significance in Britain. First, and most important, a dispute may concern "rights" or "interests." A dispute over rights exists when an employer and a worker or workers, or an employer and a trade union, disagree about the interpretation of a law, a collective agreement, or a contract of employment. An example would be when an employer and a union disagree about which of two possible job categories a worker should be placed in when the agreed categories carry different rates of pay. Such a dispute lends itself readily to some form of third-party decision: it is "justiciable." A dispute of interests exists when a trade union lodges a claim for a general increase in wages and the employer makes what the union regards as an unsatisfactory offer.

The second distinction to be noted is that between individual and collective disputes. For instance, the French labor tribunals deal basically with cases filed by individual employees, but in the Swedish labor courts the trade unions acting as the collective agent have a virtual monopoly on filing cases.

There are wide differences in the extent to which countries succeed in resolving disputes without resorting to strikes, lockouts, or other industrial action, as shown in table 1. This table shows the record for the four countries considered here, as well as the most peaceful European country of any size— Switzerland—and what is at present the European country with the most working days lost proportionally—Greece. Figures for the United States are included by way of comparison.

Table 1. Strikes and Working Days Lost

Country	All Industries and Services		Average Working Days Lost Per 1,000 Employees 1984-1993
	No. of strikes in 1993	Working Days Lost in 1993	
	I	II	III
France[1]	1,351	510,900	50
Germany[2]	N/A	592,995	40
Sweden	398	189,828	90
United Kingdom	211	649,000	240
Switzerland	3	673	Negligible
Greece	161(1991)	1,602,310	3,750
United States[3]	35	3,091,200	70

Notes:
[1] Figures exclude civil servants and other white collar employees.
[2] 1993 data represents the entire Federal Republic. Up to 1992 data represented West Germany only.
[3] Since 1981 U.S. statistics only cover strikes involving more than 1,000 workers— previously the threshold was six workers—for more than one day or shift.
Sources: ILO Yearbook of Labor Statistics, 1994; and Derek Bird, "International Comparisons of Labor Disputes," *Employment Gazette*, London, December 1994.

Even taking account of the many qualifications which must be made in assessing strike statistics, it is evident that there are considerable differences in the extent to which countries are successful in mediating conflict. If other industrial countries were added to the comparison shown in table 1, it would be seen that Spain, Canada, and Italy are high in workdays lost (580, 350, and 310, respectively in column III), while Austria and Japan are very low, and would be classified as "negligible" in column III.

Labor disputes are included in the rule-making of certain international organizations and individual nations. The countries considered in this chapter are not only members of the International Labour Organization (ILO), as is the United States, but are also members of the Council of Europe and the European Union. The relevant activities of these organizations will be summarized here.

The ILO has a worldwide responsibility for establishing labor standards. These are formulated after lengthy research and discussion and have to be approved at one of the annual (tripartite) conferences of the organization. They are in the form of "conventions" (175 of them as of 1994), which member countries (170 in 1994) are invited to ratify. Ratification has the effect of making the conventions binding on the country concerned. The International Labour Office has an extensive system of oversight, keeping the application of the conventions under review.[1] The ILO also promulgates "recommendations" (182 as of 1994), which do not give birth to obligations but provide guidelines for action.

Three conventions and two recommendations are of particular interest to the subject of this chapter. Conventions 87 and 98 deal with freedom of association and the right to organize and bargain collectively. Convention 154 is concerned with the promotion of collective bargaining, and states that "bodies and procedures for the settlement of labor disputes should be so conceived as to contribute to the promotion of collective bargaining." Recommendation 92 says that machinery should be made available to assist in the prevention and settlement of disputes and Recommendation 130 deals with "examination of grievances within the undertaking with a view to their settlement." The provisions of each of these guidelines are reasonable enough and make no demands that industrial relations experts would regard as excessive. Typical is the suggestion in Recommendation 130 that grievance procedures "should be as uncomplicated and rapid as possible."

The Council of Europe adopted a European Social Charter in 1961.[2] The charter invites its "contracting parties" to promote joint consultation, negotiating machinery for the regulation of terms and conditions of employment by means of collective agreements and voluntary arbitration for the settlement of labor disputes. It calls on them to recognize "the right of workers and employers to collective action in cases of conflicts of interest, including the right to strike, subject to obligations that might arise out of collective agreements previously entered into."[3]

The European Union, though markedly interventionist in industrial relations, is not authorized[4] to deal with the right to strike or lockout. Nevertheless, its executive agency, the European Commission, has conducted a survey of its member countries on their laws affecting strikes and the prevention and settlement of industrial conflict.[5]

In each of the four country discussions in this chapter, the following topics are addressed: the industrial relations background of the country, the structure of collective bargaining and related grievance procedures, the laws relating to strikes, and the role of the state in managing and resolving disputes. It should be noted that the Federal Mediation and Conciliation Service (FMCS) and the National Labor Relations Board (NLRB), the two major federal organizations used to settle disputes in the United States, do not correspond to European institutions and services. We now turn to the countries to be reviewed, starting with Britain.

II. Britain

A. The Industrial Relations Background

Britain is the country where the industrial revolution occurred. And although it has not suffered political upheaval for several centuries or foreign occupation since the eleventh century, it would be a mistake to expect it to have a neat and tidy system of industrial relations. The structure of British trade unions is particularly untidy. It is a mixture of general, industrial, craft and occupational unions of all shapes and sizes. British trade unions have been losing members continuously since their peak in 1979. Some unity is provided by having one central body, the Trades Union Congress (TUC), with which the great majority of unions are affiliated. Employers' associations are mostly industry-based, headed by a single central body, the Confederation of British Industry.

For more than a century, collective bargaining has been used to determine wages and working conditions, the dominant level gradually becoming industrywide, but then, from the 1960s, moving down to the enterprise or workplace level. Collective agreements are not legally binding. They may contain a "peace clause" stating that there should be no departure from normal working during the life of the agreement, but this too is not legally binding either. Britain has never made any clear distinction between disputes of rights and interest disputes, or between individual and collective disputes.

A peculiarity of British practice has been the extent to which grievance procedures have been used for bargaining. Thus, the existence of collectively negotiated rates of pay in an establishment has not stopped unions from claiming increases for groups of their members. Since many agreements are open-ended and multiunionism in enterprises has been widespread, numerous British managements have found themselves in almost continuous negotiation, notably in the 1960s and 1970s. Today, with declining union membership, union amalgamations, the decline of industrywide bargaining, and greater resistance by employers to fragmented bargaining, sectionalism is now much less marked.

In the years immediately after the Second World War, the British considered their industrial relations system one of the best in the world. There were relatively few disputes and industrywide bargaining was supplemented by grievance procedures and a network of joint consultative committees within enterprises. British governments were content to leave industrial relations largely to employers and trade unions. In the decade of the 1960s, however, with the growth of worker militancy and with unprecedented low unemployment, the industrial relations system came under more and more criticism for the prevalence of unofficial strikes and restrictive practices, and for the consequences of fragmented bargaining. From 1969 on, successive governments sought to improve the situation, generally unsuccessfully, until the advent of the Conservative governments that governed Britain from 1979 to 1997.

The central debate in the 1960s and 1970s was between the Labour Party governments who supported the voluntarist approach and the Conservatives who supported the legalistic approach. The British tradition of volunteerism was based on employers and unions regulating their own affairs with a minimum amount of legislation. Its advocates viewed this as something of much value, which should be preserved. In contrast, others considered a firm new legal framework essential to overcome the problems which had come to pervade the system. Between 1980 and 1993, after both Conservative and Labour legislation in the 1970s, a series of eight Conservative laws sought to recast the system. The approach, learning from earlier failures, was to proceed incrementally, with pauses after each change, rather than attempting one comprehensive reconstruction, which was tried with the ill-fated Conservatives' Industrial Relations Act, 1971. If the new legislation has not changed the hearts and minds of British workers, it has certainly made workers and their trade unions think carefully before striking.

B. Enterprise Dispute Resolution Procedures

The general mechanisms for resolving disputes in Britain are collective bargaining and grievance procedures. The use of collective bargaining has been declining and by 1990 it covered less than half of the employed population.[6] The major change over the years has been the decreasing use of multiemployer bargaining, though it remains an important form.[7] The third Workplace Industrial Relations Survey (WIRS3), carried out in 1990, found a substantial reduction in multiemployer bargaining over pay. Multiemployer bargaining was the main method of pay determination in only a quarter of the workplaces surveyed. As a result of the decline in union membership, and derecognition of unions in some enterprises, the proportion of workplaces in private industry where pay was determined at the workplace level by management increased between 1984 and 1990 from 33 percent to 44 percent for manual workers, with a smaller increase for nonmanual workers.[8] Thirty-eight percent of all establishments specified recourse to arbitration at the end of their procedures for resolving disputes on pay and working conditions.[9] In the public sector, the considerable extent of privatization and decentralization have led to smaller bargaining units.

As to grievance procedures, there is no standard model. But they are ubiquitous throughout industry. They generally provide a series of steps to resolve disputes that sometimes end in meetings involving an employers' association and union official and sometimes end in arbitration. WIRS3 found that 94 percent of managers reported that they had some form of grievance procedure.[10]

C. Services of the State

Parliamentary concern about disputes dates back to the Cotton Arbitration Act, 1800, and other early arbitration measures, and to inquiries such as that made by the Select Committee on Masters and Operatives (Equitable

Councils of Conciliation), 1856. The most durable were the arrangements made under the Conciliation Act, 1896, and the Industrial Courts Act, 1919. Under this legislation the minister of labour was given power to advise disputants and to hold inquiries into disputes. An arbitrating body, the industrial court, was established, to which the minister could refer a case for arbitration if the parties consented and any relevant procedure had been exhausted. The advisory service kept in touch with the development of disputes and was available to give help, including conciliation, to disputants, when asked to do so. The inquiry power provided for courts of inquiry and committees of investigation. "court" was a misnomer since the body did not have normal judicial powers. When faced with an important and obdurate dispute the minister could appoint a chairperson (sometimes but by no means always a lawyer) and, in most cases, two or more people from union and employer circles, who would conduct hearings and then prepare a report, to be laid (technically) before Parliament. The court customarily made recommendations for a possible settlement. Usually no more than two or three such courts a year were set up and none has been established in recent years because of the role of the Advisory, Conciliation and Arbitration Service (ACAS), discussed below.

A key factor was that after a short lapse of time and after exposing their arguments to neutrals, and then to the general public through the report of the court, the parties usually saw their dispute in a new light, and were able to reach agreement. As an alternative to the court procedure a committee of investigation could be set up. This was a much lighter-weight inquiry. It worked in a manner that was similar to the court of inquiry, but its findings did not have to be sent to Parliament.

The conciliation staff maintained by the Ministry of Labour, or Department of Employment as it became subsequently,[11] experienced some difficulties in the 1960s and early 1970s since many disputes were concerned with pay claims higher than what the government considered permissible in relation to its economic policies. Unions felt that as a servant of the state the conciliator was likely to be inhibited by government policy from viewing their claims on what they considered to be their merits. This was an important reason behind the decision of the government, in 1974, to transfer the department's industrial peacemaking services to a new body, ACAS, which was given statutory form by the Employment Protection Act, 1975.

ACAS is a government-funded but independent body, headed by a fulltime chairperson who is the chief executive, and governed by a council comprising the chairperson and part-time people from union, employer, and academic circles. It offers advice and conciliation services to employers, unions, and workers and can arrange mediation and arbitration. It can conduct investigations and it issues codes of practice. It also has a duty to conciliate before a hearing in cases referred to industrial tribunals. ACAS normally requires that any procedure agreed to by the parties must be exhausted before it accepts a case. A statutory duty to advance the practice of collective bargaining was removed in 1993. In 1995 ACAS was asked to conciliate in 1,321 collective disputes. It received 91,568 requests for conciliation on employment rights issues, more than half of which had reference to unfair dismissal. The service's headquarters and regional offices handled 538,394 inquiries, most made by telephone.

Another public agency is the Central Arbitration Committee (CAC), dating from 1975 but a descendant of the Industrial Court set up under the Act of 1919. It comprises a chairperson and members with industrial experience. At the request of one or more parties to a dispute, and if all of them consent and voluntary procedures have been exhausted, ACAS may refer a dispute to the committee. Relatively little use is now made of the committee.

D. The Industrial Tribunals

The industrial tribunals were originally created by the Industrial Training Act, 1964, to deal with employers' appeals against levies[12] imposed by industrial training boards. By the Redundancy Payments Act, 1965, they were given responsibility for assessing claims concerning payments to workers dismissed through lack of work, and under the Industrial Relations Act, 1971, they acquired responsibility for dealing with workers' claims that they had been unfairly dismissed. A variety of functions related to employment were added by later legislation. The tribunals were meant to provide a flexible, informal, and relatively speedy means of settling a wide range of rights disputes. Although there is no question of replacing them, they have become increasingly legalistic, somewhat inflexible, and by no means speedy. The workload of the tribunals has increased steadily since their creation. The central and regional offices deal with approximately 12,500 hearings a year.[13]

Each tribunal consists of a chairperson who is a lawyer of not less than seven years' standing and who may be fulltime or parttime, supported by two lay members with industrial experience, one with an employer and one with a union background. The parties may appear before the tribunal themselves or they may be represented by, for instance, a lawyer or a trade union or employers' association official. Appeals from tribunal judgments may be made on questions of law, but in certain types of cases also on questions of fact, to the Employment Appeal Tribunal (EAT).[14] Thence, appeal can be made on questions of law only to the Court of Appeal[15] and from there to the House of Lords.

E. The Law Relating to Strikes

No description of the resolution of labor disputes in Britain would be complete without reference to the changed legal position of strikes under the laws passed since 1980. The long-standing position is that British workers and their unions have no right to strike as such. What they have is a negative right: they have immunity from actions in tort[16] provided that the strike is "in contemplation or furtherance of a trade dispute," a formula dating back to the Trade Disputes Act, 1906. From 1980 on, the legislation has reduced the immunity by excluding the following actions: secondary or sympathetic strikes; interunion disputes; foreign-based strikes; strikes without a previous ballot in favor;

and strikes in support of a closed shop. Political strikes are not protected. The Employment Act, 1988, removed the right of unions to discipline members who cross picket lines, and the Employment Act, 1990, required that if industrial action was organized by a union official, including a shop steward, it must either be put to a secret ballot or specifically repudiated by the union. Finally, the Trade Union Reform and Employment Rights Act, 1993, required that strike ballots should be conducted by postal voting and be independently scrutinized. Employers should have at least seven days notice of official union action and ordinary citizens were given the right to seek to restrain unlawfully organized strikes. If unions failed to observe the rules laid down, they would be open to legal action, and if they were defiant their funds could be sequestered.

In sum, the British approach to resolving labor disputes is that most are dealt with by collective bargaining, together with grievance procedures. The system is supported by public agencies (the ACAS and the CAC), to which disputants can turn for help and, for specific issues, notably disputed dismissals, the industrial tribunals and the EAT.

III. France

A. The Industrial Relations Background

Orderliness has never been a characteristic of the French industrial relations system, although this does not seem to have impeded industrial success. There are several competing confederations of unions, the largest of which is still communist in orientation. Of the other two large confederations, one is traditionally radical but not communist and the other is politically uncommitted but has become increasingly militant in the last few years. Each of these centers heads up a number of industrial unions. The rate of unionization, having severely declined since the mid-1970s, is probably no higher than 10 to 12 percent. Although they have several groupings, employers are more united than the unions and are led by a single body, the National Council of French Employers (Conseil National du Patronat Français).

Collective bargaining has grown over the years, and takes place at both the industry and the enterprise level. In 1985 it covered 92 percent of the workforce.[17] There are three main reasons for this surprisingly high figure. First, under the law of 13 November 1982, enterprises in which unions have workforce representation must negotiate annually. Second, the practice of extension allows a collective agreement to be extended by the minister of labor to cover unorganized employers and workers in the industry concerned. Third, virtually all of the fairly extensive public sector, where unionization is much higher than in the private sector, is covered by collective agreements. Committees to interpret collective agreements and conciliation committees exist formally under collective agreements but "have fallen into complete disuse."[18]

Efforts to strengthen the structure of French industrial relations have come more from successive governments than from unions or employers. Several laws have established and strengthened workers' representation at the workplace. This has resulted in an unusually complex representative system with works committees (comités d'entreprise); personnel representatives (délégués du personnel); trade union sections (sections syndicales) and representatives (délégués syndicaux); health, safety and working conditions committees (comités d'hygiène, de securité et des conditions de travail); and workers' expression groups (groupes d'expression).[19] These bodies afford a variety of means for airing grievances.

B. The Law Relating to Strikes

The right to strike is specifically recognized in the French Constitution, to be "exercised within the framework of the laws governing it." In the private sector there is generally no legal regulation of the right, provided that the subject concerned is occupational and not political. In the public sector, strikes by police, prison officers, and security personnel are prohibited. For other public sector workers, five days' notice of industrial action must be given and in some sections, such as television broadcasting and air traffic control, a skeleton service must be provided. Lockouts, with some exceptions, are generally considered under case law to be illegal.

Statistically, France is not a high-strike country, but the prominence of some strikes, notably in the public sector, plus the use of warning strikes, sometimes suggests more disruption than there is. Most French strikes are short since French unions do not normally provide strike pay.

If dispute resolution procedures are not prescribed by collective agreements or have been exhausted, a possibility exists for the parties to a dispute to turn to a public regional or national conciliation commission. Mediation can be adopted by the parties, or be set in motion by the minister of labor, the prefect (the principal representative of the state in each administrative region), or another official. The mediator is given a month to make a recommendation, which the parties are free to reject, giving their reasons, within eight days. If the matter has not been settled in conciliation or mediation it may be referred to arbitration if both parties agree. The decision then becomes binding, although the parties can contest it in the superior arbitration court (cour supérieur d'arbitrage) on grounds of illegality or being outside the arbitrator's scope of responsibility. None of these public procedures is used extensively.[20] Amadieu has summed up attempts to build effective dispute procedures bluntly: "The French system has been unable to equip itself with joint conciliation and arbitration bodies that can consider individual complaints, resolve differences in interpretation of collective agreements, and find solutions to collective conflicts before they result in strikes."[21]

C. The Labor Inspector

An agent of conciliation not mentioned thus far is the labor inspector (inspecteur du travail). This official's main responsibility is ensuring that laws, and particularly the laws pertaining to safety and health at work, are obeyed.

The inspector has no legal power to resolve grievances or strikes but may play an informal part. For example, if an employee complains of a wrongful act by an employer, advice may be given as to legal rights and means of redress. The inspector may then suggest a solution to the employer. Though no such role is prescribed by law, the inspector may also mediate in disputes, informally, at the request of the parties. Given the volume of the inspector's other work, however, little time can be given to the peacemaking function.

D. The Labor Tribunals

In contrast to collective dispute resolution procedures, the labor tribunals (Conseils de Prud'hommes) are widely used for individual rights disputes, and are generally satisfactory. This almost unique institution originated in Lyon in the eighteenth century but started its continuing life under an Act of March 1806. It was extended by a Decree of June 1809 that allowed such bodies to be set up anywhere the government considered to be desirable.[22] The present basis of the tribunals is laid down in the Acts of January 18th 1979 and May 6th 1982. The tribunals have jurisdiction over disputes arising from any individual contract of employment or apprenticeship. If small sums of money are involved, there is no appeal from a tribunal's decision but otherwise an appeal may be made to the social chambers of the courts of appeal and on to the Cour de Cassation, the highest court for civil and criminal actions. The jurisdiction of the tribunals has been given a wide interpretation, including all aspects of "the conclusion, interpretation, discharge and termination of all employment contracts."[23] Individual cases have been used to put forward claims which could result in a collective application of a decision.

In principle, the labor tribunals are divided into five sections: commerce, industry, agriculture, managerial and professional employees, and miscellaneous activities. The members are selected by employers and employees.[24] Elections are held every five years on slates of candidates proposed by unions and employer organizations. There is at least one tribunal for each tribunal de grande instance (the second tier of the ordinary court structure in France). Unlike most comparable bodies elsewhere, the tribunals comprise only employer and employee representatives. The role requirements for prud'hommes are that they should be French nationals, never convicted of certain crimes, employers or employees (or in some cases recently retired) at the time of the election,[25] and at least twenty-one years of age. No legal qualification is required.

Each section of the tribunals comprises at least one conciliation unit (bureau de conciliation) and one unit giving rulings (bureau de jugement). The procedure requires a conciliation stage, by a board of conciliation, before any judgmental hearing. Rojot cites a view that "at least two-thirds of all cases are concluded via conciliation, within four months of the date of filing."[26] If no agreement can be reached in conciliation, the case goes to the board of judgment, which reaches its decision by majority vote. If the board cannot agree it brings in a magistrate (juge d'instance) to preside over its meeting. Conciliation meetings are held in private, and judgmental meetings in public.

The parties have a duty to appear in person, but if they can show good cause for not appearing they may be represented, but only by a colleague in the same plant, a trade union official, an advocate, or a spouse.[27]

The low level of unionization in France and the divisions between unions have made it difficult to develop collectively agreed means of dispute resolution. The dominant form of resolving collective interests disputes—collective bargaining—has been shaped by successive laws, while individual rights disputes are a matter for the labor tribunals. In France, in contrast with the other countries considered here, the institutions and practices of conflict resolution have had considerable input from government.

IV. Germany

A. The Industrial Relations Background

In 1945 Germany had to start afresh to create an industrial relations system. In several respects the system that evolved incorporated elements of the system which operated under the Weimar Republic that preceded the Nazi takeover of 1933. It also contained several new features and amounted to a well-designed and integrated whole. Apart from additions to strengthen industrial democracy, the system has experienced no fundamental change since its creation, and it has served Germany well.

The main trade union structure comprises sixteen industrywide unions, united in a single central body, the German Trade Union Federation (Deutsche Gewerkschaftsbund, or DGB). Other trade union centers exist for white-collar workers and civil servants, and there is a smaller federation with a Christian orientation. Industry-wide employers' associations belong to a central organization dealing with labor matters, the German Employers' Confederation (Bundesvereinigung der Deutschen Arbeitgeberverbände, or BDA).

Wages and working conditions are determined by collective bargaining conducted by industry at the regional or national level, though there is some enterprise-level bargaining. As in France, collective agreements may be extended by the minister of labor. Matters on which employers and workers are deemed to have common interests are handled within the enterprise by the employer and the works council, an elected body of workers commonly including nonunion as well as union members. The works council has an obligation to strive to keep the peace and to cooperate in good faith with the employer. It has important rights to information, consultation, and co-determination. In principle it plays no part in collective bargaining. Broadly speaking, therefore, matters involving major conflicts are kept out of the enterprise, and management-worker interaction promotes a cooperative relationship within it.[28]

B. Codetermination

An understanding of the German form of industrial democracy, or co-determination (Mitbestimmung), is essential for understanding the industrial relations system as a whole. The German company board is usually two-tiered, with a supervisory board of nonexecutive directors (the Aufsichtsrat) and a management board of full-time directors (the Vorstand). A series of laws determine worker/union representation on the supervisory board by enterprise size. In coal, iron, and steel, representation is 50 percent in enterprises employing more than 1,000 workers. In other companies employing 2,000 or more workers, representation is also 50 percent, but with qualifications that virtually ensure that the shareholders' representatives have the last word. In other companies with 500 or more workers, worker/union representatives have one-third of the places on the supervisory board. In coal, iron, and steel, one member of the management board, the labor director, is practically a trade union nominee. Just as board representation ensures that the workers' viewpoint is not lost in the supervisory board's overview of company strategy, the works council, as already mentioned, ensures representation at the workplace level. In principle unions have no control over the works councils but so many council chairpersons and members belong to trade unions that, again, a mainly cooperative situation exists.

C. The Law Relating to Strikes

The legal position of strikes and lockouts in Germany has been developed by the federal labor court (Bundesarbeitsgericht) and the constitutional court (Bundesverfassungsgericht). In effect the right to strike is a union right, not a worker's right. Union rules commonly prescribe a 75 percent majority in pre-strike ballots before calling a strike. A strike must respect the peace obligation implicit in collective agreements. It must be a last resort and it must not be an excessive instrument to effect its purpose. Civil servants do not have the right to strike. Lockouts are regarded as a defensive, and not an offensive weapon; they must be proportional to the extent of the action to which they are a response.

To sum up, German industrial relations are the subject of comprehensive and detailed legal specification. Such a framework might not suit other countries but it does mean that everyone concerned knows what is and what is not permissible. The pieces fit together and there is no doubt that the system has contributed to the smooth working of German industry.

As to disputes, the principle of Tarifautonomie (bargaining autonomy for employers and unions) ensures that it is mainly up to employers, unions, and workers to sort out their differences themselves. Industrial and trade union leaders have built effective structures providing mediation in collective interests disputes and arbitration for disputes between an employer and a works council. Legislators have provided labor courts for disputes of rights.

D. Collective Interest Disputes

Control Council Law 35, of August 1946, advised employers' associations and trade unions to provide procedures for the settlement of collective labor disputes and obliged the minister of labor of each land (State) to establish a conciliation commission. Public conciliation would come into play only if private procedures did not exist or had failed. In 1949 the central employers and union organizations told the federal labor minister that they preferred private to public conciliation and prepared a model of their own. This model was approved in the Margarethenhof Agreement of September 7th, 1954. If negotiations reached an impasse, the agreement recommended affiliates to establish that the claim should be referred to a mediation commission comprising equal numbers of representatives from the employers' association and trade union concerned. One of the representatives might take the chair or there might be an independent chairperson. Such committees have been adopted in most industries.

Proposals for settlement made by a commission are not binding unless that has been agreed upon in advance, but if they are accepted they then have the same effect as a collective agreement. If the commission cannot find a solution, or if its proposal is not accepted, the peace obligation which applies in German collective bargaining is at an end and a strike can begin.

E. Disputes between an Employer and a Works Council

For disputes between an employer and a works council, an arbitration committee (Einigungstelle) is provided. It is normally constituted for particular cases but it may be a standing body. The makeup of the body is left to the parties concerned, each nominating its representative members, both from inside and outside the firm. The neutral chairperson is jointly decided, but if the parties cannot agree the labor court makes the appointment. In fact an overwhelming majority of chairpersons are qualified judges of labor courts. Hearings are in private. Decisions are adopted by majority vote, with the chairperson abstaining in the first round of voting. The committee is required to consider the interests both of the enterprise and of the workers concerned. Either party may dispute the award of the committee by appealing to the labor court, but only on a matter of law, not of substance.[29] In other words, the court would only rule on whether the decision of the committee had been properly determined and conformed to German law.

German law provides no specific machinery for addressing grievances in an enterprise, but in fact there are a variety of options for raising a complaint. The worker may raise it with the appropriate level(s) of management, or can seek the help of a works council member or of the works council itself, in the expectation that the council will take it up with the employer. In this last case the matter could be taken on to the arbitration committee. If it is a rights matter the worker can take it up with the labor court.[30]

F. Labor Courts

The mediation commissions and the arbitration committees are the responsibility of the employers and unions, but disputes of rights are heard by labor courts (Arbeitsgerichter), which are statutory bodies. The courts, though separate from ordinary courts, are part of the German judicial system. Set up under the Labor Courts Act, 1953, revised in 1979, the district courts are supplemented by appellate labor courts and a federal labor court, seated in the city of Kassel. The courts are composed of panels of professional judges supported by lay judges, drawn from employer and union circles. The professional judges, at all three levels, are appointed for life. The courts deal with both individual and collective disputes of rights. Cases are first considered in a conciliation meeting in which the chairperson tries to guide the parties to a settlement. If no settlement is reached, the case goes forward to a hearing by the court at a later date. The most frequent subject of cases is dismissal, followed by pay. Cases may be brought by an individual employee, a works council, a trade union, an employer, an employers' association, or a state agency, though in practice the vast majority of cases are brought by the workers' side. The parties may put their case themselves or they may be represented by a union or employers' association official or by counsel; in hearings of the federal court, legal representation is required. The peace obligation precludes industrial action being taken on the kinds of issues handled by the labor courts.[31]

In Germany, therefore, collective interests disputes are resolved by collective bargaining, adding conciliation when necessary. In contrast, collective and individual rights disputes are handled mainly by the labor courts. Of the four countries considered here, Germany has the most logical structure for dealing with labor disputes, which is directly related to the good record of industrial peace which the country enjoys. Substantial strikes do occasionally take place in Germany, but usually only on issues of interests when negotiation has been exhausted and mediation has failed. The small number of such strikes is evidence of the success of the system.

V. Sweden

A. The Industrial Relations Background

The early history of Swedish industrial relations gave no evidence of the enviable record of industrial peace that the country was subsequently to enjoy. It was not until the Basic Agreement ("Saltsjöbaden Agreement") was signed in 1938 by the manual workers' trade union federation (Landsorganisation i Sverige, or LO) and the employers' confederation (Svenska Arbetsgivareföreningen, or SAF) that cooperation could be said to have replaced conflict as the hallmark of the system.

The Basic Agreement set out a framework to govern the relationship between the parties, including the handling of disputes. Together with the active labor market policy based on the Rehn-Meidner model (named after the two LO economists who devised it), the agreement forms the basis of what came to be known as the "Swedish Model." Throughout the 1950s and 1960s, this model was perhaps the most effective industrial relations system of any industrial country, including Germany.

The characteristics of the Swedish model were as follows:

1. Few, powerful, independent central bodies on each side.
2. Employer respect for trade union rights and interests and union respect for private ownership in a free market economy, for managerial rights, and for the need for rationalization and efficient management.
3. That government should do only what the parties cannot do themselves, chiefly to provide an appropriate economic framework and to finance a national manpower policy.[32]
4. Maintenance of industrial peace.[33]
5. Highly developed negotiation and consultation procedures.
6. The active labor market policy of support for labor mobility providing exceptionally low levels of unemployment.
7. Employers' tacit acceptance of LO's policy of reducing differences in pay (the "solidaristic wage policy").

In the mid-1950s, the collective bargaining part of the model evolved to produce an articulated system: there were central national agreements to which industrywide and enterprise agreements had to conform.

The Swedish model began to deteriorate at the beginning of the 1970s with a wave of worker militancy and a growing tendency for LO to attack managerial prerogatives in the name of industrial democracy. The LO pressed government for legislation which the employers saw as contrary to the "spirit of Saltsjöbaden." Although the industrial relations system still has many strengths today, the Swedish model is widely regarded as dead. There are now four characteristics of Swedish industrial relations. First, there is a high level of unionization (around 83 percent) dominated by LO and two white-collar union centers. Second, there are strong employer organizations, but since the central employers' confederation terminated its bargaining role in 1990, the level at which bargaining occurs remains uncertain but tends to be industrywide. Third, there is a somewhat higher level of strikes than in the past. Fourth, unemployment, which was kept below 4 percent until the early 1990s, has risen substantially with the deterioration of the Swedish economy.

A major result of the union attack on managerial prerogatives in the 1970s was the Codetermination at Work Act (Lag 1976 om Medbestämmande i Arbetslivet, or MBL), which was fleshed out for the private sector by the Development Agreement of 1982. The MBL entitles the union to negotiate on almost any issue relevant to the relationship between the employer and the union members (section 10 of the act). This might apply, for example, to "personnel reallocation, the giving of notice, recruitment, managerial appointments, new working methods, new production, the preparation of the budget and organizational change."[34] Section 11 places the onus on the employer to initiate negotiations with the union before deciding on any major change in activities, working conditions, or terms of employment.[35] A safeguard is provided for the employer, however, so that a decision may be implemented if there are urgent reasons to do so. Should the employer fail to open negotiations, or refuse to negotiate, the labor court (see below) may award damages.[36] The MBL also provides (section 33) that, in disputes over the interpretation of a codetermination agreement, priority is given to the union's view until the matter has been finally tried by the labor court. The union has a right of veto where the employer wishes to subcontract certain work.

B. The Law Relating to Strikes

Strikes and lockouts are both legal in Sweden. In fact Sweden is one of the few countries, and the only one of the four considered here, where lockouts are significant. The right to strike was extended to public employees in 1965, but does not cover political strikes. Unions and employers are required to give at least seven days' written notice to each other before action is taken (MBL, section 45). Unofficial strikes are not uncommon in Sweden. When they occur the organization concerned is obligated to try to bring them to an end.

There are, however, qualifications to the right to industrial action. Thus the MBL forbids action if it is a breach of a collectively agreed peace obligation or if the action has as its goal any one of the following:

1. to exert pressure in a dispute over the validity of a collective agreement, its existence, or its correct meaning, or in a dispute as to whether a particular procedure is contrary to the agreement or this Act
2. to bring about alteration of the agreement
3. to effect a provision which it is intended will come into operation when the agreement has ceased to apply, or
4. to support some other party who is not himself permitted to take industrial action" (section 41)

Any action taken must conform to the rules of the organization concerned. Action is permitted during the life of an agreement if it is concerned with matters not covered by the agreement; if it is secondary action in support of legal primary action; if it is to secure unpaid wages; or if it is aimed at securing a codetermination agreement.

C. Collective Interest Disputes and the Mediation Service

Collective interests disputes are normally resolved by collective bargaining. The stress placed by Swedish unions and employers on the peaceful resolution of differences has ensured that, despite some increase in recent years, days lost through strikes or lockouts are relatively low.

A national mediation service, with mediators for different regions, was introduced as long ago as 1906 and was revised by an Act of 1920. It now comes under the MBL (section 46ff). The national mediation office monitors industrial negotiations and, when requested, or on its own initiative, appoints mediators to act in disputes which threaten to result, or have already resulted, in industrial action. The mediators are usually experienced lawyers, serving in a part-time capacity. In major disputes the government may appoint a special mediator or a mediation commission. The mediators have no power to postpone action although they are usually able to persuade the parties to do so, or to revoke action which has already started. Their task is to facilitate settlement of the dispute and they have no power to insist on solutions. A mediator may propose, but not insist on, arbitration,[37] though arbitration is little used in Sweden, except for resolving piecework disputes.

D. Rights Disputes

Rights disputes, or those concerned with the application of legislation or collective agreements, may not be pursued through industrial action. Some may be handled by the common courts of first instance but most, if they are not settled by negotiation between the parties, go to the labor court (Arbetsdomstolen, or AD). In cases brought direct to the court there is no appeal from its decisions. In cases which have gone to the ordinary court, the labor court serves as a court of appeal.

The labor court was set up by the Labor Courts Act, 1928, to interpret the provisions of collective agreements, though it has some other functions. Employers and unions are free, if they wish, to make other arrangements for settling disputes about collective agreements. If they go to the court they must first have tried to settle the case themselves through their own procedures. The chairperson and vice-chairperson of the court are experienced judges. There are also three neutral members who are not associated with employers, or with trade unions. The remaining thirteen members are lay people that come from union or employer circles. Most cases are judged by a court of seven—the chairperson and two other official members and two from each side of the lay members. After receiving written and oral arguments, the court seeks to conciliate between the parties. If conciliation fails, a hearing goes ahead and the court makes its determination.

For disputed dismissals, the case must be brought by the employee's trade union. If the union will not represent its member, the case has to be taken to an ordinary court. The remedy for unjustified dismissal is annulment of the decision to dismiss, or damages.

Although the volume of strikes has increased appreciably in recent years, it is still quite low compared with the volume in many other countries. The quality of workplace relations remains generally good. A commission appointed some years ago concluded that the system of mediating conflict was basically sound. Consistent with the rest of Swedish industrial relations, the system gives prominence to collective organizations rather than individuals. Cases raised by nonunion workers go to ordinary courts, not the labor court.

VI. Conclusions and Directions for Future Research

A. *Some Comparisons*

The differences between the four European countries reviewed here, and between them and the United States, suggest that each country has crafted means of dispute resolution to fit its own unique history and industrial relations system. The European countries discussed, like the United States, resolve the vast bulk of their collective labor disputes by collective bargaining. But there are several major differences between their practices and those of the United States. First, the issue of union recognition is a minor one in Europe. Second, none of the four countries has the low level of coverage of collective bargaining present in the U.S. This leaves five-sixths of the employed population to make the best deal they can with their employer without the aid of a union, as Feuille points out in chapter 2. Third, much European bargaining, at least in the continental countries, is conducted at the industry level rather than the company level. Fourth, in addition to procedures available within the enterprise, there are means in all of the countries discussed except Sweden for individual workers to pursue at least some grievances through special public procedures. Due to the 83 percent rate of unionization in Sweden, however, relatively few workers lack union protection.

Finally, in the unionized sector in the U.S. collective bargaining agreements not only prescribe grievance procedures in the enterprise, but in a large majority of cases also provide for referral to arbitration as the final step. No European country uses arbitration as it is practiced in the U.S. to any great extent, and there is no European equivalent of the Steelworkers Trilogy. In Britain, where little distinction is made between rights disputes and interest disputes, the ACAS arranged only 136 arbitrations in 1995. A smaller number of arbitrations are probably arranged without using the ACAS. There is also some small use of the Central Arbitration Committee. In recent years a few British firms have adopted final offer selection arbitration, sometimes called "pendulum arbitration," which requires the arbitrator to decide in favor of the final position of either the employer or the union. The arbitrator thus is prohibited from "splitting the difference" between the two positions. Arbitration is possible in France but is rarely used. In Germany it is used in disputes between an employer and a works council. Arbitration is very uncommon in Sweden, and is used primarily in the newspaper and construction industries, and in piecework disputes.

In all of the four countries, as in the unionized sectors of the United States, collective interest disputes are handled through collective bargaining, either at the central, industrywide, enterprise, or workplace levels. The industrywide level is dominant in Germany, is used in most bargaining rounds in Sweden, and though still important in France, has now been largely supplemented by enterprise bargaining. In Britain, enterprise and workplace bargaining have to a large extent superseded industrywide bargaining.

For grievance procedures and workplace rights disputes, the variety of arrangements is considerable. In all of the countries the great majority of disagreements are resolved within the enterprise by management and worker representatives. Britain has no specific legislated form of worker representation, but does have a well developed shop steward system and the possibility for grievances to be processed through ACAS. Additionally, the industrial tribunals offer facilities to both union and nonunion workers to handle dismissals and certain other matters. France offers a range of legislated forms of workforce representation, supplemented by the labor tribunals and the labor Inspector. Germany primarily uses its works councils. These are supplemented by referring disagreements between a works council and management to arbitration and allowing some forms of disputes to be taken to the labor court. Sweden has the provisions of the MBL and a labor court.

History and usage in several countries offer examples of management-worker bodies that are given merely consultative rights. This structure leaves decision making in the hands of the employer and, in some cases, precludes these bodies from dealing with matters subject to collective bargaining. In contrast, the German and French bodies are established by statute and endowed with rights to information, consultation, and in some cases co-determination. One example illustrates how far their powers may extend. When collective layoffs are necessary in Germany the works council cannot block them, but the management has an obligation to propose measures to mitigate the adverse effects on the workers. A "social plan" must be developed. If the works council considers the management's proposal inadequate, the case can be referred to the arbitration committee. Thus, the relevance of the works council to disputes is not only that it is a means of resolving differences which arise between management and workers, but also that it embodies the co-operative aspects of the industrial relationship. It therefore becomes a vehicle for establishing trust between management and workers. The develop-ment of cooperation and trust in turn contributes to the goal of reducing disputes through proactive prevention.

Though extravagant claims for works councils are not justified, their contribution has, to say the least, been a positive one. Consequently, interest in works councils has grown in other countries which do not have such bodies. But given the well-known difficulties of transplanting institutions between countries with different industrial relations systems, the establishment of works councils in countries with well-established systems is problematic. This is particularly true where the industrial relations system is based on ad-versarial relationships and dispute management procedures and institutions.

Nowhere in Europe are ordinary courts of law used to any appreciable extent to resolve labor disputes, but judicial-style labor courts or tribunals are widespread. Whether or not such arrangements are more appropriate than practices built cooperatively over time by employers and unions is an interesting question. In their favor, they can offer equal protection to a large part of the labor force, union and nonunion alike. They substitute judicial reason for what might otherwise be a trial of strength. Their negative features commonly include a degree of formality, inflexibility, and slowness that contrasts unfavorably with procedures created cooperatively within industry. These procedural differences reflect differences in goals. Labor courts focus on making an objective determination based on interpretation of the letter of the law or collective bargaining agreement. In contrast, self-determined procedures developed by industry focus on finding a mutually satisfactory way for the parties to work together. Be that as it may, the relevant bodies in France, Germany, and Sweden work satisfactorily enough, though in Britain the industrial tribunals have been much criticized because of the formality involved and the time it takes to settle cases. The British tribunals are currently under review to determine how they can be improved, but there is no question of abolishing them.

It is somewhat surprising that at a time when many industrial relations systems have been undergoing appreciable change, there have been no significant changes in the way in which labor disputes are mediated in the countries reviewed here.[38] The only conclusion that can be drawn from the stability of existing arrangements is that the countries concerned consider them to be broadly satisfactory. Certainly, there is no evidence of any substantial dissatisfaction that might lead to change.

The role of the state varies somewhat in these four countries. The basic rationale for state involvement is that stoppages of work inevitably inconvenience many people, sometimes seriously. Thus, it is in the public interest for state peacemaking services to be readily available to reduce that inconvenience and costs to the national economy. Leaving aside the labor courts and industrial tribunals, which are primarily judgmental bodies for rights disputes rather than advisory and conciliatory bodies, Britain has its successful ACAS, and France has the labor inspectorate, even though its role in disputes is small. For constitutional (the bargaining autonomy principle) and historical reasons, the German federal government offers no advisory or conciliation services. For the German states, however, Control Council Law No. 35, of August 1946, is still in force[39] and requires the labor ministry of each state to establish a conciliation commission to help resolve collective disputes. Disputes can only be submitted if both parties agree. Sweden has its mediation arrangements.

It is difficult to find parallels for the American public agencies in the European countries, although the FMCS has something in common with the British ACAS. The NLRB has no equivalent. The reason is that none of the countries considered in this chapter has adopted the main features of the American Wagner/Taft-Hartley system, in which union recognition occurs through application to a public institution and that institution rules on a basic industrial relations code of unfair labor practices.

B. Disputes in Essential Services

The involvement of the government becomes particularly critical when a dispute arises that is viewed as seriously damaging to the national interest. There are two notable aspects of this. First, various categories of worker may be excluded from the right to strike. These commonly include the armed forces and police, but in various countries at various times they have included and sometimes still include groups such as prison staff, water supply personnel, air traffic controllers, and workers employed in electricity and gas supply.

The second aspect is what government can do about a stoppage of work in essential services, bearing in mind that experience has shown the serious difficulty of acting against large numbers of strikers. Some Draconian measures have been used. For instance, a French government faced with a strike of railroad locomotive engineers ordered them into the army and put them back on their locomotives on soldiers' pay. The use of military personnel to do strikers' work is another possibility. In Britain the Emergency Powers Act, 1920, as amended in 1964, enables the government to govern with special powers if essential supplies for the community are threatened, and to use army personnel for work of national importance. Troops have been used in Britain to drive ambulances and in the early postwar years to load and unload ships. France has used soldiers to clear garbage in Paris. In a strike in Germany the post office used that portion of its staff which had civil servant status, and thus did not have the right to strike, to do strikers' work. (The Constitutional Court later condemned this practice.) Although the legal position in Germany is not clear, opinion suggests that essential supplies and services must continue during a strike.[40] The German Trade Union Federation (DGB) has promulgated instructions that in the event of a dispute, workers should do what is necessary to safeguard industrial installations and to supply essential goods and services.[41] In Sweden the Basic Agreement between the employers and union originating in 1938 protects essential work.

Special caution is required concerning industrial action in relation to national security, law and order, and the care of the sick, as well as where action might cause major disturbance to the economy or to food supplies, or which might be regarded as inhumane. But government does reserve the right to intervene, one method being to declare the relevant collective agreement still in force, rendering industrial action unlawful.[42] Another practice is to require that in the event of a strike a minimum service should be provided for the public. This has been done in France, Belgium, and Portugal.[43]

In the U.S. the equivalent of the European procedures are the series of steps established in the Taft-Hartley Act for disputes deemed likely to imperil the national health or safety. These procedures have not been used since 1978.

C. Directions for Future Research

As the references following this chapter show, the field of resolution of labor disputes in Western Europe is amply documented, but there are still areas that call for attention. For instance, it would be useful to learn more about what shifts are occurring in the causes and subjects of disputes. What has been the impact of privatization, deregulation, and structural adjustment? In what ways are the use of present procedures changing as a result of these general movements and the accompanying shifts in employment and skill distribution of the workforce?

This chapter has not attempted to deal with the disputes procedures of former Communist countries in Central and Eastern Europe for the good reason that they have been undergoing reconstruction and in many respects are still in flux. As these countries have been able to draw on other countries' experience, and that of international organizations, it would be valuable to know precisely what has emerged,[44] and how it relates to the experience in Western Europe and the U.S. Studies that would be valuable include surveys of the laws adopted and employer-union agreements made concerning strikes (including strikes in essential services), collective bargaining and grievance procedures, labor courts and conciliation, and mediation and arbitration; and comparative field studies of the operation of these laws and procedures in the various countries.

As ever, it is better to prevent disputes than to resolve them, which calls primarily for good management. This is not the place to review the characteristics of good human resource management, but one essential feature is the existence of an effective and speedy grievance procedure. The Marsh et al. (1981), Hanami/Blanpain (1987 and 1989), and Smith et al. (1992) texts listed in the references provide useful explanations about the practical operation of these procedures. Still, there is room for more comparative research using, for example, similar enterprises in different countries as a base for examining how, and with what success, different types of grievances are managed and resolved.

Notes

1.   See L. Betten, *International Labour Law. Selected Issues* (Deventer: Kluver, 1994), 396–414.

2.   This should not be confused with the so-called Social Charter of the European Union (1989), which of itself has little or no legal significance.

3.   For more discussion of the legal significance of the charter, see A. de Roo and R. Jagtenberg, *Settling Labour Disputes in Europe* (Deventer, Netherlands: Kluwer, 1994), 348–55.

4.   Ibid., 364.

5.   T. Treu, *The Prevention and Settlement of Industrial Conflict in the Community Member States* (Luxembourg: Commission of the European Communities, 1984).

6.   N. Millward et al., *Workplace Industrial Relations in Transition* (Aldershot: Dartmouth, 1992).

7.   Ibid., 218.

8.   Ibid., 222.

9. Ibid., 210.

10. Ibid., 186.

11. The Department of Employment was abolished in July 1995. Its functions were distributed among other departments, mainly the Department of Education which became the Department of Education and Employment, and the Department of Trade and Industry.

12. The levy was a tax against which employers could claim rebates on the basis of the amount they spent on training. The purpose was to ensure that employers either carried out adequate training or paid others to train employees.

13. B. Hepple and S. Fredman, *Labour Law and Industrial Relations in Great Britain*, 2d ed. (Deventer, Netherlands: Kluwer, 1992), 63.

14. The Employment Appeal Tribunal (EAT) comprises a judge and either two or four lay members.

15. In Scotland the Court of Session (Inner House) replaces the Court of Appeal used in England and Wales.

16. Hepple says that the immunity applies to any person ". . . inducing breach of contract of employment or . . . interfering with business." (Hepple and Fredman, 42).

17. "Collective Bargaining: Levels and Coverage," *Employment Outlook* (Paris: OECD, 1994), 185.

18. J-F Amadieu, "Industrial Relations: Is France a Special Case?" *British Journal of Industrial Relations* 33, no. 3 (September 1995): 359.

19. Expression groups were introduced by an Act of August 1982, one of the four "Auroux" laws of that year. They give workers an opportunity to express their views on work content and organization, and on working conditions.

20. J. Rojot, "The Role of Neutrals in the Resolution of Interest Disputes in France," *Comparative Labor Law Journal* 10, no. 3 (spring 1989): 324–38.

21. Amadieu, "Industrial Relations," 349.

22. Roo and Jagtenberg, 132–33.

23. Ibid., 139.

24. In December 1992 nearly fourteen million employees and employers were on the register of eligible voters.

25. J. Rojot, "France," *Comparative Labor Law Journal* 9, no. 1 (1987): 68–81.

26. Ibid., 74.

27. Roo and Jagtenberg, 142.

28. In fact there are plenty of disagreements within enterprises, but overall the basis of cooperation holds.

29. M. Weiss, "Federal Republic of Germany," *Comparative Labor Law Journal* 9, no. 9 (1987): 161–63.

30. Ibid., 103.

31. Ibid., 96–102.

32. This active labor market policy stressed vocational guidance, training, placement, and relocation as an essential complement to unemployment benefit for workers losing their jobs.

33. This characteristic reflected a preference for pragmatic compromise rather than confrontation.

34. S. Edlund and B. Nyström, *Developments in Swedish Labour Law* (Stockholm: The Swedish Institute, 1988), 47.

35. Ibid.

36. Ibid., 48.

37. F. Schmidt, *Law and Industrial Relations in Sweden* (Stockholm: Almqvist and Wiksell, 1977), 205.

38. Though the British enactments of 1980–93 considerably changed the legal position of strikes, and have helped to reduce the volume of overt industrial action, they did not set out to change the methods of resolving disputes.

39. E. O. Smith et al., *Third Party Involvement in Industrial Disputes* (Germany and Britain: Aldershot: Gower, 1992), 35.

40. Weiss, "Federal Republic of Germany," 143.

41. A. Pankert, "Settlement of Labour Disputes in Essential Services,"

International Labour Review 119, no. 6 (1980): 725.

42. R. Fahlbeck, "The Role of Neutrals in the Resolution of Interest Disputes in Sweden," *Comparative Labor Law Journal* 10, no. 3 (spring 1989): 391–410.

43. Pankert, "Settlement of Labour Disputes," 732.

44. See "Preventing and Resolving Industrial Conflict, Labour Market and Social Policy," (OECD Occasional Paper No.11, Paris, 1993).

Suggestions for Further Reading

General

Aaron, B., ed. 1969. *Dispute Settlement Procedures in Five Western European Countries.* Los Angeles, Calif.: UCLA Institute of Industrial Relations.

Aaron, B., and K. W. Wedderburn, eds. 1972. *Industrial Conflict.* London: Longman.

Aaron, B., ed. 1971. *Labor Courts and Grievance Settlement in Western Europe.* Berkeley, Calif.: University of California.

Bernstein, I., et al., eds. 1955. *Emergency Disputes and National Policy.* Madison, Wis.: Industrial Relations Research Association.

Betten, L. 1993. *International Labour Law. Selected Issues.* Deventer: Kluwer.

Bird, D. 1994. "International Comparison of Labour Disputes in 1993." *Employment Gazette*, 433–39.

Birk, R. 1993. "The Law of Strikes and Lockouts." In R. Blanpain and C. Engels, eds., *Labour Law and Industrial Relations in Industrialized Market Economics.* Deventer: Kluwer.

Blain, N., et al. 1987. "Mediation, Conciliation and Arbitration." *International Labour Review*, March–April.

Blenk, W., ed. 1989. *European Labour Courts: Current Issues.* Geneva: ILO.

_____, ed. 1993. *European Labour Courts: Industrial action and procedural aspects.* Geneva: ILO.

Bronstein, A., and C. Thomas, eds. 1995. *European Labour Courts:*

International and European labour standards in labour court decisions and jurisprudence on sex discrimination. Geneva: ILO.

Cullen, D. E. 1968. *National Emergency Strikes.* Ithaca, N.Y.: New York State School of Labor and Industrial Relations.

Edwards, P.K. 1992. "Industrial Conflict: Themes and Issues in Recent Research." *British Journal of Industrial Relations* 30 (3): 361–404.

Essenberg, B. 1986. *Labour Courts in Europe.* Geneva: International Institute for Labour Studies.

European Industrial Relations Review. 1989. *The Regulation of Industrial Conflict in Europe.* London: Industrial Relations Services.

Givry, J. de, and J. Schregle. 1968. "The Role of the Third Party in the Settlement of Grievances at the Plant Level." Pp. 129–47 in *Industrial Relations: Contemporary Issues,* ed. B. C. Roberts. London: Macmillan.

Gladstone, A. 1993. "Settlement of Disputes over Rights." Pp. 455–79 in *Comparative Labour Law and Industrial Relations in Industrialized Market Economies,* ed. R. Blanpain and C. Engels. Deventer: Kluwer.

Goldman, A. 1993. "Settlement of Disputes over Interests." Pp. 481–500 in *Comparative Labour Law and Industrial Relations in Industrialized Market Economies,* ed. R. Blanpain and C. Engels. Deventer: Kluwer.

Hanami, T., and R. Blanpain, eds. 1987. *Industrial Conflict Resolution in Market Economies.* (Canada, Great Britain, Sweden) Deventer: Kluwer.

_____, eds. 1989. *Industrial Conflict Resolution in Market Economies* (Australia, Germany, Italy, Japan and the U.S.A.). Deventer: Kluwer.

Jacobs, A.T.J.M. 1993. "The Law of Strikes and Lock-outs." Pp. 423–53 in *Comparative Labour Law and Industrial Relations in Industrialized Market Economies,* ed. R. Blanpain and C. Engels. Deventer: Kluwer.

Marsh, A., et al. 1981. *Workplace Relations in the Engineering Industry in the United Kingdom and the Federal Republic of Germany.* London: Anglo-German Foundation.

Pankert, A. 1980. "Settlement of Labour Disputes in Essential Services." *International Labour Review* 119 (6): 723–37.

Roo, A. de, and R. Jagtenberg. 1994. *Settling Labour Disputes in Europe.* Deventer: Kluwer.

Smith, E. O., et al. 1992. *Third Party Involvement in Industrial Disputes* (Germany and Britain). Aldershot: Gower.

Sweeney, K., and J. Davies. 1997. "International Comparison of Labour Disputes in 1995." *Labor Market Trends* 105 (4) (April): 129-34.

Trebilcock, A., ed. 1995. *European Labour Courts: Remedies and Sanctions in Industrial Action.* Geneva: ILO.

Treu, T. 1984. *The Prevention and Settlement of Industrial Conflict in the Community Member States.* Luxembourg: Commission of the European Communities.

International Labour Organization. 1980. *Conciliation and Arbitration Procedures in Labor Disputes.* Geneva: ILO.

OECD. 1994. "Collective Bargaining: Levels and Coverage." *Employment Outlook.* Paris: OECD, 167–94.

_____. 1993. "Preventing and Resolving Industrial Conflict, Labour Market and Social Policy" (Occasional Paper No. 11, Paris).

Britain

Chang, D. 1936. *British Methods of Industrial Peace.* New York: Columbia University Press.

Hepple, B., and S. Fredman. 1992. *Labour Law and Industrial Relations in Great Britain,* 2d ed. Deventer: Kluwer.

McCarthy, W.E.J. 1990. "The Case for Labour Courts." *Industrial Relations Journal* 21 (2): 98–111.

Millward, N., et al. 1992. *Workplace Industrial Relations in Transition.* Aldershot: Dartmouth.

Schulze-Gaevernitz, G. von. 1900. *Social Peace,* 2d ed. New York: Swan Sonnenschein.

Sharp, I. G. 1950. *Industrial Conciliation and Arbitration in Great Britain.* London: George Allen and Unwin.

Wood, Sir J. 1989. "The Role of Neutrals in the Resolution of Interest Disputes in the United Kingdom." *Comparative Labor Law Journal* 10(3) (spring): 411–28.

Wood, Sir J., et al. 1987. "United Kingdom." *Comparative Labor Law Journal* 9(9): 198–211.

France

Amadieu, J-F. 1955. "Industrial Relations: Is France a Special Case?" *British Journal of Industrial Relations* 33(3) (September): 345–51.

Despax, M., and J. Rojot. 1987. *Labour Law and Industrial Relations in France.* Deventer: Kluwer.

"France, Conseils de Prud'hommes: Role and Operation." 1988. *European Industrial Relations Review* 168 (January): 18, 19.

"France: Collective Bargaining Reform." 1993. *European Industrial Relations Review* 108 (January): 22–3.

McPherson, W., and F. Meyers. 1966. *The French Labor Courts: Judgement by Peers.* Urbana, Ill.: University of Illinois Press.

Rojot, J. 1987. "France." *Comparative Labor Law Journal* 9(1) (fall): 68–81.

_____. 1989. "The Role of Neutrals in the Resolution of Interest Disputes in France." *Comparative Labor Law Journal* 10(3) (spring): 324–38.

Germany

Berghahn, V.R., and D. Karsten. 1987. *Industrial Relations in West Germany.* Oxford: Berg.

Weiss, M. 1987a. "Federal Republic of Germany." *Comparative Labor Law Journal* 9(9): 82–98.

_____. 1987b. *Labour Law and Industrial Relations in the Federal Republic of Germany.* Deventer: Kluwer.

_____. 1989. "The Role of Neutrals in the Resolution of Interest Disputes in the Federal Republic of Germany." *Comparative Labor Law Journal* 10(3) (spring): 339–55.

Williams, K. 1988. *Industrial Relations and the German Model.* Aldershot: Avebury.

Sweden

Edlund, S., and B. Nyström. 1988. *Developments in Swedish Labour Law.* Stockholm: The Swedish Institute.

Fahlbeck, R. 1989. "The Role of Neutrals in the Resolution of Interest Disputes in Sweden." *Comparative Labor Law Journal* 10(3) (spring): 391–410.

Fahlbeck, R. 1987. "Sweden." *Comparative Labor Law Journal* 9(9): 177–97.

Johnston, T. 1962. *Collective Bargaining in Sweden.* Cambridge, Mass.: Harvard University Press.

Ministry of Labour (Sweden). 1988. *The Swedish Act on Co-determination at Work.* Stockholm: Ministry of Labour (Sweden).

Schmidt, F. 1977. *Law and Industrial Relations in Sweden.* Stockholm: Almqvist and Wiksell.

Part Three

New Perspectives on Negotiation

9

FAIRNESS, JUSTIFICATION, AND DISPUTE RESOLUTION

Kristina A. Diekmann, Ann E. Tenbrunsel,
and Max H. Bazerman

I. Introduction

As social beings, we are highly motivated to act in a fair and appropriate manner. We are also highly self-interested and strive to satisfy our own preferences. Consequently, we often face a conflict between what we want and what we think is fair. How do people resolve this tension between self-interest and fairness? This question is particularly important in negotiation situations where negotiators are motivated to do as well as possible but, at the same time, where fairness concerns are critical to the maintenance of ongoing relationships and the management of disputes. In this chapter we address this issue by reviewing economic and behavioral decision theory perspectives on negotiation, assessing the limitations that these perspectives have placed on understanding fairness in negotiation, and proposing the incorporation of fairness into negotiation models. First, we review research that has documented systematic ways in which concerns for fairness affect decision making and negotiation. Second, we offer our theoretical account for how people incorporate fairness concerns into their decisions. Our primary argument is that people are constrained by fairness, but will often resolve the tension between fairness and outcome maximization in favor of outcome maximization when they can justify doing so. Our discussion will be illustrated by examples explaining the impact of fairness issues on negotiations involving job offers, performance evaluation and compensation, managerial behavior, and union contract negotiations.

II. Theoretical Overview

Economists studying negotiation start with the basic, theoretical assumption that people have stable, well-defined preferences and make choices that are consistent with those preferences. A central tenet of virtually all economic theory is that a person will choose the course of action that maximizes his or her expected preferences or utility. Economic and game theoretic perspectives of negotiation have made important contributions to negotiation research. First, such models offer powerful analytic tools for negotiators in highly structured, but limited interactions. Second, game theory has catalyzed a vast amount of empirical research aimed at validating its predictions. This economic perspective has given negotiation researchers a unique benchmark of optimality to use in evaluating the processes and outcomes of a successful negotiation. Third, economic theories have provided many qualitative predictions that are very stable. In general, people do seek to maximize their perceived outcomes.

One important criticism of economic models of negotiation is that the assumptions on which they are based have been shown repeatedly to be incorrect.[1] In contrast to economic models, a behavioral decision theory (BDT) perspective on negotiation has been developed which focuses on identifying the ways in which individual judgment systematically deviates from rational models of behavior in the context of negotiation. This research has suggested that negotiators tend to be inappropriately affected by the positive or negative frame in which risks are viewed[2] (i.e., whether something is framed in terms of gains or losses), to anchor their number estimates in negotiations on irrelevant information,[3] to rely too heavily on readily available information,[4] to be overconfident about the likelihood of attaining outcomes that favor themselves,[5] to escalate commitment to a previously selected course of action when it is no longer the most reasonable alternative,[6] and to overlook the valuable information that is available by considering the opponent's cognitive perspective.[7] Negotiators also tend to assume that negotiation tasks are necessarily fixed-sum and thereby miss opportunities for mutually beneficial trade-offs between the parties.[8]

While BDT offers a variety of proven critiques of economics, it shares a common assumption with economic theory—that individuals are trying to maximize their outcomes. This paper argues that this assumption is not accurate because it ignores concerns for fairness. It explores the implications of individuals sacrificing their own outcomes for fairness concerns for both the economic and BDT models of negotiation.

III. Evidence That People Care About Fairness

A central theme of this chapter is that concern for fairness results in behavior that systematically deviates from what we would expect from a purely rational decision model. We argue that fairness is a critical component of negotiation outcomes and should be incorporated into the field. People are not just outcome maximizers: people care about fairness and will often forgo more profitable outcomes in favor of more fair outcomes. Numerous authors have identified several ways in which concerns for fairness result in behavior that is inconsistent with rational economic behavior.[9] First, fairness considerations can lead people to question decisions dictated by traditional supply and demand considerations. Second, fairness considerations can lead negotiators to accept joint outcomes that are inefficient and suboptimal because they leave both parties worse off than they would have been had fairness considerations been ignored. Third, fairness considerations affect resource allocation decisions, often resulting in resources being divided equally and outcomes not being maximized. Finally, and perhaps most significantly in terms of the challenge presented to standard conceptions of economic rationality, fairness considerations can lead to inconsistencies in expressed preferences.

A. Fairness and the Violation of Supply/Demand Considerations

Kahneman, Knetsch, and Thaler have persuasively documented the impact of fairness concerns on the laws of supply and demand.[10] Subjects in these studies were asked to evaluate the fairness of a hardware store raising the price of snow shovels from $15 to $20 the morning after a large snowstorm. Despite the economic rationality of raising the price of snow shovels given the increased demand, 82 percent of subjects viewed such behavior as unfair. Even those subjects who deemed raising the price to be fair appear to be concerned with fairness. An informal analysis of these subjects reveals that in two similar situations they would not believe it fair to raise the price of generators after a hurricane and certainly not fair to "sell" organs for transplantation to the highest bidder. Kahneman and his colleagues illustrate quite clearly that these responses are not consistent with economic theory concerning supply and demand. Concerns for fairness, it appears, provide a valid explanation for violations from the supply and demand equilibrium.

B. Fairness and Violations to Pareto Optimality

Concerns for fairness can also lead to inefficiency in competitive situations. Several researchers have demonstrated in a series of experiments using "ultimatum games" that fairness considerations led individuals to an outcome that made them worse off than they would have been had they not taken fairness into consideration.[11] In a study conducted by Guth, Schmittberger, and Schwarze, player 1 divided a known, fixed sum of money any way s/he chose.[12] Player 2 could accept the offer and receive his/her portion of the money as divided by player 1, or reject the offer, leaving both parties with nothing. According to game theoretic models, player 1 should offer player 2 only slightly more than zero dollars and player 2 should accept any offer greater than zero dollars. This was not what actually happened. Subjects in the role of player 1 demanded on average less than 70 percent of the available funds, regardless of whether they were first time players or players who played the game one week earlier. Subjects in the role of player 2 often rejected offers that were less than an equal share, leaving both parties with nothing 20 percent of the time. These were Pareto inefficient results because there were other possible agreements that would have made one party better off without reducing the outcome to the other party. People in the role of player 2 expect more than just a little and will not hesitate to punish those in the role of player 1 who demand too much. Furthermore, it seems that people in the role of player 1 understand that others will sacrifice gains rather than accept "unfair" allocations. Again, we see that acting in accordance with purely economic models may not be rational in a world where fairness considerations play a critical role and where one's opponent may be following systematic patterns of behavior that deviate from purely rational economic theory.

C. Fairness and Equal Allocations

Concerns for fairness also manifest themselves in resource allocation situations. In these situations, people often advocate equality without necessarily maximizing their self-interest. People often follow an equality norm even when they could justify taking more than an equal share by following the contribution rule. At times, people engage in a "politeness ritual" whereby they make equal allocations, even though they contributed more than others, in order to present the self as being as neutral and impartial as possible.[13] For example, allocators such as division directors will tend to divide a bonus equally between themselves and another person, such as another division director, even when differences in their division's performance could "justify" taking more than an equal share.[14] In a negotiation, this desire to maintain an impression of fairness often results in an agreement that "splits the difference" rather than one that attempts to maximize an individual's outcome. Messick and his colleagues argue that equality is a social decision heuristic that is readily and automatically used without careful deliberation.[15]

D. Fairness and Inconsistency

The previous sections explain how fairness considerations lead to behavior that is inconsistent with traditional economic models. Given the revealed importance of fairness, many researchers argue that fairness has utility to decision makers[16] and as such should be included in a rational model of decision making. But even this more flexible definition of rationality that includes nontraditional variables such as the difference between one's own outcome and that of another party falls short of accurately predicting people's behavior. One of the reasons is that preferences for fairness are not consistent across situations.

Inconsistencies in preferences for fairness have been documented in a variety of situations. Responses seem to be inconsistent when people are asked to rate certain outcomes versus when they are asked to make actual choices.[17] People care far more about social comparisons such as comparing their outcome with those of others when rating a specific outcome than when choosing among various outcomes. Bazerman, Loewenstein, and White found that when subjects rated the acceptability of various outcomes, they were more likely to rate an outcome that had a lower payout to the self, but equal payout in comparison to another person, as more acceptable than a higher payout to the self, but less in comparison to another person.[18] But when choosing between these two outcomes, subjects were more likely to chose the higher, but unequal outcome. For example, 70 percent of subjects rated $400 for self and $400 for the other party more acceptable than $500 for self and $700 for the other party. But when choosing between these two options, only 22 percent of subjects chose $400 for self and $400 for the other party over $500 for self and $700 for the other party. The authors argue that when joint outcomes are evaluated separately, other parties' outcomes become the referent point because there is no other referent point available.[19] But when choosing between two outcomes, people can use one of their own outcomes to evaluate the other. They no longer need the outcomes of others as referents and thus seem less affected by social comparisons when making choices.

It seems that the reason for this inconsistency is not the ratings/choice distinction, but whether the parties evaluated one or two options at a time. In a follow-up study, White and Bazerman examined the choice behavior of potential subjects who were recruited to participate in a forty-minute experiment run by a colleague.[20] One group of potential subjects was offered seven dollars to participate in the experiment knowing that other subjects would also be paid seven dollars. A second group of potential subjects was offered eight dollars to participate in the same experiment, knowing that other subjects (arbitrarily chosen by the last digit of their social security number) would be paid ten dollars. A third group was offered the choice of (1) participating in an experiment in which everyone would be paid seven dollars, (2) participating in an experiment in which they would be paid eight dollars and others would be paid ten dollars, or (3) not participating. While significantly more subjects in the first group chose to participate (72 percent) than in the second group (55 percent), the majority of subjects (56 percent) in the third group chose to participate in the experiment in which they would be paid eight dollars while others would be paid ten dollars (16 percent chose the experiment in which everyone received seven dollars; 28 percent chose not to participate in either). When subjects were choosing between participating or not participating in one experiment (groups 1 and 2), they were influenced by the outcomes of others. But when subjects were given multiple experiments in which to participate, the outcomes of others became less important. Subjects were able to compare their own outcomes without turning to the outcomes of others.

These findings have been generalized to a more realistic and readily identifiable context. In a study conducted by Bazerman, Schroth, Shah, Diekmann, and Tenbrunsel, second-year MBA students who were in the process of recruiting for jobs were given several scenarios that described a job offer they had received from a consulting firm to which they had to respond given an approaching deadline.[21] Subjects were told to imagine they had one (or two) job offers which expired today. The two job offers were as follows:

> Job A: The offer is from company 1 for $75,000 a year. It is widely known that this firm pays all starting MBAs from top schools $75,000 . . . (additional descriptive information about the firm).

> Job B: The offer is from company 2 for $85,000 a year. It is widely known that this firm is paying some other graduating students from the same school $95,000 a year . . . (additional descriptive information about the firm).

One group of subjects was given twelve scenarios of different single job offers and asked whether they would accept each of the individual job offers (single condition). Another group of subjects was given six scenarios in which they had pairs of job offers (jobs A and B were combined for one of these pairs) and was asked which, if any, job they would accept (dual condition). The six pairs included the same twelve jobs as in the single condition and in each case set up a comparison between equality and the maximization of outcomes to the self.

As expected, subjects given one job offer at a time were more likely to accept the lower, equal paying job than the higher, unequal paying job, but when choosing between the two, subjects were more likely to accept the higher, unequal paying job. In the example of jobs A and B above, of the subjects who accepted one of the jobs in the single condition, 69 percent accepted job A and 31 percent accepted job B. In contrast, of the subjects who accepted one of the two jobs in the dual condition, 17 percent accepted job A and 83 percent accepted job B. It seems that people's concern for fairness had a much greater impact on their decisions in the single-choice context than in the multiple-choice context.

It seems that this pattern occurs not only with social comparison information, but also with other types of social information. In a second study, the researchers substituted procedural justice information (i.e., information concerning how fairly they would be treated in the process by which outcomes are allocated) for social comparison information. They then asked MBA students to make choices on either six single job offers or three pairs of job offers in the same format as described in the first study. The pairing of jobs was set up to create a trade-off between obtaining procedural justice or maximizing salary. An example of one of the pair of job offers is as follows:

Job A (low salary, high procedural justice): The first offer is from company 1 for $60,000 a year. . . .New associates are given the opportunity to participate in decisions typically made by upper management. . .new associates are allowed to voice their preferences regarding client and project assignments. . . .The firm encourages all consultants, both junior and senior, to voice their opinions for changes and improvements to the company's policies. . . .

Job B (high salary, low procedural justice): The second offer is from company 2 for $75,000 a year. . . . New associates are assigned by senior partners to specific clients, projects, and engagement teams in which a senior partner is in charge and are not allowed to request changes. Decisions involving company policies including MBA training, job objectives, career advancement, and salary increases are made by senior management. The new MBAs are not encouraged to voice their opinions or objectives. . . .

In the single condition, of the subjects who accepted one of the two jobs listed above, 72 percent accepted job A and 28 percent accepted job B. In contrast, in the dual condition, of the subjects who accepted one of the two jobs, 38 percent accepted job A and 62 percent accepted job B. The results of the two studies suggest that people use social information (whether social comparison or procedural justice information) to make sense of outcomes when they lack a way to directly assess the worth of the outcome itself. This implies that concerns for fairness depend on the amount of information the decision maker has. The more relevant information available concerning the decision, the less concerns for fairness will have an impact on one's decision.

IV. Using Justification to Resolve the Tension between Self-Interest and Fairness

This evidence clarifies that while people care about maximizing their own outcomes, they also are concerned with being fair. Being perceived as fair is critical in gaining social approval. By behaving in what is perceived as a fair manner, people enhance their self-image and projected social image.[22] Although people may be genuinely concerned with being fair, they often will be less concerned with being truly fair than with being perceived as fair because of their self-interest motivation. For instance, Greenberg found in a survey of 815 managers that these managers were more concerned with appearing to be fair than with actually being fair.[23] In such cases, the concern with developing an impression of fairness operates at the level of conscious awareness. In other cases, these impression management processes may be semiautomatic, over-learned responses that involve little if any conscious deliberation.[24]

Our view is that impression management concerns are critical in the resolution of tension between self-interest and fairness. We argue that when the two motives of self-interest and fairness are in competition, people will deviate from what they perceive as fair in the direction of outcome maximization to the extent that the outcome maximization behavior is justifiable. People use justifications to support their self-serving behavior and still maintain the impression that they are being fair. Justifications are defined as explanations of social behavior where the individual accepts responsibility for a given action but denies any negative attributions resulting from that action.[25] Justifications can reduce the conflict between self-interest and fairness by providing oneself and others with reasons that support self-interested behavior. By providing decision makers the impetus to choose the hedonically preferred outcome while still maintaining the appearance of fairness, justifications can help people convince themselves that they are decent human beings.[26]

Justifications are asserted to be the most salient consideration in any decision.[27] When faced with uncertainty, people make choices based on reasons.[28] Indeed, people have a need to seek and provide reasons for their decisions.[29] Providing reasons can enhance one's self-esteem and one's appearance of being competent.[30] Furthermore, providing reasons is consistent with our perception of being rational human beings.[31] For instance, Simonson found that when consumers were indifferent about two alternative brands (brands A and B), the introduction of a third brand (brand C) which was dominated by one of the original two brands (brand A) increased the likelihood that brand A would be chosen over brand B. The introduction of brand C provides consumers with reasons for choosing brand A (namely that it is superior to brand C).[32]

Returning to the research previously detailed in this chapter on job choice conducted by Bazerman and his colleagues, when subjects were faced with a single job offer where they would be paid less relative to others, they may have faced difficulty in justifying their acceptance of the offer because it was unfair. But when they received two job offers simultaneously, they had an available justification that one job paid more than the other job and thus was acceptable.[33]

Not only do justifications provide the impression that we are rational human beings with reasons for preferring one option over another, they also provide the impression that we are fair. One of the reasons that justifications are so important is that justifications can help mitigate any negative consequences of an action.[34] Justifications, or "social accounts," are used to minimize the expression of moral outrage and retaliation from one's victims.[35] Mitigating the negative consequences of one's behavior is particularly important when one is held accountable for this behavior, so much so that justification becomes the primary influence on one's decision when one is held accountable for that decision.[36] In recognition of the importance of justification, Messick and Sentis propose a model that incorporates justification as a central element in evaluating fair decisions.[37]

When evaluating how fair other people are, we are strongly affected by the justifications that are provided. Bies & Shapiro found that the presence of a causal account claiming mitigating circumstances for an unfair act reduced the perception by others of unfairness.[38] In their experiment, subjects assumed the role of an arbitrator in a conflict between a manager and his subordinate. According to the case, the manager was accused of stealing his subordinate's ideas. When subjects were given a causal account for this action, which included mitigating factors, they perceived less unfairness than when no causal account was given. The findings were replicated in a field study where people's perception of fairness regarding their boss's rejection of a budget request or proposal were much more fair when a justification was provided than when not.

At times, the use of accounts or justifications reflects a person's honest desire to be fair. At other times, these accounts are provided purely as a means to manage the impression of fairness and to distort the truth. It is difficult, however, to know when people are honestly using justifications and truly believe their behavior is fair, or are strategically using justifications to maximize their outcomes because they think they can get away with their self-serving behavior because their justifications deceive others that it is fair.

The importance of justifications, particularly when people behave in a self-serving manner, has been demonstrated in research on resource allocation decisions. Diekmann, Samuels, Ross, and Bazerman found that subjects whose performance differed along two dimensions in relation to another person (i.e., performing better on one dimension, but worse on the other dimension), rated receiving an equal allocation to be perfectly fair, but rated receiving an unequal, larger share to be more fair than the comparable unequal, smaller share even though their performance, although different, was equivalent.[39] Furthermore, those whose performance differed and who received an unequal, larger share justified the fairness of such advantageous inequality. In contrast, evaluators who received an unequal, smaller share did not justify the fairness of such disadvantageous inequality even when they had different performance. In general, subjects justified inequality when they had an adequate reason, such as different performance, and were motivated to do so, e.g., they would receive a larger share of the resource. If people cared only about fairness, they would perceive both advantageous and disadvantageous inequality as being equally unfair.

Advantageous inequality, however, seems to be more acceptable and thus more likely to be justified as being fair.

It is quite common for all negotiators in a conflict to suggest viable solutions that are self-serving but to justify them based on abstract fairness criteria. For example, self-serving, biased attention to available information in a conflict situation affects negotiators' perception of what constitutes a fair settlement.[40] The interesting question then becomes, "When do violations of fairness occur in negotiation contexts?" In other words, when does self-interest manifest itself? We argue that self-interest manifests itself in negotiation situations and other decisionmaking contexts more when people are able to justify their self-interest as fair and when people believe that their self-interest motivation is hidden. Thus, identifying the sources of justification is the first step in understanding when we would expect to see deviations from fairness in a negotiation setting. In the following sections, we present three such sources of justification: ambiguity, groups, and anonymity.

V. Ambiguity and Justification

One factor that is important in the ability to justify self-serving behavior is ambiguity. Fairness is very subjective and thus what is truly fair is often ambiguous. People often interpret uncertainty in a manner that favors themselves while still maintaining, in their eyes, the perception of fairness. In a negotiation situation, individuals have been found to exhibit "egocentric interpretations of fairness," or judgments that are biased in a manner that favors themselves. For example, in negotiations over disputes that may be referred to arbitrators for resolution, such as disputes that emerge from collective bargaining agreements, negotiators overestimate the probability that the arbitrator will accept their final offer.[41] Similarly, expectations of an arbitrated award are biased in a self-serving manner, with individuals believing that an arbitrator will be more likely to settle in their favor.[42]

The primary cause of egocentric interpretations may be selective, egocentric recall of information. Thompson & Loewenstein argue that egocentric biases in bargaining situations are the result of selective recall of facts that support an egocentric interpretation.[43] In their study, representatives of a teachers union and a board of education played their respective roles in a simulated teacher contract dispute. Representatives from each group recalled significantly more facts that supported their own position than facts that supported the position of the other party. Loewenstein, Issachoroff, Camerer, and Babcock argue that biased recall occurs even when both parties have identical information.[44] Subjects assigned the role of plaintiff or defendant in a legal dispute were given the same case materials and were told that a judge presiding over the case had also reviewed the same materials. Results demonstrated that both defendants and plaintiffs recalled more arguments from the case favoring their own position and that plaintiffs' estimates of the judge's award were significantly higher than defendants' estimates.

Thus, even when two parties engaged in dispute resolution have identical information, individuals selectively interpret that information to support, or justify, their position. In negotiations, these egocentric interpretations of fairness can result in unnecessary impasses where both parties firmly believe that their proposed agreement is the most fair. Thompson and Loewenstein concur, stating that "breakdowns in interpersonal conflict resolution occur when two parties simultaneously attempt to attain their own egocentrically biased position of fairness—a mutually incompatible goal. The paradox of such situations is that both parties believe they are making good faith efforts to arrive at a fair solution".[45]

Interpreting information in a self-serving manner is exacerbated when that information is uncertain. Hsee provides an interesting illustration of how people use uncertainty to justify their behavior.[46] In his study, he found that people were more likely to choose a desirable but low-paying task such as proofreading personal ads in a newspaper as opposed to an undesirable but high-paying task such as proofreading used furniture ads when there was uncertainty regarding the pay. Hsee explains these results by arguing that when there is no uncertainty about the pay, one does not feel justified in choosing the more desirable, but low-paying task. When uncertainty exists, however, one can reinterpret the uncertainty regarding the pay in favor of the more desirable task. Thus, individuals have the tendency to interpret information in an egocentric manner. Uncertainty provides a justification for egocentric interpretation, allowing individuals to feel that their self-serving and unfair behavior is justified.

VI. Groups and Justification

Another source of justification for self-serving behavior may be membership in a group. For example, Diekmann found that when subjects were allocating a scarce resource, they were more self-serving when allocating to their group than when allocating to only themselves.[47] After completing a task in a group of three people or by themselves and receiving feedback on their performance in relation to another group or person, subjects took a significantly larger percent of the available resource when dividing between their own group and a competing group than when dividing between themselves and another person. Taking more for one's group seems to be more legitimate than taking more for oneself, even though one benefits in both cases. Implicit in the act of allocating to one's group is the justification that other people will benefit: there exists the possibility that taking more for one's group may reflect the individual's genuine concern with the welfare of fellow group members and not just greedy behavior. One's self-interested motivation is less obvious. No additional justification needs to be offered since the justification already exists in the behavior. In negotiation contexts, when people are representing their group, they may be able to make higher demands and get a better deal simply because they have an added justification that their fellow group members are benefiting. The problem arises when one's opponent in the negotiation is also representing his/her group. The two negotiators may make overly extreme demands, both believing that these demands are fair and will be perceived as fair by others, resulting in increased competitiveness between the parties and frequent breakdowns in the negotiation.

The study conducted by Diekmann also provides another illustration of the importance of justifying self-interested behavior. Subjects allocating to their group were also more likely to overweight their performance in relation to that of their competing group, thereby justifying taking more of the available resource. This pattern of justification occurred in both the self- and group-allocation conditions: the more people took (regardless of whether it was for themselves or for their group), the more they justified this by overweighting their performance and the fairness of taking more.

VII. Anonymity and Justification

A third factor that appears to be important is the effect of anonymity on allocation decisions. In the same study by Diekmann described above, subjects who allocated to themselves were more likely to take more when the allocation was completely private and anonymous than when it was public.[48] It appears that subjects took more for themselves because no one else knew that they took more, revealing the importance of managing the impression of being fair. These individuals in turn justified their self-interested allocation by claiming they performed better and deserved more, even though their decision was completely private and anonymous. This indicates that people need to justify their behavior not only to others but also to themselves. It is interesting to note that very few subjects took a full 100 percent of the resource when allocating to self or group in private or in public. Even in the case where no one else would know if they took more, subjects were still constrained by fairness. While most negotiation situations are "public" to some degree, there are some situations where the negotiation is less "public." Thus the degree to which an organizational dispute is public or not public may profoundly affect the degree to which the disputants engage in self-serving behavior.

What seems clear from the research outlined in this chapter is that people care about managing the impression of being fair and that justification plays a critical role in this impression management process. Regardless of whether justifications reflect true beliefs or strategic behavior, they shift the focus away from fairness and allow people to maximize their outcomes without necessarily appearing to do so. This creates a tremendous problem, particularly in the negotiation contexts such as those discussed above that involve a great deal of uncertainty and where there are many factors that allow individuals to justify self-serving interpretations of fairness.

What becomes even more problematic when negotiators justify their self-serving interpretations of fairness is that they may initially use these justifications in a strategic manner to distort the truth, but they may eventually start to believe these accounts as being true. When the parties in a negotiation start to negotiate, their conflicting, egocentric interpretations may exacerbate the conflict, with the parties escalating to their egocentrically determined fair solution. The end result may be unnecessary impasses, spoiled relationships, and/or increased costs as the conflict is taken to the courts. Gaining knowledge of these justification processes may facilitate our ability to prevent such escalation and eventual breakdown in the negotiation process.

VIII. Conclusions and Implications for Future Research

Behavioral decision theory has provided a number of breakthrough discoveries, and has fueled new research approaches across a wide variety of applications.[49] In our own work, the research approach and values of this literature have enabled us to identify a large set of systematic mistakes that are made by negotiators. This chapter has provided an opportunity to extend this list by focusing on the unique roles of fairness concerns and justifiability in a judgmental perspective on negotiation.

This chapter has examined the impact of fairness on creating barriers to negotiated agreements. Justifications provide individuals in a dispute setting with the means to act in a self-interested manner. The more justified a given behavior, the more likely it is that the behavior will be enacted.[50] The availability of justifications results in decisions or actions that deviate from fairness, but which are perceived as fair by the actor.

Future research should investigate the different types of justifications that a negotiator can utilize to create the impression of being fair. These justifications might include mitigating factors, better performance, and the claim that other people may benefit. Identifying the different types of justifications will help us understand why negotiations often quickly turn into excessively competitive battles. This, in turn, will enable us to predict when negotiations can be expected to result in suboptimal agreements and eventual impasses.

Notes

1.   M. A. Neale and M.H. Bazerman, *Cognition and Rationality in Negotiation* (New York: Free Press, 1991).

2.   M. A. Neale and M.H. Bazerman, "The Effects of Framing and Negotiator Overconfidence on Bargainer Behavior," *Academy of Management Journal* 28 (1985): 34–49; and M.H. Bazerman, T. Magliozzie, and M. A. Neale, "The Acquisition of an Integrative Response in a Competitive Market," *Organizational Behavior and Human Performance* 34 (1985): 294–313.

3.   M. A. Neale and G.B. Northcraft, "Experts, Amateurs, and Refrigerators: Comparing Expert and Amateur Decision Making on a Novel Task," *Organizational Behavior and Human Decision Processes* 38 (1986): 305–17; and G. B. Northcraft and M. A. Neale, "Expert, Amateurs, and Real Estate: An Anchoring-and-adjustment Perspective on Property Pricing Decisions," *Organizational Behavior and Human Decision Processes* 39 (1987): 228–41.

4.   M. A. Neale, "The Effect of Negotiation and Arbitration Cost Salience on Bargainer Behavior: The Role of Arbitrator and Constituency in Negotiator Judgment," *Organizational Behavior and Human Performance* 34 (1984): 87–111.

5.   M. H. Bazerman and M. A. Neale, "Improving Negotiation Effectiveness under Final Offer Arbitration: The Role of Selection and Training," *Journal of Applied Psychology* 67 (1982): 543–48.

6.   Neale and Bazerman, *Cognition and Rationality*.

7.   M. H. Bazerman and J. S. Carroll, "Negotiator Cognition," in *Research in Organizational Behavior*, ed. B. Staw and L. L. Cummings (Greenwich, Conn.: JAI Press, 1987), 9: 247–88.

8.   M. H. Bazerman, T. Magliozzie, and M. A. Neale, "The Acquisition of an Integrative Response in a Competitive Market" *Organizational Behavior and Human Performance* 34 (1985): 294–313.

9.   D. Kahneman, J. L. Knetsch, and R. H. Thaler, "Fairness as a Constraint on Profit Seeking: Entitlements in the Market," *American Economic Review* 76 (1987): 728–41; and W. Guth, R. Schmittberger, and B. Schwarze, "An Experimental Analysis of Ultimatum Bargaining," *Journal of Economic Behavior and Organization* 3 (1982): 367–88.

10.   Kahneman, Knetsch, and Thaler, "Fairness as a Constraint."

11.   W. Guth, R. Schmittberger, and B. Schwarze, "An Experimental Analysis of Ultimatum Bargaining," *Journal of Economic Behavior and Organization* 3 (1982): 367–88.

12.   Ibid.

13.   G. Mikula, "On the Role of Justice in Allocation Decisions," in *Justice and Social Interaction: Experimental and Theoretical Contributions from Psychological Research*, ed. G. Mikula (New York: Springer-Verlag, 1980); and T. Schwinger, "Just Allocations of Goods: Decisions among Three Principles," in *Justice and Social Interaction*, ed. Mikula.

14.   K. A. Diekmann, S. M. Samuels, L. Ross, and M. H. Bazerman, "Self-Interest and Fairness in Problems of Resource Allocation: Allocators versus Recipients," *Journal of Personality and Social Psychology* 73 (1997): 1061–74.

15.   D. M. Messick, "Equality as a Decision Heuristic," in *Psychological Perspective on Distributive Justice: Theory and Applications*, ed. B. Mellers (Cambridge: Cambridge University Press, 1993); and S. T. Allison and D. M. Messick, "Social Decision Heuristic in the Use of Shared Resources," *Journal of Behavioral Decision Making* 3 (1990): 195–204.

16.   D. M. Messick and K. P. Sentis, "Estimating Social and Nonsocial Utility Functions from Ordinal Data," *European Journal of Social Psychology* 15 (1985): 389–99; and G. F. Loewenstein, L. Thompson, and M.H. Bazerman, "Social Utility

and Decision Making in Interpersonal Contexts," *Journal of Personality and Social Psychology* 57 (1989): 426–41.

17. M. H. Bazerman, G. F. Loewenstein, and S. B. White, "Reversals of Preference in Allocation Decisions: Judging an Alternative versus Choosing Among Alternatives," *Administrative Science Quarterly* 37 (1992): 220–40.

18. Ibid.

19. Ibid.

20. S. B. White and M. H. Bazerman. "The Inconsistent Evaluation of Comparative Payoffs in Labor Supply and Bargaining." *Journal of Economic Behavior and Organizations* 891 (1996): 1–14.

21. M. H. Bazerman, H. A. Schroth, P. P. Shah, K. A. Diekmann, and A. E. Tenbrunsel, "The Inconsistent Role of Comparison Others and Procedural Justice in Reactions to Hypothetical Job Descriptions: Implications for Job Acceptance Decisions," *Organizational Behavior and Human Decision Processes* 60 (1994): 326–52.

22. H. T. Reis, "The Nature of the Justice Movement: Some Thoughts on Operation, Internalization, and Justification," in *Social Comparison, Social Justice, and Relative Deprivation,* ed. J.C. Masters and W. P. Smith (Hillsdale, N.J.: Lawrence Erlbaum, 1987).

23. J. Greenberg, "Cultivating an Image of Justice: Looking Fair on the Job," *Academy of Management Executive* 2 (1988): 155–58.

24. B. R. Schlenker, *Impression Management: The Self Concept, Social Identity, and Interpersonal Relations* (Monterey, Calif.: Brooks/Cole, 1980); and J. T. Tedeschi and P. Rosenfeld, "Impression Management Theory and Forced Compliance Situations," in *Impression Management Theory and Social Psychological Research,* ed. J.R. Tedeschi (New York: Academic Press, 1981).

25. J. T. Tedeschi and M. R. Reiss, "Identities, the Phenomenal Self, and Laboratory Research," in *Impression Management Theory,* ed. Tedeschi.

26. E. Aronson, *The Social Animal* (San Francisco: W.H. Freeman & Co., 1972).

27. P. E. Tetlock, "Accountability: The Neglected Social Context of Judgment and Choice," in *Research in Organizational Behavior,* vol. 7, ed. L. L. Cummings and B. M. Staw (Greenwich, Conn.: JAI Press, 1985).

28. A. Tversky. "Elimination by Aspects: A Theory of Choice," *Psychological Review* 79 (1972): 281–99; and I. Simonson, "Choice Based on Reasons: The

Case of Attraction and Compromise Effects," *Journal of Consumer Research* 16 (1989): 158–74.

29. P. E. Tetlock, "The Impact of Accountability on Judgment and Choice: Toward a Social Contingency Model," in *Advances in Experimental Social Psychology*, ed. M. Zanna (New York: Academic Press, 1992).

30. P. E. Tetlock, "Accountability: The Neglected Social Context of Judgment and Choice," in *Research in Organizational Behavior*, vol. 7, ed. Cummings and Staw.

31. R. Abelson, "The Choice of Choice Theories," in *Decision and Choice*, ed. S. Messick and A. Brayfield (New York: McGraw Hill, 1964).

32. I. Simonson, "Choice Based on Reasons: The Case of Attraction and Compromise Effects," *Journal of Consumer Research* 16 (1989): 158–74.

33. Bazerman, Loewenstein, and White, "Reversals of Preference," *op. cit.*

34. S. Bok, *Lying: Moral Choice in Public and Private Life* (New York: Pantheon Books, 1978).; and D.L. Shapiro, "Has the Conflict-Mitigating Effect of Explanations Been Overestimated? An Examination of Explanations' Effects under Circumstances of Exposed Deceit," working paper, University of North Carolina's Research Council, 1992.

35. R. J. Bies, "The Predicament of Injustice: The Management of Moral Outrage," in *Research in Organizational Behavior*, ed. Cummings and Staw, 9:289–319.

36. A. P. Brief, J. M. Dukerich, and L. I. Doran, "Resolving Ethical Dilemmas in Management: Experimental Investigations of Values, Accountability, and Choice," *Journal of Applied Social Psychology* 21 (1991): 380–96.

37. D. M. Messick and K. P. Sentis, "Fairness, Preference, and Fairness Biases," in *Equity Theory: Psychological and Sociological Perspectives*, ed. D. M. Messick and K. S. Cook (New York: Praeger, 1983).

38. R. J. Bies and D. L. Shapiro, "Voice and Justification: Their Influence on Procedural Fairness Judgements," *Academy of Management Journal* 31 (1988): 676–85.

39. Diekmann, Samuels, Ross, and Bazerman, "Self-interest and Fairness," *op. cit.*

40. L. L. Thompson and G. F. Loewenstein, "Egocentric Interpretations of Fairness and Interpersonal Conflict," *Organizational Behavior and Human Decision Processes* 51 (1992): 176–97.

41. M. H. Bazerman and M. A. Neale, "Improving Negotiation Effectiveness under Final Offer Arbitration: The Role of Selection and Training," *Journal of Applied Psychology* 67 (1982): 543–48.

42. L. Babcock, G. Loewenstein, S. Isaaccharoff, and C. Camerer, "Biased Judgments of Fairness in Bargaining," *American Economic Review* 85 (1992): 1337–43

43. Thompson and Loewenstein, "Egocentric Interpretations."

44. G. F. Loewenstein et al., "Self-serving Assessments of Fairness and Pretrial Bargaining," *Journal of Legal Studies* 22 (1993): 135–59.

45. Thompson and Loewenstein, "Egocentric Interpretations," 194.

46. C. K. Hsee, "Elastic Justification in Decision Making: How Tasks Irrelevant but Tempting Considerations Influence Decisions," *Organizational Behavior and Human Decision Processes* 62 (1995): 330–37.

47. K. A. Diekmann, "'Implicit Justifications' and Self-serving Group Allocations," *Journal of Organizational Behavior* 18 (1997): 3–16.

48. Ibid.

49. A. Tversky and D. Kahneman, "Judgment Under Uncertainty: Heuristics and Biases," *Science* 185 (1974): 1124–31; and D. Kahneman and A. Tversky, "Prospect Theory: An Analysis of Decision under Risk," *Econometrica* 47 (1979): 263–91; and R. M. Dawes, "Social Dilemmas," *Annual Review of Psychology* 31 (1988): 161–91; and T. Gilovich, *How We Know What Isn't So* (New York: Free Press, 1991).

50. P. A. M. Van Lange, "The Rationality and Morality of Cooperation," diss., Amsterdam, 1991.

10

RELATIONSHIPS BETWEEN DISPUTANTS
AN ANALYSIS OF THEIR
CHARACTERISTICS AND IMPACT

Leonard Greenhalgh and Deborah I. Chapman

I. Introduction

When scholars have studied disputes, they traditionally have focused on the conflict situation. For example, in a two-person case where A wants something, but B is somehow interfering with A's getting it, the dispute is analyzed in terms of conflicting preferences (they cannot both get all of what they want) and the rules governing the interaction (both A and B are constrained from simply taking what they want). For decades, dispute resolution scholars have worked on refining their ability to predict dispute outcomes by measuring the parties' preferences[1] and factoring in the process of dispute resolution (the use of power, negotiation, and conflict resolution tactics). Unfortunately, this way of analyzing disputes ignores the relationship between the parties. As a consequence, the effective management of disputes is limited by the omission of this central determinant of the process and outcome of most real-world disputes.

The importance of relationship characteristics can be seen in the everyday situation of a buyer interacting with a seller. Economic theory tells us that both are motivated to make as good a deal as possible. In economic parlance, this means they want to maximize their utilities and minimize their disutilities. Also, both must act within the constraints of law and social mores, e.g., neither party should engage in misrepresentation or coercion. Let us consider the case of a man who wants to sell a car. The man has bought a new car and is about to sell his five-year-old car. He can sell it to his daughter, now eighteen and about to go away to college; he can sell it to the used car dealer across the street from his office; or he can advertise in the newspaper and sell it to a stranger. In dealing with the daughter, he may offer the car at a price below what he could get for it in alternative transactions, motivated by his instinctual support of her. She might respond by counteroffering a higher price, to avert negative feelings of guilt and dependency now that she believes she ought to be self-sufficient. They may compromise on book value, with an interest-free, delayed-payment provision. The motivation for each party is not to maximize economic utility, but to avoid destabilizing the relationship.

If the daughter does not want the car, the man's negotiation with the used car dealer would be quite different. Let us assume that he responds to stereotypes of used car dealers as being untrustworthy, and takes a defensive stance at the outset. The negotiation is a psychological strain and he emerges having sold the car for a little more than book value. He is convinced that the dealer "got the better of him"; otherwise, he reasons, the dealer would not have agreed to that price. We should note that most negotiation theory would predict opposite results because the car is identical across the two transactions, as is the seller's personality and need for money. But the father got a "better deal" from the used car dealer and is *less* happy about it. Much of the difference is attributable to the relationship, yet this variable is absent from most dispute resolution theory.

The third scenario is a negotiation with the stranger responding to the newspaper advertisement. This would be affected by the relationship that forms in the process of negotiating for the car. If a positive relationship quickly developed, the negotiation would proceed more like the negotiation with the daughter. If a distrustful, adversarial relationship developed, then the negotiation would proceed more like the one with the used car dealer.

In contrasting this man's tactics in selling the car to his daughter, a stranger, or a used car dealer, it is worth noting that if the man approached each of these negotiations in the same way, most clinical psychologists (and, indeed, most scholars of human behavior) would diagnose the behavior as pathological. So it seems that many scholars understand the importance of relationships, and take relationships into account when dealing with their own everyday disputes, even though they do not include relationships in their theories of dispute resolution.

The neglect of this factor is baffling. Indeed, one is reminded of the adage: "we don't know who first discovered water but we're sure it wasn't a fish." Scholars conduct their daily lives steeped in relationships, but when they study disputes, they typically contrive a stimulus scenario that isolates the dispute from its relationship context. Thus, in the typical laboratory study, subjects are given a situation that will shape their preferences, then directed to follow a process essentially dictated by the researcher (e.g., "You have twenty minutes to *negotiate* a deal"). In real-life situations, by contrast, the typical dispute is experienced not as an opportunity to improve one's utilities, but rather as an unpleasant strain in an ongoing relationship. The choice of which process is appropriate to address the dispute will be made on the basis of what is compatible with the relationship.

This chapter explores the issues linking the choice of a dispute resolution process and the nature of the interpersonal relationship of the parties. This impact of the characteristics of the relationship on the choice of power, negotiation, or conflict resolution to handle a dispute, the process by which each option is implemented, and the success of the implementation are discussed. The limitations of the current dispute resolution literature in analyzing the role of relationships in making this choice are reviewed. We then report the findings of our exploratory research on the impact of relationships on dispute management processes. This research is based on interviews with persons involved in disputes who were asked to identify relationship characteristics they considered during the dispute process. These characteristics are discussed and the implications for future research are identified.

II. Dispute Resolution Processes

The three alternative processes for addressing disputes between parties are power, negotiation, and conflict resolution. Power is typically defined as the ability to induce someone to do something that he or she would not do in the absence of influence. From this definition, it is obvious that power presupposes conflict: what is in dispute is that one is unwilling to do what the other wants. Power, if it is available to a disputant, can be used to gain *compliance* with an outcome that is beneficial to the party using power.

The second alternative, negotiation, involves gaining *commitment* to a course of action that will settle the dispute. Commitment differs from compliance in the extent to which it is voluntary. A voluntary commitment binds the individual, group, or larger collectivity to a course of action. The commitment may be a result of acceding to a settlement as the best that can be achieved under circumstances of interdependence: "I wanted 100 percent of the pie but I realize that giving me the whole pie involves too much of a sacrifice by the other party; so I'm willing to settle for 50 percent." It may also be the result of problem solving: "We can divide this pie so that each of us gets all of what we want: I want the crust and you want the filling." The quality of the settlement can be judged in terms of the strength of the commitment by both parties, as well as its efficiency, that is, whether either party "left money on the table."[2]

The third alternative, conflict resolution, is a persuasive process that involves shaping the way the parties think about the dispute. An objective stimulus is made meaningful when individuals interpret the situation. Interpretations that set people in opposition are de-emphasized in favor of interpretations that foster reconciliation. For example, issues that are viewed as dichotomous "matters of principle" are reconceptualized with a focus on their divisible elements. The focus of attention shifts from "either I get my way or you get your way" to such perspectives as how broad the scope of this change is, how soon it gets phased in, or who pays what portion of the cost. The result is that the dispute can be reframed as a mutual problem to be worked out.[3]

The three alternatives for addressing disputes are conceptually distinct from each other but are rarely used in isolation. Negotiators use conflict resolution techniques to make intractable issues more negotiable, and power to back up conflict resolution when one party is recalcitrant.

The use of these alternative processes is causally intertwined with the relationship between the parties. Characteristics of the relationship will influence the *choice* of power, negotiation, or conflict resolution, the *process* by which each of these alternatives is implemented, and the *success* of the implementation. The parties' experience with the way the dispute is handled will determine the subsequent relationship, completing the causal loops summarized in figure 1.

Figure 1. Reciprocal Effects of Relationship-Characteristics and
Mechanisms for Addressing Disputes

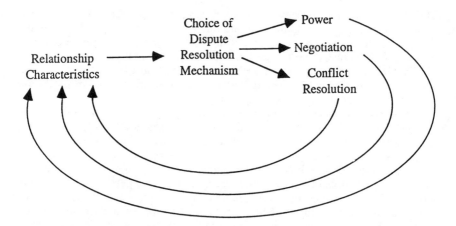

Consider first the impact of a relationship's characteristics on the decision to use negotiation and on the effectiveness of this effort. When the relationship is maximally adversarial, the parties are unlikely to negotiate, as in the case of a feud. The feuding parties' motivation is not to remove the strain in the relationship, but to impose costs on the other party even when there are significant costs to oneself. A suicide bomber is an extreme example of the willingness to endure self-sacrifice to hurt the other party. In contrast, when the relationship is multifaceted, strong, positive, and enduring, the motivation to negotiate will be strongest. The parties will not want to leave a dispute unaddressed because the conflict will fester and impair their relationship. Similarly, the parties will be wary of using their available power because forcing compliance engenders resentment and motivates the coerced party to change the relationship in ways that foster future autonomy. Greater autonomy necessarily means reduced interdependence and therefore a weakening of the bonds that tie the parties.

In addition to shaping the *choice* of negotiation as the means of addressing a dispute, relationships will also determine the *effectiveness* of the negotiation process. Effectiveness in negotiation primarily reflects the success of information-gathering.[4] The parties are well aware of their own situation, interests, aspirations, expectations, and constraints, so the real challenge is to gain such information about the other party. Disclosing information is risky.

While it facilitates beneficial solutions to disputes in positive relationships, it leaves the negotiator vulnerable to exploitation in relationships in which one party experiences no qualms about pursuing self-interest without regard for the other party's welfare. In short, the effectiveness of information exchange depends on the degree of trust, a key characteristic of relationships. Trust, in turn, depends on other relationship characteristics, as well as previous experience in negotiating with the other party, particularly whether the other party frames the dispute in win-lose terms.[5]

Therefore, the choice and effectiveness of conflict resolution as the means of handling a dispute are determined by the relationship between the parties and, in particular, by the level of trust. If party A believes that party B views the relationship as instrumental (that is, B is perceived to view the relationship solely as a means of achieving self-gain), then A will experience little trust. B's persuasive messages will be perceived as manipulative rather than helpful, and B's persuasion efforts will be rebuffed. At the other extreme, if A believes that B views the relationship as one in which B feels a responsibility to look out for A's interests, messages intended to foster conflict resolution will be treated with less suspicion as to motive. Thus, the trusted person will "get the benefit of the doubt."

Moreover, in relationships with strong positive bonds, especially the bonds of trust, similarity, and concern for each other's welfare, people are likely to want to work together to find a solution as well as to find a solution that is maximally satisfying to both parties. Working together—the *process* of being on the same side of the table—will be as important to them as the outcome. In such a case, conflict resolution is an obvious choice. Both alternative methods of dealing with conflicts keep the parties on opposite sides of the table, as separate individuals with their own agendas. As a result, no matter how "friendly" a negotiation is, the parties remain adversaries. In conflict resolution, the parties find a way to put aside what divides them, and deal with issues on which they are able to agree. For example, take the case of labor-management committees. These groups are able to take a domain of issues and deal with them constructively, even when there is an adversarial context of collective bargaining. The negotiating teams do not deny or minimize their differences at the bargaining table, but treat the set of issues being addressed by the labor-management committee as "separate from" what is going on in the divisive context of contract negotiations.[6]

Sometimes, when the relationship between the two primary parties is too strained to allow them to engage directly in conflict resolution, a third party can use these cognitive adjustment tactics very effectively. In such cases, the effectiveness of the effort depends on the prestige, bias, motives, and trustworthiness of the party attempting the intervention, all of which reflect relationship characteristics. To illustrate this, suppose we return once again to the father we described in the earlier example. He and his wife have decided to divorce and are deadlocked on a number of issues. When they think about and talk about the issues in dispute, their cognitions are polarized. Making concessions is difficult because each of them is hypersensitive to what they are giving up in a settlement. In other words, they construe the situation as a zero-sum endgame with high stakes. Furthermore, there are problems with the *process* of their interaction. They are not civil toward each other because years of suppressed anger surfaces in their interactions. The lack of civility makes concessions even more difficult because concessions carry with them a loss of social face. They each see this as an act of submission in their battle of wills.

The daughter, now a young adult, has relationships with her parents that are somewhat independent of their relationship with each other. The daughter's relationship with each of them enables her to persuasively reshape their cognitions, accomplishing the conflict resolution necessary for progress in agreeing to the division of assets. She can discuss the objective economic utility of concessions with each parent and the mutual loss involved in litigation ("only the lawyers will benefit"). She can make suggestions for compromises that the couple may be too grudging to offer to each other.

In practice, the daughter's effectiveness in conflict resolution will depend less on her persuasive skill than on the characteristics of the relationship she has with each parent. If both parents value their long-term relationship with her, they will try to avoid doing or saying things that will jeopardize their own parent/daughter relationship: they will try to be "reasonable" with her. Furthermore, it is likely they still will experience a parental role relationship with her that leads them to want to nurture and protect her. This parental role discourages divisive tactics that will indirectly hurt the daughter. The daughter therefore has some strong advantages when intervening in the interparental dispute. Her effectiveness in conflict resolution, however, will depend on how she *manages* the relationship she has with each parent. She must remain trusted as a neutral third party so the perceived relationship does not change to that of a member of a rival coalition. This will likely exacerbate rather than mitigate the divisive feelings ("Hey, this isn't fair: you're taking sides against me, after all I've done for you").

Finally, the choice of power as a means of settling a dispute is both affected by and has an effect on the relationship between the parties. In this case, the parties have to be especially careful about their choice of tactics because the act of inducing compliance further strains, and in some cases, can transform the relationship. Using power, in other words, may "solve" the original dispute but in doing so may leave an even larger problem in its place. The relationship strain that arises from power use is perhaps most obvious in the parent/child relationship. Imagine that the father wants the daughter to do something she is unwilling to do. When he expresses his wishes, and she her resistance, they both experience the strain, cognitively and emotionally, as conflict. He orders her to do it, imposing the legitimate power inherent in his role as parent. She continues her resistance, thereby increasing the relationship strain. Escalating his influence attempt, he threatens punishment, at this stage in the form of withheld approval signified by his changed tone of voice. This implies a deliberate degradation in the quality of his relationship to her. She continues to resist, further straining the relationship because she has implicitly signaled that the loss of approval is less important to her than the outcome she hopes to gain in the dispute. Escalating further, he threatens stronger punishment, perhaps the loss of utility (e.g., her allowance or privileges) or the experience of physical pain (e.g., a spanking). Overwhelmed by his use of power, she now complies. The relationship has been transformed, at least temporarily, from the loving-father/loving-daughter dyad that existed before the dispute arose to a domineering-father/subjugated-daughter dyad.

A second kind of problem can arise when one person uses power in a domain or a way that is inappropriate to the relationship. When this happens, the other party may focus on the abuse of power more than the issue in dispute. Sexual harassment follows this causal chain. Let us assume that M, a male manager, is sexually interested in F, a female relatively new to the firm whom he hired several months ago as his assistant. F is not sexually interested in M but is eager to do well in this job. In the course of their working together, M has often asked F to accompany him on business trips and in fact has asked her on occasion to go to his apartment and pack his bag for him. On one such trip, M ordered adjoining rooms and insisted that they meet in her room before and after seeing their client. At the end of the first day, as F was leaving her room, M suggested that she leave her side of the door unlocked in case he needed to retrieve some papers. F was shocked at the request. As she paused to think of the proper response, she remembered their dinner conversation in which he had told her about her predecessor—a woman who, in his view, was a militant feminist—who had been pushed out of the firm for insubordination. Nevertheless, she refused, suggesting that he take all the papers with him. Back in the office the following week, she finds that M's behavior toward her has changed. He has stopped informing her of meetings she is expected to attend, he openly criticizes her in front of others, and he begins giving the good assignments to others in the department. At the end of her ninety-day probationary period, his review of her performance states that F is uncooperative, fails to meet her responsibilities, and does not show any initiative. His recommendation is to replace her. Upon learning of his recommendation, F decides to press charges of sexual harassment.

From an analytical standpoint, the power dynamics are as follows: M wants sex from F, but F is not interested in M as a sex partner. M tries to overcome her resistance by using the power inherent in his organizational role. She cognitively transforms the dispute from an incompatibility of interests to a matter of principle with high stakes. In her view, M has no right to use his managerial power to exert influence in the sexual domain. Furthermore, the influence attempt becomes loaded with meaning, and emotion, as yet another instance of the exploitation of women in Western society. The relationship has become transformed from boss-subordinate to defendant-litigant, with little hope of re-establishing the original working relationship. The employee will probably be transferred to another department after the case is "resolved" by higher authorities.

III. The Study of Dispute Resolution

It is obvious from everyday experiences such as those described above that the characteristics of relationships can have an enormous impact on how a dispute is addressed, and that the ongoing relationship is in turn affected by the process by which the dispute was handled. As we noted earlier, however, dispute resolution scholars have given virtually no theoretical or empirical attention to the effects of—and on—relationships. Instead, major paradigms have evolved that neglect this important variable.

Early scholars approached dispute management from an economic viewpoint, particularly game theory.[7] These researchers posited a simple unidimensional relationship involving utility gain and loss: from this perspective, the relationship between the parties can be totally described in the payoff matrix. Other aspects of human interdependence and connection are defined as being beyond the scope of this paradigm. As a result, the noneconomic dimensions of relationships are simply not studied. Economists defend their approach by arguing that if preserving the relationship is important to disputants, they will somehow factor the value of relationship preservation into their aggregate utility function, i.e., total utility of an outcome is the sum of its economic utility plus its noneconomic utility. The economic study of negotiations has undeniably yielded a wealth of knowledge about negotiator choices. Indeed, the key proponents of game theory were awarded the Nobel Prize in 1994 in recognition of their contribution to science.

The game-theoretical framework has also shaped the paradigm developed by social psychologists studying dispute resolution, as evidenced by their emphasis on studying conflicts that can be fully defined by a payoff matrix. But these scholars (at least indirectly) acknowledged the potential influence of negotiator relationships by attempting to eliminate their effects. Laboratory simulations are usually designed to decontextualize negotiation situations, depicting them as pure transactions between parties who have no interpersonal history or future. In the real world, purely transactional negotiation is extremely rare, but experimental social psychologists are interested in investigating basic psychological phenomena and the lack of external validity does not necessarily diminish the scientific value of their findings. Relationship effects are controlled in the process by which individuals are assigned to dyads. Investigators typically eliminate pairings where significant prior relationships exist to "minimize error variance due to factors exogenous to the experiment."

In practice, however, these experimentalists do *not* control the effects of relationships because relationships form during any interpersonal interaction. Strangers have a relationship comprising, at a minimum, points of common identity, whether it be sophomores at the same college, residents of the same town, or people who volunteered for the same study. Furthermore, their relationship begins with the impressions they form at the first encounter and can evolve very rapidly as the experiment progresses. So even if there were simply a stranger-to-stranger relationship at the outset of the negotiation experiment, it would likely change into something more complex by the time the experiment concluded.

To illustrate the de facto evolution of relationships among "strangers," we can return to the example cited earlier of the college-aged daughter. She is enrolled in an introductory psychology class with 200 students at a large university. The research requirement of the course is to participate in a laboratory study of negotiation. When she shows up at the lab, she is paired with another student, and asked if she has a prior relationship with the other subject. She answers no, and the experiment proceeds. If the other subject is a slightly more attractive, somewhat condescending woman, the initial impression will likely inspire a strong competing dynamic that will rapidly shape the relationship. If the other subject is a domineering woman, the relationship may rapidly turn into a struggle for control, the daughter being predisposed to be reactive on this dimension by her recent experiences in adolescence. If the other subject is a handsome young man, a flirtatious dynamic may dominate the relationship and the negotiation interaction being studied. In each of these cases, the most powerful determinant of the process and outcomes will have gone unmeasured. Our view is that there is no such thing as "no relationship" in a social-psychological experiment, but rather only the probability that an important variable has not been taken into account.

Research conducted under the economic and social-psychological paradigms has yielded considerable knowledge of negotiation phenomena.[8] At the same time, the dominance of these paradigms in negotiation research has left us with little understanding of the role of relationships in negotiations. We believe this neglect has been unfortunate. The antidote begins with a multifaceted account of how people experience relationships. Once this perspective is understood, then an instrument can be developed to empirically measure the relative importance of the multiple facets of relationships.

IV. How We Define Relationship

Elsewhere we have defined a relationship as "the meaning assigned by two or more individuals to their connectedness or coexistence."[9] This definition recognizes that relationships exist at the level of the dyad or larger collectivity, but are *experienced* by individuals. Because a given individual's experience of the relationship will be affected by such factors as temperament, socialization, and personal history, this experience is asymmetrical between parties to the relationship.

The situation is made even more complex with the addition of structured roles for the two individuals. Take, for example, a boss-subordinate dyad. Here, even setting aside differences in personality and emotional experience, the imbalance in power between the two parties will almost inevitably create a difference in their respective views of the relationship. An exchange of favors is one example. When the boss asks the subordinate to do something to help him or her out, the subordinate complies because it is a role demand that has economic consequences in the future. When the subordinate asks the boss for a favor, he or she experiences it as an act of supplication. If the boss grants the wish, it is experienced as magnanimous by the subordinate. Similarly, a traditional wife-husband dyad is likely to exhibit asymmetry when describing their relationship. The wife is likely to use words that refer to her emotional needs and the extent to which she feels connected to her husband. The husband, on the other hand, is likely to use words that refer to each person's responsibilities and rights, and the set of rules that govern their interdependence. In fact, the popular press has noted that even if they use the same words, they often mean quite different things.[10]

Given that our definition refers to *assigned* meaning, we must pay special attention to what characteristics of relationships are salient in a particular interaction. Imagine that the daughter referred to earlier is driving the car she bought from her father while away at college. She gets into an accident on the way home from a date, injuring her boyfriend who was not wearing his seat belt. In order to recover his medical costs from her insurance company, he has to sue her. Consider the complex nature of their relationship. He is her lover and potential future husband, her enemy in court, her tutor in her biology course where she met and started dating him, her informal tutee for his language class, part of a network of mutual friends, an ally in supporting the varsity teams, a roommate sharing an apartment who does not do the same share of housework, a competitor in tennis, and a fellow member of the college's Environmental Action Club.

All of these aspects of the relationship are very real to her, but not all of them are salient at a given point in time. In court, on the court, in class, and in bed, the two deal with incompatible wishes in vastly different ways. The relationship does not change from situation to situation, but some aspects of it become more salient as a result of context. In addition, in this case, the car accident has had an effect on the couple's relationships with others which further strains their own relationship. His lawsuit has transformed his relationship with her family, because they cannot reconcile the boyfriend role with the plaintiff role. They close ranks protectively and reject him as an enemy. At the same time, his family withdraws their acceptance of her. She injured him in the car accident. His family cannot reconcile inflicting bodily harm on him with the girlfriend role. They close ranks protectively and reject her as an enemy.

If we want to understand and manage the dispute that has the young couple in court, we have to understand all of these relationship dynamics. Unfortunately, the field of conflict management has not yet developed the concepts, models, and theories necessary to even label the forces operating.

V. The Literature on Relationships

The most comprehensive summary to date of the bargaining literature by Rubin and Brown[11] showed that relationships between negotiators had largely been ignored up to that point in time. Although their key individual difference variable—interpersonal orientation—implies the importance of relationships, Rubin and Brown do not recognize relationships as an important construct per se. Other prominent works have explored constructs that are proxies for relationships between negotiators, without giving adequate attention to the underlying construct. For example, the classic work by Walton and McKersie[12] devoted a section to "attitudinal structuring," the process of shaping negotiators' attitudes toward each other in a way that promotes constructive resolution of disputes. The analysis concerned attitudes, which is roughly equivalent to what we are calling the negotiator's experience of the relationship. Surprisingly, however, little follow-up research was inspired by this seminal entree to understanding the impact of particular dispositions toward the other party. Perhaps one of the reasons that the attitudinal structuring concept did not spawn a torrent of research is that attitudes, per se, do not have much appeal to the economics-trained researchers who have tended to dominate the field of labor relations.

Many studies have indirectly taken the effects of relationships into account by manipulating the time horizon variable.[13] Three time horizons have been defined. A terminal situation is one in which the parties will never interact after the transaction is completed. An episodic situation is one in which the parties focus only on the current transaction. A continuous situation assumes awareness of ongoing interaction and, by implication, an ongoing relationship between the parties. Some researchers purport to have simulated an ongoing interpersonal relationship by presenting subjects with a series of transactions in a multitrial laboratory experiment. Repeated situations are not the same thing as enduring relationship bonds, especially when the situation being repeated is experienced as a competitive game. As a result, this latter approach to research generates a serious construct validity problem.

Other studies of potential value focus on "interdependence"[14] and coalitions.[15] Interdependence is typically operationalized as whether one party can achieve its goals without the consent or cooperation of the other. Studies of coalitions have yet to fully explore the relationships which bind the coalition partners.

The call to include a consideration of relationships in our thinking about negotiation[16] gave rise to a series of studies that explore the importance of relationships as an explanatory and outcome variable.[17] But progress in conducting research on the effects of relationships has been hampered by limited understanding of the phenomenon. Scholars and practitioners need to know the *characteristics* of relationships to which people pay attention when addressing disputes. Our research makes progress in answering this basic question.

VI. Characteristics of Relationships: Research Findings

We began our research program with exploratory field research in which we interviewed people engaged in dispute resolution. We learned that people *always* attend to relationships when addressing disputes, but are not equally articulate in describing the characteristics of this multifaceted, complex, interpersonal phenomenon. Therefore, we needed to design a procedure for eliciting people's experience of relationship characteristics that would be as effective with people who talk about relationships as a dominant topic of conversation as it is with people who deal with relationships more implicitly.

Our approach to the research drew on the work of George Kelly,[18] who showed that the "definition of the situation" to which people react could be broken up into a set of personal constructs, i.e., the elements of the conceptual framework by which people understood complex phenomena. The method we used for construct elicitation was to ask interview subjects to describe the similarities and differences in their relationships, while the interviewer wrote down the characteristics these subjects were describing.[19] The content of the responses was then analyzed. The resulting information was not only illuminating in itself, but also became the foundation for the development of a scale to measure the characteristics of relationships.

This phase of the research yielded fourteen distinct constructs or dimensions of relationships. Respondents had identified stimulus individuals in organizational, social, and family relationships. The dimensions they used to describe their relationships were essentially the same irrespective of setting. These dimensions are shown in table 1.

The left column in table 1 lists the dimensions that arose in our interviews. The center column shows the frequency of mention expressed as a percentage, e.g., 91 percent of the respondents talked about common interests. The right column of the table shows whether or not that dimension has been identified as important in other scholars' attempts to operationally define relationships as a multifaceted variable. It also confirms that no previous researcher has identified the spectrum of characteristics that respondents consider important in assessing relationships.

The fourteen dimensions can be grouped into four categories. They are: attraction, or the other party's appeal to the respondent; rapport, or the comfort the parties have in dealing with each other; bonding, or the robustness of the relationship when it encounters strain; and the breadth of the relationship, i.e., its perceived scope and time horizon.

A. Attraction

This grouping includes the degree to which the focal individual sees that they have much in common (common interests), likes the other (affection), finds him or her stimulating (stimulation), and is romantically interested (romantic interest).

Common Interests. Most of the respondents differentiated relationships on the basis of "how much they had in common" with the other party. Their notion resembles the social psychologist's concept of similarity and refers to the degree to which there is a sharing of values, interests, beliefs, and activities. The link to cohesion in the relationship seemed to involve their sense of common identity, or sense of "belonging" in the same group or dyad. Another link seemed to be self-validation. It is ego-enhancing to find someone who thinks and feels about the world the same way. Note that this dimension is somewhat independent of the stimulation dimension. Respondents did not necessarily find people with whom they had much in common interesting.

In general, fewer conflicts arose in relationships where the parties had a lot in common. There were fewer differences of opinion, fewer disagreements over decisions that affected both parties, and a tendency to view situations from the same perspective. When conflicts did arise in such relationships, the parties avoided using divisive tactics.

Table 1. Comparison of Empirically and Theoretically Derived
Dimensions of Relationships

DIMENSION	EMPIRICAL: FREQUENCY OF CONSTRUCT RESPONSE (%)	THEORETICAL: INCLUSION IN EXISTING MODELS*
Attraction		
Common Interests	.91	B, D, E
Affection	.60	D, F
Stimulation	.27	
Romantic Interest	.14	
Rapport		
Trust	.87	F
Disclosure	.76	C, D, F
Empathy	.71	F
Acceptance	.68	F
Respect	.62	F
Bonding		
Alliance	.44	A, B, C, D
Competitive Dynamics	.32	
Positive Exchange	.20	E, F
Breadth of Relationship		
Scope	.91	A, B, C, D, E, F
Time Horizon	.27	C, E

* Key to Sources
A Wish, Deutsch, and Kaplan, 1976
B Kelley, 1979
C McCall, et al., 1970
D Hinde, 1979
E Kelley, et al., 1983
F Davis and Todd, 1985

Sources: See note 20

Affection. This dimension reflects the quality and intensity of emotional reaction, ranging from love to hate, that the individual experiences in the relationship. When referring to this dimension, respondents made the following kinds of statements: "I really like the other person," "She really hates me," or "I don't know why, but we just don't like each other." Liking, according to respondents' accounts, is one of the relationship characteristics that can form instantly. This reinforces our earlier argument that pairing strangers in laboratory studies does not create a "no relationship" condition. Respondents identified such instances colloquially in referring to good or bad "chemistry" between them and people they had met for the first time. They also identified experiences in which they had "learned to like" or "grown fond of" someone. Interestingly, respondents viewed liking as different from similarity, or what we refer to as having things "in common" with others. Thus, the tendency of social psychologists to virtually equate similarity and liking seems inconsistent with common experience.

Our respondents agreed that positive affect clearly strengthens the bond between people and has an impact on how they react to a strain in the relationship. It also clearly affects the meaning they assign to the outcome and process of the negotiation. Take, for example, the case of two junior managers working in the same department. One makes a comment in a meeting with superiors that implicitly criticizes the other and causes a loss of face. If the offended manager likes the other, the offense might be forgiven. Not so if there is dislike: the same behavior will probably be interpreted as a self-serving attempt to undermine a rival, rather than a display of poor judgment. The degree of liking thus affects how meaning is assigned to behavior, which in turn affects the future relationship.

Stimulation. Another cohesive force in relationships appears when one or both individuals experience the other as interesting or intellectually challenging, and the interaction with that person as having learning value. The converse of stimulation, thus defined, is boredom. In our interviews, respondents described stimulation with phrases such as, "This person is really exciting to be around" or "This person is never dull—she always has an interesting perspective on things" or "He always pushes me to do new things, things I never would have done on my own." Conversely, respondents described boredom as, "I hate to say this, but time passes very slowly when I'm around her. In fact, to be honest, I dread spending extended time together even though I feel very close to her. Five minutes on the phone every few days is plenty."

Stimulation can be important when conflicts strain relationships because people have less attention span when dealing with a boring relationship partner and may be less motivated to resolve it. One respondent reported a good overall working relationship with a peer, but felt strains mounting as conflicts went unaddressed. He was afraid to surface problems because he did not want his coworker to "drone on" about the issue. Instead, he compartmentalized the relationship to involve business interactions and kept himself looking busy so as to limit social conversation.

Romantic Interest. This dimension refers to physical attraction and is different from, though usually correlated with, affect. Romantic interest makes interaction rewarding, i. e., from an operant conditioning standpoint, people are likely to repeat interactions with others when the interaction is romantically intriguing. This is a complex dimension of relationships because it may be unilateral or bilateral; overt, covert, or tacit; and it may be experienced, suppressed, or repressed.

Bilateral romantic interest may enrich or complicate relationships, depending on the circumstances. For example, the greatest potential exposure to romantic partners for most adults is at work, because that is where they spend the greatest amount of time interacting with others. Under idyllic circumstances, romantically entwined coworkers can "get married and live happily ever after." Under the more real-world circumstances reported by our respondents, however, there are barriers to acting on bilateral romantic interest: perhaps one or both are married; perhaps there are strong norms proscribing office romances; or perhaps the perceived risks of taking the next steps are too high, as in many cases of same-sex attraction.

Unilateral romantic interest can but does not necessarily destabilize relationships. Individuals ultimately have little control over whether they become romantically interested in another; they can only control how the interest gets expressed. Unreciprocated interest can strain relationships when it generates feelings of rejection and resentment, but it can also strengthen relationships when properly managed. Our respondents found others' unilateral romantic interest in them to be ego-enhancing, so long as the person "respected the boundaries" that had been set up and was not being an interpersonal nuisance. They were likely to strengthen relationships with people who were attracted to them, because they found the attention rewarding.

Attraction is overt when the person unambiguously expresses it to the object of his or her romantic interest, it is covert when no clue is communicated, and it is tacit when the message is transmitted in a way that requires interpretation. Tacit messages, in other words, are ambiguous. Tacit expressions allow the interested person to save face if the other person reacts negatively. They also allow the object of the romantic interest to ignore the message if it generates discomfort.

Finally, romantic interest may be a dynamic of a relationship that is not accurately experienced by the person who is smitten, leading to complicated interactions. Many people repress feelings of attraction, usually due to taboos or fear of rejection. Repression occurs when the psyche does not permit conscious experience of thoughts and feelings. When fear of rejection motivates repression, this can be a great strain on relationships: the attracted person rejects the romantic object before this person has a chance to reject him or her. This phenomenon is difficult to identify because the person is not aware at the time of repressing a romantic reaction. Suppressed romantic interest is less of a strain on a relationship because it is consciously experienced. The person is aware of his or attraction but is determined not to act on it.

If the romantic interest dynamic is well managed in a relationship it tends to facilitate dispute settlement. Attraction tends to motivate ingratiating behavior, which reduces the utility sacrifice in concessions; and, if the romantic attention is ego-enhancing, the person receiving the attention will be motivated to use relationship-preserving tactics.

B. Rapport

The second group of dimensions involves the comfort the parties have in dealing with each other. Included in this grouping are trust, disclosure, empathy, acceptance, and respect.

Trust. Trust consists of cognitions regarding three facets of behavior: reliability, interpersonal integrity, and altruism. Reliability involves the predictability of the other's behavior. One respondent illustrated this facet in describing a substance-abusing friend: "I know he means well, but I just can't rely on him to be there for me." Consistency is another form reliability takes. Deep trust requires a response that can be "counted on" irrespective of mood, whims, forgetfulness, or context. The second facet of trust, interpersonal integrity, involves whether the relationship partner will keep confidences, tell the truth, resist the temptation to achieve self-gain through cheating, and honor commitments. The third facet, altruism, concerns the motive to look after the other person's best interests. The antithesis of altruism may be self-serving impulses, indifference to one's welfare, or insensitivity.

There seems to be a multiplicative relationship between the three facets: if any one of the facets were rated low, overall trust would therefore be rated low. Someone who is self-serving may be experienced as untrustworthy, for example, despite being rated as reliable and having high interpersonal integrity. In the words of a respondent, "He was reliable all right: looking out for himself all the way!" Similarly, a person who was unreliable yet of high interpersonal integrity might be described as someone who "means well, but you just can't depend on her."

We found trust to be one of the most important relationship characteristics when respondents talked about dealing with disputes. Negotiation is a persuasive process, so trust will determine how messages are interpreted. It also affects the parties' willingness to divulge information about their situation, needs, and constraints, virtually a prerequisite for arriving at integrative solutions. Distrustful negotiators were unwilling to reveal detail for fear that it might be used to exploit them. Trust was also important in conflict resolution: for example, the third-party role requires that the intervenor is seen as unbiased. One has to trust someone to have some confidence that one will be treated fairly.

Disclosure. This relationship characteristic refers to the openness with which the parties deal with each other. An intimate relationship, in this sense, is one in which the parties disclose information that is "sensitive" in terms of revealing areas of vulnerability. Respondent comments relevant to this dimension include: "I tell her everything," "He's always on his guard when we talk," or "In contrast to what I was telling you about women that I'm close to, I can't really be myself when he's around." In a low-disclosure relationship, the parties may spend a great deal of time together, sharing activities and interests, but never reveal how they feel, emotionally or with respect to values. Relationships display varying degrees of bilaterality on this dimension, although nonreciprocated disclosure creates relationship strains because one party has taken the social risk of making himself/herself vulnerable while the other has not.

Disclosure is a central element of rapport because high disclosure involves low social barriers. In fact, within cultural boundaries, confiding is an effective rapport-building tactic. Respondents felt closer to people who had been "open and honest" with them.

In dispute resolution, disclosure is most obviously helpful for discovering integrative solutions because disclosure reveals interests. It also has a modeling effect whereby the other party tends to copy the discloser's behavior. The modeling is backed up by the reciprocity norms of social exchange: "I have told you about my own situation and areas of vulnerability: now it's your turn." These dynamics counteract "gaming" tendencies in dispute resolution whereby the parties "play [their] cards close to the vest." Furthermore, disclosure affects dispute resolution because it fosters trust and communicates expectations about interpersonal integrity. If one party is being candid about areas of vulnerability, the other party faces responsibilities to manage that information in a way that respects the rights of the disclosing party. The discloser, in effect, has both shown trust and elicited trust, and the relationship must adjust accordingly. Put succinctly, "one does not exploit a confidant."

Empathy. Empathy is the ability to see something as it looks from the other party's viewpoint. It is a property of relationships because it determines the degree to which people are self-centered rather than relationship-centered. Low empathy means that the individual lacks the ability, willingness, or insight to take the other party's perspective.

There are degrees of bilaterality in empathy, partly because empathic ability is a personality variable.[21] The predisposition to be empathic bodes well for working relationships, but its converse—empathic insensitivity—does not have to be a problem since one can compensate by teaching the other party how the situation looks from one's own perspective. Empathic inducement is, indeed, a useful and often effective persuasive technique. For example, the question, "What would you do if you were in my shoes?" can be disarming, and challenges the other party to obtain the information necessary to answer the question. Used tactically, it can be a useful device for fostering integrative negotiated solutions. It induces the person to actively think about the other party's interests, situation, and constraints as well as his or her own.

Acceptance. Our respondents were attuned to their need for unconditional positive regard and their quest to find it in relationships. As such, they were typical people who want to be accepted for who they are, not on condition that they do particular things or live up to particular standards imposed by the other party.

Our respondents did not feel fully accepted if they sensed they were being judged by the other party. Acceptance was mentioned by virtually all respondents as being a primary component of their closest relationships. Their descriptions took the form: "I can always just be myself without worrying what he will think of me"; "She takes me for what I am and doesn't try to change me"; or, conversely, "I just can't be myself around him: I feel pressure to behave in certain ways that aren't really me." Acceptance also characterized relationships in which there was a high degree of disclosure, for understandable reasons: disclosure is difficult when one fears being judged.

Respect. This final aspect of rapport involves the extent to which the parties see each other as having a valid value system and living up to it. In essence, respect involves judgments of integrity in a broader context than the interpersonal integrity we discussed when explaining trust. Respect allows conflicting value systems to coexist, and the cognitive adjustments necessary to deal with the dissonance involved are built into our descriptions of such differences: "I respect her point of view. I happen to see the world differently, and make my choices accordingly; but she, too, has to make the decision that's right for her, and I'll accept it as a thoughtful choice."

It is informative that courage is the quality we admire when bestowing respect. Courage involves living by one's value system when there are costs such as sacrifices in popularity or personal gain, or risks, e.g., known potential sacrifices. The converse, cowardice, implies a lack of courage in living up to one's value system and elicits disrespect.

Respect facilitates dispute resolution because it permits toleration of differences. Respect is also surprisingly independent of some of the more global relationship dimensions, such as overall liking. People were as comfortable saying, "I like him but I don't respect him" as they were saying, "I respect him greatly but I also dislike him intensely." Some respondents reported high trust in people for whom they had no respect: "He doesn't stand for much, but he always looks out for me." Finally, although respect shows a tendency to become bilateral, unbalanced respect is a stable relationship characteristic.

C. Bonding

The third group of dimensions describes how robust the relationship is. Colloquially, we might refer to some relationships as "casual" and others as "strong" when using dimensions in this grouping. Robustness refers to the relationship's ability to survive strains undamaged. The component dimensions are the sense of alliance, the competitive dynamics, and the positive value of the exchange.

Alliance. Each party can characterize the other on a continuum from ally to enemy. As in the case of affection, the midpoint may be either indifference or ambivalence. In the positive range, being considered an ally reflects loyalty. One way loyalty is experienced is in terms of the risk that the other person might abandon the relationship: "He's really just a 'fair-weather friend' who'd sacrifice the relationship in a minute if someone else came by with more to offer." Another facet of loyalty is whether the person would be supportive in the absence of monitoring: "She is very nice in dealing with me, but I don't know what she'd say behind my back if others were critical, which often happens in this business." Loyalty is also experienced in terms of public commitment to the relationship. Strong alliances are visible to others because the loyal person takes a supportive stance. The stance is often nonverbal and symbolic, such as standing behind or alongside the speaker when announcements of potentially unpopular decisions are being made, but also may be explicit and verbal.

Enemy status is often masked: it is one thing to consider oneself another's enemy, and another thing altogether to openly declare it. The masking is greatest when the enmity is weak because there are risks to declaring oneself another's enemy. The first is the risk of attack. An enemy is someone who is motivated to induce suffering. Thus, when the other party declares this motive state, it is rational to attack one's enemy first, and then take a defensive posture to reduce the effectiveness of retaliation. The second is the risk of generating additional enemies. The status of being a declared enemy evokes in-group/out-group behavior in which alliances form protectively around enemies. This pits larger groups against each other, when the enmity may have started out as interpersonal in scope. The third is the risk of organizational reproach. Many organizations subscribe to an implicit order model[22] in which having someone as an enemy is seen as dysfunctional. These factors make the enmity side of the alliance dimension difficult to handle.

Unlike many other characteristics of relationships, the alliance dimension is almost purely bilateral. If party A declares party B an enemy, party B will consider party A an enemy. There are few cognitive adjustments other than denial that will allow imbalanced definitions of the situation to coexist. Conversely, if one party treats the other as an ally, social norms make it hard to respond with exploitation or rebuff without enduring guilt and shame, so there is a tendency to accept offers of alliance when they are viewed as sincere.

Competitive Dynamics. Respondents described competitive tensions as impediments to the relationship, a factor that "gets in the way" of constructive interactions. The negative cast arose from several sources: a fear of being shown inadequate or foolish; the risk of divisiveness that would interfere with getting the job done; or suspicion that the other person would undermine him or her in order to look better by comparison.

Overt competing was actually a rarity in our respondents' experiences. They knew that they were supposed to be collaborating in business and social relationships. Yet beneath that veneer of collaboration there was keen awareness of competitive tensions: "If I did something, I *knew* he would try to go one better. It was sickeningly predictable." Respondents were also aware of the extent they got drawn into competing: "I don't know who started it, but I always have to do better than him." Women were less aware of being drawn into competing, but nevertheless the dynamic was often there: "We're friends on the surface, but we'll never be really close because we're always trying to beat each other one way or another." They were not as stoic as men in accepting competing as "part of the game" in interpersonal relationships, but saw it as an unfortunate occurrence that sometimes cannot be prevented: "It's like the common cold of relationships."

The effect of competing dynamics on the way people resolve disputes is obvious. First, the parties are even more likely than noncompeting negotiators to fall prey to the "fixed pie error"[23] by which negotiators frame the problem as a struggle for a share. Second, concession-making will be difficult because a concession to a competitor is, by definition, viewed in zero-sum terms. Third, there is likely to be an emphasis on assessing the utility of settlements relative to the other negotiator, rather than irrespective of the other negotiator. This leads the negotiators to focus on winning instead of problem solving.[24] Finally, the stakes involved in the dispute will be magnified because in addition to the objective issues, negotiators take into account self-esteem utility involved in prevailing over, or losing to, a rival.

Positive Value of the Exchange. Assessments of exchange involve the tangible benefits the parties derive from their association. Respondents illustrated this dimension with comments such as, "Look. I get lonely. He's someone to spend time with"; "She brings home a weekly paycheck, and that's what gets me though school"; and "It was a business deal: nobody could match his quality at that price." In talking about this dimension, respondents were articulate about what benefits the other party received in return. At the same time there was a pattern to the responses that suggested that the salience of this dimension was inversely related to the depth of the relationship: the shallower the relationship, the easier it was to describe in terms of exchange. In deep relationships, even between business representatives, exchange was either not mentioned at all or brought up only when serious exchange imbalances caused equity concerns.

Our field research indicates that exchange seems to be a minor consideration when people consider their relationships, despite the fact that it is the foundation of so much social science.[25] People do not normally look at relationships—even in business—from the perspective of the history and current balance of the benefits each party provides. In limited interactions, to be sure, indebtedness could be an important dimension of the relationship. In long-term relationships, however, the history of exchange is likely to be complex and multifaceted. When such exchanges are primarily positive, the effect is cohesive, to the point where the relationship is *intrinsically* valued and the parties lose track of the exchange balance.

D. Breadth of the Relationship

The last grouping of constructs reflects differences in conceptualizations of the relationship both in scope and along the time dimension or time horizon.

Scope. Relationships vary in terms of how pervasive they are: scope refers to the breadth of the relationship's domain. A narrow-scope relationship is usually one that has little significance to the parties beyond its functional value or role relationship. One respondent illustrated the scope dimension very vividly.

> I have two sisters and they both live in [my home town], less than two miles from where I was living. I don't know Karen at all. I see her at family get-togethers but I don't know her any better than I know you [referring to the interviewer]. Actually I know you better. At least we're having a real conversation here. Anyway, my other sister, Marie, is my best friend. I mean it. We tell each other everything. We lend each other money, go on double dates together, cook for each other, everything. She's teaching me German. She also sticks up for me

all the time, and I'll do the same for her. But Karen. . . .You know, if we weren't related, we'd be total strangers.

Scope has shown itself to be a dimension that is largely independent of longevity. Some relationships start narrow and stay narrow. Many others grow and recede. Some start with broad scope (for example many organizational roles—such as "boss"—and familial roles—such as "in-law") and over time recede to relationships having narrower scope (such as when there is psychological withdrawal or geographic relocation).

In our field research, we found respondents motivated to address conflicts proactively and fairly in broad-scope relationships because there was "so much at stake." They also referred to the "reservoir of goodwill" that could be drawn upon in broad-scope relationships to ensure that the process was constructive, concessions easy to grant, and apologies easy to make.

Time Horizon. In describing relationships, some respondents focused on immediate events, and were able to disconnect these from the history of interaction or the future relationship. Others contextualized all their thinking in the relationship as an ongoing entity. This difference was sometimes stark, and had little to do with the objective situation. One woman described a relationship as on going that had formed when she learned job details from the woman she was replacing. The period of overlap was one afternoon, the day before the predecessor left the job to work for a different company in Hong Kong. When questioned about why she considered the relationship to be ongoing, she seemed baffled that the interviewer had asked the question. She explained: "OK, so she's in Hong Kong and I'm in New York, but it's ongoing as far as I'm concerned, and, I'm sure, as far as she's concerned as well. Maybe she'll call me. She's got the number here. If she does, we'll just pick up where we left off. I don't know."

Other people can easily dissociate the current interaction from an objective long-term relationship. The interaction is treated as a transaction and the person chooses power and negotiation tactics as if the outcome of the immediate situation is the only factor to be taken into consideration. One man explained: "[My coworker in the group] had just as much opportunity as I did to take advantage of the situation. Maybe she'll learn from this—that each time an issue comes up and it can go her way or my way, it's a new ball game and she's going to have to look out for herself. Nothing's going to get handed to her." He was describing a relationship which had become permanently strained as a result of a dispute that had arisen in a long-term relationship.

Our field research suggests that there is probably more asymmetry in perceived time horizon than any other relationship characteristic. One party can have an extreme long-term view and the other can have a purely transactional view. In fact, this difference frequently falls along gender lines.[26] Obviously the discrepancy in time horizon leads to frustrations, but the differences have often become so familiar to people by adulthood that they have learned to accept the different viewpoint and can compensate for it and thereby be effective in their everyday interactions. The asymmetry is least tolerated, however, by those with a long time-horizon perspective involved in a close relationship with a transactionally oriented partner.

Time horizon has an enormous effect on how disputes get resolved. Sometimes the relationship is viewed in terms of its salience to particular transactions: "I know we had been working together for years, but this meeting was about the particular deal, and that's what the relationship was about at that time. The relationship *was* the deal. At another point in time, it might be another deal, but at the time, the deal was all that was relevant. That's not so hard to understand, is it?" At other times, the relationship supersedes any transaction: "We had to agree on something to get us moving forward. We didn't really know what we were getting into because the technology was unproved and nobody knew what was happening in the market: it was changing too fast. But we trusted those people and knew we'd be able to work things out as they came up." Dispute resolution is easier to resolve when the parties contemplate the ongoing relationship. The parties are more aware that the tactics they use in addressing the dispute have future consequences, so they are less likely to use power, more likely to seek integrative solutions, and find it easier to make concessions because concessionary behavior obliges the other party to reciprocate in future negotiations.

VII. Conclusions and Implications for Future Research

This article has shown relationships between negotiators to be an important factor in understanding how disputes are resolved between individuals, groups, and larger collectivities such as organizations and even nation-states. The logic of looking at interpersonal relationships when the dispute involves large institutions is that the agents are the point of contact. The ability to resolve disputes between institutions is often at the mercy of their agents' relationship. The relationship affects the *process* by which the dispute gets addressed. How each party construes the relationship affects his or her willingness to share information, make concessions, apologize, risk losing face, make commitments without contractual assurances or penalty clauses, forgive past infractions, and implement the agreement in a spirit of goodwill.

The research findings described in this paper show that we can, indeed, determine the characteristics or dimensions of relationships that are salient to typical business negotiators. These dimensions do not exactly match what economists and other social scientists studying negotiations have posited to be salient. In particular, economic exchange proved to be of minor importance to our respondents, even though they were all experienced businessmen and businesswomen enrolled in an MBA program. This discrepancy should stimulate a theoretical debate among scholars. Our position in that debate would be that economic exchange theory is useful when negotiators are preoccupied with economic exchange, and that empirical research should be devoted to investigating the conditions under which such preoccupation arises. In most of the business relationships described by our respondents, however, other noneconomic relationship characteristics were more important in the joint decision-making context.

In identifying the characteristics of relationships to which people pay attention, we have laid the groundwork for two major streams of research. First, a relationship-characteristics or dimensions inventory can be used to distinguish strong relationships from weak ones. This allows us to examine, for example, the causes and consequences of strong boss-subordinate, labor-management, and cross-functional relationships. Second, this inventory could be used to empirically distinguish the different characteristics of relationships and allow us to isolate the effects of various dimensions. For example, when and how does trust really make a difference? How does romantic interest affect concession behavior? When teams negotiate with other teams, how does heterogeneity of relationships affect process? What kinds of personalities are able to disregard the "attraction" cluster of dimensions? The potential for addressing important research questions is enormous.[27]

The need to understand how relationships affect conflict resolution has never been more pronounced. In an increasingly global and gender-diverse business system, negotiators will have to know how to manage relationships as well as claim value. Yet cross-cultural comparisons of negotiators[28] and cross-gender comparisons of masculine and feminine negotiators[29] show differential concern for building and preserving relationships. Furthermore, concern for the quality of relationships is likely to be more important in future business deals because there is a growing shift from a hierarchical and contractual mode of organizing toward one characterized by strategic alliances. Thus, if relationships prior to actual negotiations are important to the success of integrative bargaining, and the process is important to the future of the relationship, then this research on relationships has strong implications for (1) the people we select as negotiators, (2) the models we adopt for best practice, and (3) how we teach people to be effective negotiators.

Notes

1.   See, for example, J. Nash, "The Bargaining Problem," *Econometrica* 18 (1950): 155–62; or L. Greenhalgh, S. A. Neslin, and R. W. Gilkey, "The Effects of Negotiator Preferences, Situational Power, and Negotiator Personality on Outcomes of Business Negotiations," *Academy of Management Journal* 28 (1985): 9–33.

2.   A thoughtful review and synthesis of negotiation alternatives can be found in the book, *Strategic Negotiations* (Boston: Harvard Business School, 1994), by R. E. Walton, J. Cutcher-Gershenfeld and R. B. McKersie.

3.   For further information on cognitive adjustments that foster dispute resolution, see L. Greenhalgh, "Managing Conflict," *Sloan Management Review* 27, no. 4 (1986): 45–52.

4.   See R. J. Lewicki, J.W. Minton, J. A. Litterer and D. M. Saunders, *Negotiation,* 2d ed. (Burr Ridge, Ill.: Irwin, 1994); Walton, Cutcher-Gershenfeld and

McKersie, *Strategic Negotiations* (Boston: Harvard Business School Press, 1994).

5. See M. H. Bazerman and M. A. Neale, *Negotiating Rationally* (New York: Free Press, 1992) or L. Greenhalgh, "The Case Against Winning in Negotiations," *Negotiation Journal* 3 (1987): 235–43.

6. For example, see R. B. McKersie, L. Greenhalgh and T. D. Jick, "The CEC: Labor-Management Cooperation in New York," *Industrial Relations* 20, no. 2 (1981): 212–20.

7. See, e.g., Nash, "The Bargaining Problem."

8. Good reviews of this literature can be found in Bazerman and Neale, *Negotiating Rationally*; H. Raiffa, *The Art and Science of Negotiation* (Cambridge: Harvard University Press, 1982); J. Z. Rubin and B. R. Brown, *The Social Psychology of Bargaining and Negotiation* (New York: Academic Press, 1975); Lewicki et al., *Negotiation*.

9. L. Greenhalgh and D. I. Chapman, *The Influence of Negotiator Relationships on the Process and Outcomes of Business Transactions,* working paper, Amos Tuck School of Business Administration, Dartmouth College, 1994.

10. Deborah Tannen summarizes these differences in *You Just Don't Understand: Women and Men in Conversation* (New York: Ballentine, 1990).

11. Rubin and Brown, *The Social Psychology of Bargaining.*

12. R. E. Walton and R. B. McKersie, *A Behavioral Theory of Labor Negotiations* (New York: McGraw-Hill, 1965).

13. For example see D. H. Pruitt and J. Z. Rubin, *Social Conflict* (New York: Random House, 1986); L. Thompson, "Negotiation Behavior: Empirical Evidence and Theoretical Issues," *Psychological Bulletin* 108 (1990): 515–32.

14. H. H. Kelley, *Personal Relationships* (Hillsdale, N.J.: Erlbaum, 1979); H. H. Kelley et al., *Close Relationships* (New York: Freeman, 1983).

15. See J. K. Murnighan, "Organizational Coalitions: Structural Contingencies and the Formation Process," *Research on Negotiation in Organizations* 1 (1986): 155–73.

16. L. Greenhalgh, "Relationships in Negotiations," *Negotiation Journal* 3 (1987): 235–43.

17. For examples, see L. Greenhalgh and R. M. Kramer, "Strategic Choice in Conflicts: The Importance of Relationships," in *Organizations and Nation*

States: New Perspectives on Conflict and Cooperation, ed. R. L. Kahn and M. N. Zald (San Francisco: Jossey-Bass, 1990); J. J. Halpern, *Bonded Rationality: The Rationality of Everyday Decision Making in a Social Context*, working paper, New York State School of Industrial and Labor Relations, Cornell University, 1994; G. F. Lowenstein, L. Thompson, and M. H. Bazerman, "Social Utility and Decision Making in Interpersonal Contexts," *Journal of Personality and Social Psychology* 57 (1989): 426–41; E. A. Mannix, Negotiation and Dispute Resolution in Small Groups: The Effects of Power, Justice Norms, and the Anticipation of a Future Relationship," working paper no. 76, Dispute Resolution Research Center, Northwestern University, 1991; G. B. Northcraft and N. A. Neale, "Negotiating Successful Research Collaboration," working paper no. 78, Dispute Resolution Center, Northwestern University, 1991; H. Sondak and M.C. Moore, "Relationship Frames and Cooperation," *Group Decision and Negotiations* 2 (1993): 103–18; L. Thompson and T. DeHarpport, "Effects of Relationship, Task Expectancy, and Communal Orientation on Interpersonal Conflict," working paper, Department of Psychology, University of Washington, 1991; M. Tuchinsky, J. E. Escalas, M. C. Moore, and B. H. Sheppard, "Beyond Name, Rank and Function: Construal of Relationships in Business," working paper, Fuqua School of Business, Duke University, 1994; K. L. Valley, "Relationships and Resources: A Network Exploration of Allocation Decisions," working paper, Dispute Resolution Research Center, Northwestern University, 1991.

18.   G. A. Kelly, *The Psychology of Personal Constructs* (New York: Norton, 1955).

19.   More specifically, the first stage of the research was to establish the dimensions along which people (rather than theorists steeped in the current paradigms) think about and assess relationships. Personal constructs were systematically identified by means of a variant of the repertory grid technique (F. Fransella and D. Bannister, *A Manual for Repertory Grid Technique* [New York: Academic Press, 1977]). The technique involves presenting respondents with salient stimuli then recording the constructs they use in describing their reactions to the stimuli. Saliency of the stimuli was assured by allowing respondents themselves to pick their own real relationships to analyze.

In this phase of the research, fifty MBA students participated in construct-elicitation interviews. Their ages ranged from twenty-five to thirty-two and they typically had between two and five years of post-baccalaureate organizational experience. These respondents were asked to write, on separate index cards, the names of eight people with whom they had some sort of interpersonal relationship. These became the stimuli for eliciting the personal constructs respondents employed when thinking about relationships.

Next, using G. A. Kelly's (*op. cit.*) method of triads, respondents were directed to pick a set of three stimulus cards at random, and describe how relationships with two of them were similar, and how the other differed. As the respondent spoke, the interviewer performed content-analysis of the responses, listing the personal constructs used to describe the relationships. The process was repeated with new combinations of three stimulus cards until no new constructs emerged. Then the interviewer showed the list to the respondent to verify the validity of the content analysis, thereby assuring that the set reflected the respondent's rather than the interviewer's construct set. Finally, the respondent was asked to rank-order the list of elicited constructs from most to least important. Interviews averaged one hour in duration.

We were confident that the diversity of respondent-chosen stimuli was sufficient to elicit the full set of constructs because of the large number of respondents in this laborious phase of the research. But as a check on the possibility of bias arising from an all-student respondent population, a second group was interviewed. A convenience sample of twenty respondents from the community was drawn, emphasizing diversity in age and socioeconomic status. The results were strikingly similar; no new constructs emerged. Thus we are confident that we have evoked the full set of dimensions, and that the findings can be generalized beyond a graduate student population.

20. M. Wish, M. Deutsch and S. J. Kaplan, "Perceived Dimensions of Interpersonal Relations," *Journal of Personality and Social Psychology* 33 (1976): 409–20; H. H. Kelley. *Personal Relationships*; G. J. McCall, M. M. McCall, N. K. Denzin, G. D. Suttles, and S. B. Kurth, *Social Relationships* (Chicago: Aldine, 1970); R. A. Hinde, *Towards Understanding Relationships* (New York: Academic Press, 1979); H. H. Kelley et al., *Close Relationships*; K. E. Davis and M. J. Todd, "Assessing Friendship: Prototypes, Paradigm Cases and Relationship Description," in *Understanding Personal Relationships*, ed. S. Duck and D. Perlman (Beverly Hills: Sage Publications, 1985), 17-38.

21. For example, see M. A. Neale and M. H. Bazerman, "The Role of Perspective Taking Ability in Negotiating Under Different Forms of Arbitration," *Industrial and Labor Relations Review* 36 (1983): 378–88; L. Greenhalgh and R. W. Gilkey, "Clinical Assessment Methods for the Laboratory: The Study of Narcissism and Negotiator Effectiveness," working paper, Amos Tuch School of Business Administration, Dartmouth College, 1994.

22. W. R. Nord, "The Failure of Current Applied Behavioral Science—A Marxian Perspective," *Journal of Applied Behavioral Science* 10 (1974): 557–78.

23. M. A. Neale and M. H. Bazerman, *Cognition and Rationality in Negotiations* (New York: Free Press, 1991).

24. See L. Greenhalgh, "The Case Against Winning in Negotitions," *Negotiation Journal* 3 (1987): 235–43.

25. For example see Blau, 1964.

26. L. Greenhalgh and R. W. Gilkey, "The Effects of Relationship Orientation on Negotiators' Cognition and Tactics," *Group Decision and Negotiation* 2 (1993): 167–86.

27. Greenhalgh and Chapman, *op. cit.*

28. Such as K. Avruch, P. W. Black and J. A. Scimecca, eds., *Conflict Resolution: Cross-Cultural Perspectives* (New York: Greenwood, 1991); M. N. Davidson, "The Effects of Racioethnicity on Managers' Beliefs About Coping with Discord in Working Relationships," paper presented at the 1994 Academic of Management Annual meeting, Dallas, Tx. Working paper No.304, Amos Tuck School, Dartmouth College, 1994; R. M. March, *The Japanese Negotiator* (New York: Kodansha International, 1988); S. Sudweeks, W. B. Gudykunst, S. Ting-Toomey and T. Nishida, "Developmental Themes in Japanese-North American Relationships," *International Journal of Intercultural Relations* 14 (1990): 207–33.

29. Greenhalgh and Gilkey, "The Effects of Relationship Orientation."

11

THROUGH THE LOOKING GLASS
NEGOTIATION THEORY REFRACTED THROUGH THE LENS OF GENDER

Deborah M. Kolb and Linda L. Putnam

The White Queen offers Alice a biscuit to quench her thirst, but tells her she cannot have jam. "I don't care for jam," Alice says. "That's good," the White Queen responds, "because the rule is jam tomorrow and jam yesterday but never jam today." "It must sometimes be jam today," says Alice. "No, it's jam every other day and today isn't every other day," concludes the Queen.

Through the Looking Glass
Lewis Carroll

I. Introduction

Not so long ago, negotiation was viewed as a rather sordid affair, associated with haggling, dickering, bartering, niggling, swapping, and backroom deal making. It is now recognized as a widespread, serious social activity for solving problems on a grand and modest scale.[1] Interest and research on the topic have exploded as negotiation has permeated and even been equated with most social interactions,[2] including those at the workplace.

A mere twenty-five years ago, academic work on negotiation was primarily confined to economists interested in game theory and its applications,[3] collective bargaining in labor relations,[4] international diplomacy,[5] and the social psychology of the prisoner's dilemma.[6] Scholarly interest has not only grown exponentially, but has extended into fields such as communications, cognitive psychology, law, management, and anthropology, among others.

Despite the apparent diversity in approaches such growth might signal, much of the current work coalesces around basic ideas and themes summarized under the label *negotiation analysis.*[7] Work in this tradition models negotiators as parties with interests (as distinct from positions) that they seek to advance. The goal of negotiators is to improve upon available alternatives to agreement and to do so in ways that push toward efficient, mutually beneficial deals. Much of the current research investigates the various barriers to attaining these outcomes and then offers advice on how negotiators can overcome them. [8]

This chapter explores the impact of viewing negotiation analysis through the looking glass of gender.[9] There are a number of ways to investigate gender in the context of negotiations. For example, many have looked at the similarities and differences between men and women when they negotiate.[10] Our intent is different. Following contemporary feminist critique in organizational theory, we consider how the emerging framework of negotiation analysis, that is presented as neutral and natural, is not in fact gender-neutral.[11]

We argue that negotiation analysis is "gendered," i.e., it is characterized by attributes and behaviors that are more commonly associated with masculinity than femininity. First, attributes associated with masculine worldviews, such as self-interest, competitiveness, and rationality, are more prominent than those associated with feminine perspectives, such as connection, collaboration, and emotionality.[12] Second, the framework fails to take account of how a negotiator's position in a social hierarchy, a hierarchy that tends to be gendered and characterized by power differentials, might influence expectations about what possibilities exist for her to negotiate successfully.[13] Finally, this framework, with its focus on inputs and outcomes, ignores or hides features of the negotiation process, where issues of gender typically get played out.

The chapter begins with an overview of the state of negotiation theorizing and its link to practice and continues with an exploration of the various ways that gender-related issues fit into existing theories. We then use a gender lens to consider two central tenets of current thinking in negotiation. First, we review the model of a negotiator as a person with agency, i.e., acting individually and autonomously. Second, we critique instrumental perspectives that see strategies and tactics only in relation to outcomes. Looking at these themes through a gender lens shows us how certain features of negotiation practice are highlighted while others are de-emphasized or hidden, and allows us to recapture elements rendered invisible. The implications for future theory, research, and the practice of dispute management at the workplace then are discussed.

II. The Field of Negotiation: The Current Status

One of the most remarkable developments in the social sciences in the last decade is the emergence of negotiation as a field of interdisciplinary research. Although the work is carried out in many disciplines using a number (although a limited number) of different research methods, there is a core set of ideas that mark much of the work. Recent models have been influenced significantly by the work of Howard Raiffa,[14] among others. They embrace the goal of *asymmetric prescription/description*. This view argues that empirical research (description) can help one party anticipate the likely behavior of the other (asymmetric prescription). Raiffa's framework provides a critical transition between earlier economic game theory and the current explosion of empirical, interdisciplinary work that Sebenius[15] calls *negotiation analysis* to highlight the rigor it seeks. At the same time it recognizes the practical realities of bargaining: "negotiation analysts" seek to "generate prescriptive advice given a (probabilistic) description of how others will behave."[16] While not all the researchers would naturally identify themselves as negotiation analysts, a common set of assumptions underlies their work.[17]

Negotiation analysts typically make a distinction between two types of bargaining. One type, variously described as zero-sum, distributive, or positional negotiations, is contrasted with mutual gains, integrative, or interest-based negotiations.[18] The former, distributive bargaining, is usually characterized by a single issue, such as price or wages. Negotiation then is primarily a process of compromise or *splitting the pie.* Success goes to the distributive bargainer who starts with high demands, concedes slowly, exaggerates the value of concessions made, minimizes the benefits of the other's concessions, conceals information, argues forcefully, and can outwit the other person.[19]

When negotiators engage in integrative bargaining, on the other hand, they seek to increase the payoffs to both parties. Starting with interests rather than positions, integrative bargaining involves the open sharing of information to identify interests and needs, the use of creative problem solving techniques to accommodate these interests, and making trades and exchanges based on complementary values and interests.[20] Success in integrative negotiation is a joint activity where both parties can communicate well enough and be creative enough to find exchanges they can make with the goal of agreements that meet the needs of all parties.

The relationship between these two models is the subject of some debate within the field. Some argue that they are totally separate. In a popular vein, *Getting to YES* captures the separate model. This book is highly critical of what it calls positional bargaining, or what others might call distributive negotiations. It proposes a number of now-familiar principles that purport to shift negotiations from win-lose or zero-sum to those that are win-win or joint-gain.

The research community generally sees these two models as intertwined in a paradoxical way.[21] Tactics that promote one approach undercut or interfere with the other. To openly communicate one's interests, for example, in pursuit of mutual gains, can leave one open to exploitation by the distributive bargainer. There is an inescapable tension between the competitive moves for individual gain and the cooperative behaviors necessary for coordinating mutual agreement. This mixed-motive quality of negotiations, called the *bargainers dilemma,* has been the subject of scholarly inquiry focused on the question of what interferes with achieving integrative or optimal agreements.[22] Other barriers to reaching integrative agreements include negotiators who are overconfident about their positions and abilities to persuade others, value positive outcomes differently from negative ones, devalue concessions from others, and make assumptions that all negotiations are zero-sum and involve splitting the proverbial pie.[23]

The lure of prescription in the field is strong. Consistent with Raiffa's concept of asymmetric prescription-description,[24] the advice that researchers typically give is asymmetric, i.e., it is offered to an individual negotiator to help in the selection of specific strategies and tactics. Advice covers opening offers and responses, strategic choices about personal negotiating style and stance, methods of creative problem solving, and ways to overcome barriers to mutual gains agreements.

III. The Study of Gender in Negotiations

Gender is a complex topic in negotiations. There are three major approaches used in the field to frame the issues: first, the study of individual differences between men and women based on observation and research; second, comparing "masculine" and "feminine" approaches to negotiation; and third, using a gender-relations perspective that defines gender as a belief system that influences all social interactions.

The first approach, the study of individual differences, has dominated the research for a significant period of time. Sex differences are relatively easy to measure, so biological sex becomes a variable that is frequently assessed. What people look for is whether men and women use different tactics and/or reach different kinds of agreements. The results are equivocal. For example, the belief that women are more collaborative than men is borne out in some studies but not in others.[25] Some research finds that women are more attentive to relationships and care about building and preserving them.[26] Generally, women are oriented more to actions of others and set strategy in relation to the actions of others, whereas men are more focused on task and their own positions.[27] Negotiation tactics may also differ with men being more positional and women more flexible.[28] The outcomes achieved by men and women may also differ in terms of substantive issues and relationships, equality versus equity, and the short term versus the long term.[29] Others find no direct main effects attributable to sex.

Context can affect the results. For example, more differences are likely to show up in negotiations with strangers, between negotiators of the same sex, and in less intense conflicts.[30] Others suggest that gender is an artifact of situation and intertwined with power and position, i.e., that differences in negotiating style and stance that we attribute to gender might be either the result of gendered power differences or an interaction of power and gender.[31] Although positional power, e.g., a vice president or a secretary, has been shown to be a better predictor of difference than gender, power seems to exert differential effects on men and women. Higher power men act in a more aggressive and assertive manner and tend to use more "take it or leave it" strategies. High-powered women are not as aggressive or assertive. Indeed, one of the differences is the degree to which women feel their power is legitimated by others.[32]

These efforts to find conclusive evidence that men and women negotiate differently leave us with a confused picture. Laboratory studies, the research method of choice, produce equivocal findings. The few field studies of men and women in the area of salary and other financial negotiations do show some differences between them. Research on salary negotiation finds that women seem to realize lower returns to their salary negotiation efforts.[33] This may be because they set lower aspirations and use fewer self-promotion tactics, or because they compare their own pay to the pay of other women, who tend to be paid less than men.[34] Research on car buying finds that women and minorities pay higher prices than white males for automobiles. Not only do they achieve lower returns, but opening offers differ among these groups.[35] Here the issue is not what the negotiators themselves do but differential perceptions of what members of different groups will accept.

There is a great temptation to isolate negotiating differences by gender, but the research suggests that it is impossible to give definitive answers to questions about how men and women negotiate. But apart from the limitations of the research, there are two other reasons that this approach raises problems. First, it frames the issue of gender as one based on an individual's biological sex without any theory to explain why. Further, it minimizes the importance of social context and roles that can position men and women rather differently in a negotiation. Second, the perspective is a static one. It grafts women onto existing structures and practices.[36] Thus, whether differences are to be valued or bemoaned, the result of personal choice or situationally determined, they are understood almost entirely in the context of existing theory and practice.

A second approach to the issue of gender and negotiation is feminist standpoint theory.[37] It claims that existing theory and practice is incomplete because it has systematically excluded women's experiences. For the most part, the literature on negotiation is written from the perspective of white, Western males. Women's experiences are different for a host of reasons, including their socialization and development, their social roles and positions in society, and their responsibility for child rearing.

Several scholars have tried to develop a feminist standpoint perspective on negotiation.[38] Kolb and Coolidge[39] suggest that there are masculine and feminine approaches that frame how negotiators approach negotiations. In particular, a feminine approach would emphasize the importance of relationships, the context within which negotiations occur, efforts to establish power *with* rather than *over* another person, and a connective, not conflictual communication style. While an approach to negotiation might be considered masculine or feminine, it does not necessarily mean that it is perfectly correlated with men and women respectively. Some women use masculine approaches just as some men use feminine approaches.

There are three problems with this perspective.[40] First, feminist standpoint theory does not reflect the experiences of all men and women. Second, masculine and feminine approaches to negotiation are not equally valued or perceived equally when enacted by men and women. As many argue, since we live in a society where men have more power than women, it makes sense to assume that what is considered more worthy are those qualities associated with men.[41] Indeed, the feminist standpoint theory approach may actually reinforce stereotypes of men and women. It can lead to a priori expectations about the negotiating stance that can disadvantage those who use a feminine approach. The stereotype may be further reinforced if a woman uses the "feminine" approach.[42]

Finally, it is easy to co-opt a feminist standpoint. Northrup[43] suggests that when an expressive concern for relationships is incorporated into existing theory, it is transformed from a relational concept to one that is instrumentally used in the service of self. It becomes another way to push gender into the background and prevent it from challenging existing theory.

A third approach is one that looks at gender relations where gender is not about men and women per se. Rather, gender is viewed as a belief system that structures and gives meaning to social interactions.[44] A gender-relations perspective causes us to look at the relationships between constructs and categories associated with masculinity and femininity. These relationships presently are hierarchical and generally defined through the male experience. Bem[45] uses the term androcentrism to describe the hierarchical relationship in which the male experience becomes the norm and the female experience is seen as different and less valuable. Indeed, by rendering male as the norm taken for granted and woman as the other,[46] gender relations are established in terms of dominance and inequality. This hierarchical relationship is sustained through opposition or gender polarization[47] that permeates our language, such as male-female, instrumental-relational, individual-collective, powerful-powerless, and rational-emotional. In each polarity the element linked to the "masculine" dominates the attribute that characterizes the "feminine." Thus, it is in the enactment of the meaning that gender is created. In other words, language and action do not reflect women's and men's reality as much as they create them.

Feminist scholars reveal how these meanings are sustained in the production of scientific knowledge that renders some features as true and taken for granted as natural, while others are hidden or seen as aberrant. Our concepts of leadership, for example, focus on individual heroics and decisiveness as necessary attributes. Collaboration and power sharing, attributes that emphasize the feminine, are often defined as nonleader-like, even though they may be important attributes of leaders.[48] By questioning what is named and normal, feminist scholars expose the biases implicit in what is taken for granted as neutral and objective. Applying these concepts to negotiation theory and practice allows us to consider in what ways that theory is gendered.

IV. Negotiation Analysis through the Looking Glass of Gender

Negotiation is seen as gendered when attributes more commonly associated with one gender are valued, thereby making attributes associated with the other gender seem less valuable. In families, for example, parenting tends to be based on notions of nurturance and care associated with mothering. Hence, acts of fathering may be judged inadequate compared with these feminine attributes. Unlike parenting, however, negotiation as currently theorized is stereotypically masculine. In other words, a negotiation analysis perspective rests on those qualities that are culturally valued in males: individuality and independence, competition, objectivity, analytic rationality, instrumentality, reasoning from universal principles, and strategic thinking, among others.[49] Indeed, one could argue that the ideal negotiator is male. In the polar relationship, those attributes stereotypically labeled feminine are less valued or ignored in bargaining: community and dependence, cooperation, subjectivity, intuition and emotionality, expressivity, reasoning from particulars, and ad hoc thinking.

This has practical consequences. One is that other alternatives to the male-dominated ideal emerge as peculiar, naive, ignorant, or irrelevant. Where strategic communication, or playing close to the vest dominates, talking honestly about what you really want is to appear hopelessly naive. Where being rational and detached is valued, to act emotional and upset is perceived as disruptive. Emotions are seen to block rational thinking and make it difficult to process information, to think integratively, and to make concessions on proposals.[50] Anger is considered normal, perhaps even strategic in negotiation, whereas other emotions such as anxiety, fear, and despair are deemed injudicious to display. If these more valued features are enacted by men and the less valued by women in particular situations, then gendered expectations are further reinforced.

Negotiation analysis places certain concepts in a prominent position: the self-interested negotiator, rational judgment, exchanges and offers, and the search for efficient agreements. A gender perspective uncovers aspects of negotiation that are invisible, unexplained, suppressed, or in the background. They remain hidden because these other elements overshadow them in importance. In particular, relational, contextual, and process dimensions are hidden or invisible. By looking at what has been in the background of negotiation, a gender perspective highlights the interactive setting, rather than the individuals and what they bring to the table, as the place where the substance and process of negotiations are constructed.

Using a gender lens helps us focus on negotiation practices, that is, the meaningful actions taken and words spoken by bargainers engaged in the process of negotiation.[51] This perspective treats as dynamic and evolving the very elements taken for granted in current negotiation analysis. Thus, the identities of negotiators are worked out during negotiations as participants act on and alter their predispositions and their expectations for future interactions, and structure their working relationships. Goals, interests, and aspirations are not fixed, but are continually defined and redefined through interaction. Rationality is not an independent state of being, but is contextually and situationally defined.[52] Existing theory silences the interactive complexities of negotiation by keeping the process dimension invisible.

Our purpose here is to focus on two basic assumptions in negotiation analysis. We consider the following: (1) the negotiator as an autonomous agent who acts from a position that is distinct and separate from others, and (2) the definition of negotiation as primarily a strategic and instrumental activity. We analyze each assumption through the lens of gender by examining: (1) the centrality of the assumption in negotiation theory and research; (2) how practice, theory, and research reinforce certain ways of being and action and diminish or co-opt others; (3) what features are hidden or de-emphasized; and then (4) what other alternatives for being and acting in negotiation are possible.

This gender perspective makes it possible to envision alternatives and complements to existing theories. By revealing aspects of negotiation that are less valued and invisible, a gender perspective introduces options for expanded conceptions of negotiation that are more inclusive and less gendered. It is important to emphasize that the purpose of a gender perspective is not to substitute one model of practice for another, but to create space where new ways of thinking and acting can be openly considered.[53] Alternatives are discussed as ideas that need further development. They can, however, spark our thinking about areas worthy of further research and alert us to the need to be more eclectic in what we define as valuable research and good negotiation practice.[54]

V. The Individual Negotiator with Agency

Bakan[55] defines agency as a stance that values individualism and personal achievement. It is distinguished from a communitarian perspective where one's identity is connected to and integrally bound up with others in ongoing social relationships. Harre[56] suggests that when individuals have agency they conceive of themselves as acting as individual agents with the power to decide, to act independently, and to account for their action. To have agency means that one speaks and acts from a position that is distinct and separate from others. In contrast, to have a communitarian perspective is to emphasize the connection between self and other.

Agency is a central concept in most theories of negotiation; self-interest and individualistic orientation where one focuses exclusively on oneself exemplify this concept.[57] Negotiation typically is framed as an exchange between self-interested individuals, where each theory propounds its own ways that self-interested negotiators can meet their interests. In distributive models, the negotiator uses all means at her disposal, including threats, commitments, and bluffs, to satisfy those interests.[58] In the integrative models, the other's concerns are also to be taken into account.[59] The *dual concern* model assumes that win-win outcomes can only be achieved when both parties have concern for other as well as self.[60]

Concern for others, however, is not a notion based on connection with others, but rather a manifestation of self-interest. The concept of "enlightened self-interest" captures well the centrality of agency in negotiation. The added word "enlightened" refers to the acknowledgment by each side that the other is also likely to be pursuing a path of self-interest and that it may be possible for both to do well in the exchange.[61]

The individualistic focus of much of this psychological research is another indicator of how salient agency is in the field. In particular, negotiation studies focus on individual differences,[62] the influence of goals and aspirations,[63] and cognitive barriers and limitations to effective decision making.[64] Insights about concession making come from the patterns of individualistically oriented negotiators.[65] The degree to which one can, on one's own, overcome cognitive and other barriers and negotiate rationally further positions the individual negotiator as pivotal to our understanding about what transpires in negotiation.[66] Indeed, the most common research method, the laboratory study with its ubiquitous role play, builds into its structure an agency model of negotiations. Role players are provided with legitimate interests as a preliminary to their efforts to negotiate their differences. Generally, they are on their own and connected to any institutional setting in only the most tangential ways.[67] Indeed, most exchange models, whether they are behavioral or economic, focus on isolated individuals who are unconnected to any social structure.[68]

A. Agency and the Devaluing of Difference

Agency is a gendered concept. The observation can be made historically, legally, and psychologically that the concept of agency is masculine and not typically associated with a feminine notion of identity.[69] When we look at agency through a gender lens, two major concerns arise. First, the notion of agency is understood in light of its opposite—community. Yet negotiators who act from a sense of community are likely to have their actions judged less effective. Second, when alternative approaches that emanate from a concept of community are theorized or practiced, they tend to get incorporated into existing models in ways that co-opt them and alter their meanings significantly.

When negotiators relate to each other communally, their negotiations are likely to be seen as different and less effective. Recent research on friends, dating couples, and people who identify with each other suggests that when intimacy and caring for another are salient, people engage in different kinds of behaviors. They use behaviors that are less individualistic and self-interested.[70] Under these circumstances, there is less focus on self-interest and more on finding fair and equitable outcomes. Some claim that such equitable outcomes maximize social utility,[71] but they tend not to approach the idealized benchmark of integrative settlements and therefore are judged "suboptimal."[72] Such assessments are not neutral or objective, but are embedded in the experimental designs and moral order on which the empirical findings are based.

Behaviors that make sense when negotiators care about and feel connected to each other are mobilized in current negotiation analysis as a means to further one's self-interest. Thus, it is in a negotiator's interest to protect the "face" of others,[73] to act trustworthy,[74] and to care about what matters to others. Northrup sums it up well.[75] She suggests that when a feminine concern for relationships is incorporated into existing models, it is transformed from a relational concept tied to a concern for community to one used in the service of self. Its meaning and value are changed in the process.

B. The Invisible Elements of Agency

To succeed as a negotiator according to current negotiation analysis, one must necessarily have agency. The problem is that agency is not something you either have or do not have. Rather, to be perceived as a self-interested negotiator is to act like one and to do so in a way that persuades others.[76] This means we should study the actions taken to establish and re-establish this identity throughout a negotiation. The problem is that the model of the negotiator with agency has ignored how negotiators develop agency in the contexts of negotiations and how they establish their legitimacy as an ongoing accomplishment of bargaining.[77]

The assumptions of the negotiator with agency obscure how agency is actually accomplished: the actions taken at and away from the table, including moves that bargainers make on their own or in connection with others. Preparation, for example, so highly touted as a means to anticipate the action of others, becomes one method to establish agency.[78] Planning, then, can be as much an exercise in psychological readiness as in economic preparedness.

To be a negotiator with agency is to be positioned in the process as such. This notion of agency centers on the language and repetitive actions negotiators use to manage impressions and expectations.[79] Negotiators make their identity and reputation visible and available, sometimes on their own but also with the help of others.[80] Authority to negotiate and speak on behalf of others is made real through conversational and structural gambits.[81] Thus agency is embedded in conversational practices where negotiators construct positions for themselves and others. A negotiator's position in the process determines the platform from which she can speak.[82] Parties who are positioned positively have more leverage in constructing the major plots and themes in which the issues are embedded. A negative position leads to reactive or defensive stances. Claims of agency are always subject to disruption, challenge, and repair.[83]

The achievement of agency is sometimes a team performance.[84] All negotiators operate within the context of a social system.[85] In negotiation research the relationship of social context to negotiation process and outcome is generally narrowed to discussions of how negotiators bring their clients or constituents along.[86] The support function is invisible. McEwen[87] argues that in the rhetoric of mediation, decision makers are supposed to act autonomously; they are cut off from their attorneys and other support or institutional systems that sustain them. Once the notion of agency is made visible as a practice, then the ways that others help a negotiator find a place from which to speak are brought into focus.

Coalition-building activities can also be seen as part of the invisible work of constructing agency. Most of the work on coalitions involves dynamics in large, multiparty negotiations such as the Law of the Sea and GATT,[88] or interorganization negotiations. When agency is the concern, the focus is on how negotiators enlist behind-the-scenes support.[89] The role of teams and social networks become more important in this regard.[90]

To operate within the negotiation analysis framework means enacting the role of negotiator with agency. Negotiators are differentially positioned, often by gender, in the resources they have to be credible agents. Given the differential social constructions of gender, these approaches can never be wholly satisfactory. But a gender lens also helps us envision forms of negotiation practice that highlight interpersonal connection as the base upon which the process and agreements are built.

C. Framing a Connected Context for Negotiations

In the agency model of the negotiator, the process is characterized as a transaction between self interested individuals who may not care about their counterparts or, if they are enlightened, care about them, but primarily as a means to an end. There are other ways to think about the relationship between negotiators. One can look at how they are connected and how they foster connected contexts within which negotiations take place. Framing a connected context involves building trust, looking for ways to meaningfully engage each other, and working to understand the bases of interdependence.

Negotiators engage in rituals to build trust. Often at the outset of a bargaining session negotiators will engage in small talk about children and sports, tell stories to each other about people they know in common, or recount a good joke. These rites are efforts to develop connections. They establish and reaffirm good working relationships and some sense of shared fate even in the face of potentially difficult problems.[91] These rituals of trust building can lead to new relationships, understandings, and learning.[92]

These activities aimed at creating a socio-emotional context within which negotiators can meaningfully engage each other is part of what has been invisible in negotiations. Invisible work can take many forms.[93] It can mean arranging the many details of negotiation that bring people to the table comfortable, prepared, and feeling ready to work. It may mean meeting with them to explore mutual feelings about the negotiations and the issues. It may mean getting angry with each other to clear the air. Invisible work includes trying to establish relationships on a more personal basis and finding ways to make people comfortable and ready to work even in the most difficult of situations.

Establishing a comfortable context and working relationship is important but not sufficient for developing a connected context. Negotiators need to understand and appreciate the ways in which they are connected and how the actions of one can have an impact on the actions of the other. Talking about interdependence, asking others to consider your situation and expressing your understanding about theirs, is part of creating this connected context.[94] What is crucial is that negotiators position themselves and their counterparts as legitimate and honorable, and as people that are acting from good intentions. Only in this way is full participation possible.[95]

The approach of creating connected relationships and discovering connected interests is not as well developed as the model based on enlightened self-interests. Language is part of the problem. The notion of relationships has been hijacked and used in the service of instrumental self-interest. Further, if only one side pursues the goal of creating connected relationships, the actions can reinforce the gendered structure of negotiation or, within the norms of current practice, lead to confusion about motive and perception. This notion of negotiators who work with connected interests suggests that we need to expand our thinking beyond the idea that only individual negotiators with clearly defined self-interests come to the table. Interests are in fact discovered, defined, and revised at the bargaining table and, in the process, may be changed as well. In this formulation, the connected relationship sets the context for a different kind of negotiation that may have, as its objective, different outcomes.

VI. Negotiation as an Instrumental Activity

In the popular press, the negotiation outcomes are described in simple, bipolar terms. You either have a win-win, a win-lose, or a lose-lose outcome. Negotiation analysts have expanded that conception to focus on how negotiators achieve various outcomes, whether distributive, integrative, or some combination of the two.[96] Negotiation analysts have become quite sophisticated in describing ways that settlements are reached. In their drive to connect preferences, needs, and interests with what is ultimately attained, the processes of negotiation are seen as the instrumental means to achieve desired ends.

In negotiation analysis, the challenge is to find outcomes that represent the maximum joint gain attainable given the interests of the respective parties.[97] That outcome, often referred to as Pareto optimal, means that "neither party can do better in an alternative agreement unless the other does worse."[98] To prescribe how to reach the goal of Pareto optimality, scholars concentrate on the strategies and tactics, and the dilemmas that attend their use, which negotiators can use to maximize joint gains.[99]

Drawn from its game theory roots, negotiation is by definition a strategic endeavor directed toward the specific ends of reaching agreements and satisfying negotiators' needs.[100] Instrumental behavior in negotiation is closely intertwined with strategy and tactics. Strategies are the preformulated game plans, objectives, and approaches that guide negotiators in reaching their goals; tactics are the specific ways bargainers implement these strategies. Strategies are by definition instrumental in that the outcomes of negotiation (win-win or win-lose) are directly tied to the strategies used to attain them, e.g., concession making, contending, and problem solving. A circularity is created where behaviors such as cooperative and competitive, integrative and distributive, and creating value and claiming one's share are both strategies and outcomes in negotiation.

Barriers to implementing strategies and achieving these ends are also well studied.[101] Especially important in this regard are the limited abilities of negotiators to act rationally due to overconfidence, defining and framing issues, fixed-pie assumptions, and other cognitive barriers.[102]

A. Instrumentality and the Devaluing of Difference

Since instrumental ways of thinking and acting are seen as critical, and process defined narrowly as a path to achieving agreement, then those who pursue process goals are judged as different. Those who are seen as different are likely to have their differences undervalued and perhaps will be judged less able as well. Kolb and Coolidge[103] argue that women and others may lack a voice and a sense of place in an activity defined by strategic planning, maneuvering of positions, and fixed goals and interests. Only one study suggests that attention to interpersonal sensitivity and treating negotiation as a continuous rather than a one-shot activity makes for more effective negotiators in long-term business relationships.[104]

When most, if not all, behavior in negotiations is analyzed for its instrumental functions, then it is not surprising that alternative ways of acting are co-opted in ways that alter the intent and assumptions behind them. For example, even when scholars advise negotiators to adopt a typically "feminine" orientation, such as engaging in problem solving and emphasizing relationships,[105] these alternatives become strategies used for instrumental ends. When one negotiates, there are multiple aims beyond the instrumental ends of achieving substantive agreements.[106] Concerns about relationships, such as how people feel about each other and the trust and friendships that might develop between them, are understood primarily as instrumental to the major objective.[107] Thus, negotiators are advised to build trust with their counterparts to facilitate settlement. Face saving of self and others is defined as an impression management strategy that is necessary to attain instrumental goals.[108] Concern for relationships is transformed from an important process goal of value for its own sake independent of any outcome to an instrumental strategy valued only because it helps achieve a desired outcome.

B. What Instrumentality Renders Invisible

The interactive and communicative features of negotiation are largely invisible and under-theorized in research and practice. When the negotiation process is framed strategically from the vantage point of individual negotiators, the interaction itself is seen instrumentally: it is where interests, issues, and options are discussed and decided. In contrast, research has shown that the interaction is where interests, issues, preferences, and options actually are defined and given meaning.[109] When researchers look closely at negotiations, they discover that plans are actually developed during the negotiation process, that bargaining interests can never really be known in the absence of interaction and therefore are connectively developed, and that positions are structured and revised interactively as negotiations progress. Outcomes, therefore, are rarely traced directly to a strategic intent and plan.[110]

A more inclusive model of negotiation would focus on communicative practices such as deliberation, argumentation, and circularity. When parties deliberate, they talk inclusively about their situation and the contexts and histories that give rise to issues, positions, and demands. This kind of talk brings negotiators into each other's worlds so that the meaning of what is said becomes the base upon which movement toward agreement is built.[111] When we view goals and interests as unstable rather than fixed, then arguments and counter-arguments become forms of collective reflection.[112] Circularity is a communication technology that facilitates the development of connection, inclusiveness, and participation in a negotiation.[113] By using circular questions, negotiators explore the implications of one's action on the other, for example, what the consequences for each would be of failing to reach agreement on budgets for new programs. This kind of exploration leads to deeper understandings about issues and can result in new ideas coming to the fore. Thus, rather than persuasion and information-giving tactics, the dialogue becomes the means by which people make claims about themselves and their situation. In the process they become reflective observers of their own thinking. This practice enables negotiators to construct new interpretations of events, new possibilities for settlements, and new understandings about themselves. A focus on these interactive processes helps us appreciate the creative aspects of negotiation practice.

C. Transformation as an Alternative Process and Outcome

An instrumental model of negotiation suggests that the outcomes are predetermined by the inputs, so expected outcomes are exchanged, rearranged, and repackaged by the negotiators through the negotiation process. Yet we know that negotiations often result in vastly different outcomes than those predicted strategically at the outset. Achieving these outcomes, therefore, must involve more than brainstorming or inventing options to meet the interests and needs of negotiators. They involve collective transformations of meanings and understandings about issues and possibilities for agreement. In other words, negotiation is a process of transformation.[114] To see negotiation as a transformative process is to focus on the process through which changes in expectations, explanations, attributions, and understandings occur and to see the outcomes as inextricably related to how the dispute is defined and enacted during the process.

Transformation implies a disjuncture or break in preconceived ways of thinking about issues and demands. This understanding might reflect the ways issues develop and change and thereby evolve into problems that are different from what parties thought they were negotiating about when they began. What started as a dispute over pay becomes a problem of how to enhance quality so that customers are more satisfied. What started as a dispute over the relative shares of health insurance becomes an issue of providers and the plan itself.[115] What started as a dispute about shares of a program's profit becomes an issue of how to expand the market. What started as an issue of discipline and discharge becomes an issue of a safety program and managerial reward system in a plant.

These transformations occur because of two factors. First, understandings about causality may change. Whereas parties may blame each other at the outset for a problem, through deliberation and reflection they may come to see their problems as part of the social structures in which both are embedded. This allows them to work together to alter the situation. Parties may find joint problems to solve or, through deliberations, one may come to own the problem and thus commit to its resolution without any concession from another.

A dispute also may be transformed because parties realize that their definitions of the problem have excluded important stakeholders. Asking themselves who else belongs at the table may lead to inclusion of others who not only bring new resources to the table,[116] but also new perspectives and ways of conceptualizing the problem.[117] When these new parties join the deliberations, they may change the way the issues are understood.

On the surface, our description of transformation may sound like an embellishment of integrative bargaining, but there are three significant differences. First, transformative negotiations are rooted in historical, political, and organizational contexts. Issues are not confined to the interests of negotiators but are located in these larger contexts. Exploration of context and how it affects issues, interests, and ideas can lead to new understandings.

Second, negotiations occur in different historical contexts and time frames. Parties can explore how the past, present, and future influence the character and meaning of particular issues and demands. Issues can develop and change so that new problems are defined which differ from initial statements of positions.[118] Situations are recast in broader or more narrow terms. As both parties learn about the conflict situation together, they develop new perspectives on the situation that create a new social reality that transforms both the understanding of the conflict and the negotiated outcomes.[119]

Finally, transformation is at its core a process, not a strategy thought out and implemented by individual negotiators. This process implies a disjuncture or break in the old ways of thinking. It is a process that emerges from interactive dialogue. For example, in negotiation analysis, bargainers search for options that satisfy the individual interests of each party. They use persuasion or brainstorming tactics to discover joint gains. In contrast, transformation uses interactive dialogue that can be seen more as a form of interactive story-telling or narrative construction. Issues, interests, and options are not really discrete matters, but are instead nested in conversations and accounts that give them meaning and coherence.[120] Negotiators narrate their version of events in cohesive fashion and under a moral order that frames what is possible. In other words, negotiators tell different stories to each other in which their histories, social locations, interests, issues, and positions are found. If we can find ways to work from these accounts to develop new stories from the old, truly transformative agreements are possible.[121] Since transformation is developed jointly through negotiation interaction, it is one of the few processes that can address intractable conflicts.[122]

VII. Conclusions and Implications for Theory, Future Research, and Practice

When we look at negotiation theory, research, and practice through a gender lens, we are questioning several taken-for-granted concepts and looking at them in new ways. We have proposed an approach that enables us to analyze existing frameworks and to recover what has been hidden as a step toward developing a more encompassing and inclusive vision of negotiation. Specifically, we have used a gender lens to challenge the agency model of the individual negotiator and the instrumental definition of negotiation process to show how alternative ways of being and acting have become devalued and/or co-opted in current theory, research, and practice. A gender lens helps us to recover features of negotiation that are important but less visible, particularly the process dimensions of agency and communicative practice. These insights help us envision alternative approaches in which connected negotiations provide the bases for transformation and innovation.

There are clear implications for the development of theory, research, and practice. There are many other theoretical concepts and assumptions that could be viewed through a gender lens to uncover what is hidden and how theory might be revised by different ways of looking at the issues. Assumptions that bargainers should aspire to rationality, that negotiation is fundamentally a process of exchange, and that bargaining power depends on the alternatives to agreement would look different through a gender lens.

In order to develop alternative visions of negotiation and the possibilities for transformation, however, our approaches to research will need to be broadened as well. We will need to pay much more attention to the context of negotiations and how it positions negotiators and shapes negotiations. We will also need to understand complex negotiations as processes that involve more than money and simple tradeoffs. In addition, we will need to understand more about the varied ways that negotiators interact with each other to define themselves, their issues, and their possibilities, and how these interactions are influenced by different kinds of relationships. Finally, we need to attend more to feelings and emotions, to how meanings are constructed, to how negotiators participate in each other's experience. In other words, we need to leave room for, and then learn from, the way transformation occurs in situ.

A gender lens also implies different values of practice. These values include designing processes that are inclusive rather than exclusive, that support the equitable treatment of people in different circumstances, and that bridge differences and foster learning from diversity. The challenge is to foster these values in negotiation.

Human resource professionals are uniquely positioned to make use of the insights a gender lens offers for their dispute management activities. First, they are often charged with promoting the very values described. Helping an organization learn from its diversity and mobilizing that diversity toward goals of creativity and transformation are part of the mission of the human resource function. Second, it is under the auspices of these departments that many negotiations occur. Collective bargaining, salary negotiations, grievance and complaint handling are among its responsibilities. Human resource professionals can ask such questions as: How are these negotiations conducted? Does the process foster full participation or are certain behaviors, and therefore those who display them, positioned to advantage? Does the practice close out possibilities for enacting negotiations in new ways that benefit a wider spectrum of stakeholders?

Similar questions might also be asked about any training provided in negotiation skills. Training in negotiation skills has become increasingly popular in organizations and professional schools. Human resource professionals might use a gender lens to ask what values and forms of practice are being promoted in negotiation training. Are these the values the organization wants to promote? Are the techniques taught equally useful to all participants? What is the connection between what is taught and what the organization actually rewards?

Finally, human resource professionals are likely to be parties themselves either in negotiation or as facilitators and mediators in formal and informal disputes. These occasions provide opportunities to shape the forms negotiations will take in organizations. As such, human resource professionals need to become reflective about their own practices and the messages they convey. In the mediation role, for example, do they act in ways that empower full participation, or are they more likely to replicate existing power structures? Do they design a process that encourages broad consideration of issues or are they more likely to narrow the domain of the possible?

Looking at negotiations through a gender lens encourages us to critically evaluate how specific practices are gendered, in the sense that they reinforce masculine ways of being over the feminine. These practices limit the potential for negotiation to be a more creative way to deal with conflict at the workplace. By envisioning what a connected approach to negotiations might look like, we examine the possibilities for more participation, greater acknowledgment of interdependence, and for the process to be one in which new meanings are created that lead to transformation. These new ways are never obvious. They require a new perspective, perhaps one imported by an outsider, to highlight them for us. Let's listen to Alice again.

> The red queen admonishes Alice to speak only when spoken to. Alice observes that if everybody obeyed the rule—only speak when spoken to—nobody would say anything. Ridiculous says the Queen.

Notes

1.   P. Adler, "The Future Of Alternative Dispute Resolution: Reflections On ADR As A Social Movement," in *The Possibility of Popular Justice: A Case Study of Community Mediation in the United States,* ed. S. E. Merry and N. Milner (Ann Arbor: University of Michigan Press, 1993), 67–89.

2.   A. Strauss, *Negotiations* (San Francisco: Jossey-Bass, 1978).

3.   T. C. Schelling, *The Strategy of Conflict* (Cambridge: Harvard University Press, 1960); J. F. Nash, "The Bargaining Problem," *Econometrica* 18 (1950): 155–62.

4.   R. Walton and R. McKersie, *A Behavioral Theory Of Labor Negotiations* (New York: McGraw-Hill, 1965).

5.   W. Zartman and M. Berman, *The Practical Negotiator* (New Haven: Yale University Press, 1982); O. R. Young, *International Cooperation* (Ithaca, N.Y.: Cornell University Press, 1989).

6.   J. Z. Rubin and B. R. Brown, *The Psychology of Bargaining and Negotiation* (New York: Academic Press, 1975).

7.   M. Bazerman and M. Neale, *Negotiating Rationally* (New York: Free Press, 1991); R. Fisher, W. Ury, and B. Patton, *Getting To YES: Negotiating Agreement Without Giving In,* 2d ed. (Boston: Houghton Mifflin Company, 1991); R. Mnookin, "Why Negotiations Fail: An Exploration of Barriers to the Resolution of Conflict," *Ohio State Journal of Dispute Resolution* 8, no. 2 (1993): 235–49; J. K. Sebenius, "Negotiation Analysis: A Characterization and Review," *Management Science* 38, no. 1 (1992): 18–39.

8.   M. Neale and M. Bazerman, *Cognition and Rationality in Negotiation* (New York: Free Press, 1991); D. Kahneman and A. Tversky, "Prospect Theory: An Analysis of Decisions under Risk," *Econometrica* 47, no. 3 (1979): 263–291; Mnookin, "Exploration of Barriers."

9.   V. S. Peterson and A. S. Runyan, *Global Gender Issues* (Boulder, Colo.: Westview, 1993).

10. See D. M. Kolb and G. Coolidge, "Her Place At The Table," in *Negotiation Theory and Practice,* ed. J. W. Breslin and J. Z. Rubin (Cambridge, Mass.: Program on Negotiation, Harvard Law School, 1991), 261–77; R. J. Lewicki, J. Minton, and D. Saunders, *Negotiations* (Homewood, Ill.: Irwin, 1994).

11. M. B. Calas and L. Smircich, "Re-Writing Gender into Organizational Theorizing: Directions from Feminist Perspectives," in *New Directions In Organizational Research And Analysis,* ed. M. I. Reed and M. D. Hughes (London:

Sage, 1990), 227–53; J. Martin, "Deconstructing Organizational Taboos: The Suppression Of Gender Conflict In Organizations," *Organization Science* 1, no. 3 (1990): 339–59; D. Mumby and L. L. Putnam, "The Politics of Emotion: A Feminist Reading of Bounded Rationality," *Academy of Management Review* 17, no. 4 (1992): 465–86.

12.   J. Flax, *Thinking Fragments: Psychoanalysis, Feminism, and Postmodernism in the Contemporary West* (Berkeley: University of California Press, 1990).

13.   K. E. Ferguson, *The Feminist Case against Bureaucracy* (Philadelphia: Temple University Press, 1984).

14.   H. Raiffa, *The Art and Science of Negotiation* (Cambridge: Harvard University Press, 1982).

15.   J. K. Sebenius, "Negotiation Analysis: A Characterization and Review," *Management Science* 38, no. 1 (1992): 18–39.

16.   Ibid., 20.

17.   There are exceptions to this emerging psychological/economics/decision theory consensus, but these tend to be located in the broader field of dispute processing and resolution. Critics argue that the exclusive focus on communication tactics ignores power relations that shape communications (L. Nader, "When Is Popular Justice Popular?" in *The Possibility of Popular Justice: A Case Study of Community Mediation in the United States,* ed. S. E. Merry and N. Milner [Ann Arbor: University of Michigan Press, 1993], 435–51) that there are consequences to reducing all disputes to interests (S. Silbey and A. Sarat, "Dispute Processing In Law And Legal Scholarship" (Working Paper, Institute For Legal Studies, University Of Wisconsin, 1988), and that social and cultural contexts are crucial in accounting for the forms disputes take (S. Merry and S. Silbey, "What Do Plaintiffs Want? Re-Examining The Concept Of Dispute," *Justice System Journal* 9, no. 2 [1984]: 151–78). Empirical research on discursive practices in dispute resolution show us how interaction creates and structures the very elements negotiation analysts take for granted (S. Cobb, "Empowerment And Mediation: A Narrative Perspective," *Negotiation Journal* 9, no. 3 [1993]: 245–61; A. Firth, *The Discourse of Negotiation* [London: Pergamon Press, 1995]).

18.   Fisher, Ury, and Patton, *Getting To YES;* Walton and McKersie, *Labor Negotiations.*

19.   D. Lax and J. Sebenius, *The Manager as Negotiator* (New York: The Free Press, 1986), 32.

20.   D. Pruitt, *Negotiation Behavior* (New York: Academic Press, 1981).

21. L. L. Putnam, "Reframing Integrative and Distributive Bargaining: A Process Perspective," in *Research On Negotiation In Organizations*, ed. M. Bazerman, R. Lewicki, and B. Sheppard (Greenwich, Conn.: JAI Press), 2:3–30.

22. Lax and Sebenius, *Manager as Negotiator*; Walton and Mckersie, *Labor Negotiations*.

23. Bazerman and Neale, *Negotiating Rationally*; Kahneman and Tversky, "Prospect Theory"; Mnookin, "Exploration of Barriers."

24. Raiffa, *Art and Science of Negotiation*.

25. See Kolb and Coolidge, "Her Place at the Table" for a review.

26. L. Greenhalgh and R. W. Gilkey, "Effects of Sex-Role Differences on Approaches to Interpersonal and Interorganizational Negotiations" (Dartmouth College, 1984); R. Pinkley and G. Northcraft, "Cognitive Interpretations Of Conflict: Implications For Disputant's Motives and Behavior" (Southern Methodist University, 1989).

27. Rubin and Brown, *Psychology of Bargaining*; J. T. Spence and R. L. Heinrich, "Masculine Instrumentality and Feminine Expressiveness: Their Relationships with Sex Role Attitude and Behaviors," *Psychology of Women Quarterly* 5, no. 2 (1980): 198–205.

28. J. Halpern and J. McLean-Parks, "Vive La Difference: Gender Differences in Process and Outcomes in a Low Conflict Negotiation" (Cornell University, 1995); C. Watson and B. Kasten, "Separate Strengths? How Women And Men Negotiate" (Center for Negotiation and Conflict Resolution, Rutgers University, 1989).

29. Halpern and Mclean-Parks, "Vive La Difference"; Pinkley and Northcraft, "Cognitive Interpretations."

30. Halpern and McLean-Parks, "Vive La Difference"; L. L. Putnam and T. Jones, "Reciprocity in Negotiations: An Analysis of Bargaining Interaction," *Communication Monographs* 49 (1982): 171–91; W. J. Pikakis Smith and J. Miller, "The Impact of Close Relationships on Integrative Bargaining," (Vanderbilt University, 1993).

31. C. Watson, "Gender Differences in Negotiation Behavior and Outcomes: Fact or Artifact?," in *Gender and Conflict Resolution*, ed. A. Taylor (Cresskill, N. J.: Hampton Press, 1994), 191–210.

32. Ibid.

33. P. Gerhart and S. Rynes, "Determinants and Consequences of Salary Negotiations by Graduating Male and Female MBAs" (Working paper, #89–16, School of Industrial and Labor Relations, Cornell University, 1991); M. Renard, "Salary Negotiations and the Male-Female Wage Gap" (Ph.D. diss., University of Maryland, 1992).

34. F. Crosby, *Relative Deprivation and Working Women* (New York: Oxford University Press, 1982).

35. I. Ayres, "Fair Driving: Gender and Race Discrimination in Retail Car Negotiations," *Harvard Law Review* 104, no. 4 (1991): 817–72.

36. B. Gray, "The Gender-Based Foundations of Negotiations Theory," in *Negotiation in Organizations*, ed. R. Lewicki, B. Sheppard and R. Bies (Greenwich, Conn.: JAI Press, 1994), 4:3–36.

37. S. Harding, *The Science Question in Feminism* (Ithaca, N.Y.: Cornell University Press, 1986).

38. L. L. Burton et al., "Feminist Theory, Professional Ethics, and Gender-Related Distinctions in Attorney Negotiating Styles," *Journal of Dispute Resolution* 2, no. 2 (1991): 199–257; Kolb and Coolidge, "Her Place at the Table; Carrie Menkel-Meadow, "Portia in a Different Voice: Speculating on a Women's Lawyering Process," *Berkeley Women's Law Journal* 1, no. 1 (1985): 39–63; T. Northrup, "The Uneasy Partnership between Conflict Theory and Feminist Theory" (Syracuse University, 1994); L. Stamato, "Voice, Place, and Process: Research on Gender, Negotiation, and Conflict Resolution," *Mediation Quarterly* 9, no. 4 (1992): 375–86.

39. Kolb and Coolidge, "Her Place at the Table."

40. Frug argues that in standpoint theory, some women are excluded from the category woman. These, she suggests, are those who succeed in the male-dominated world. See M. J. Frug, "Re-Reading Contacts: A Feminist Analysis of a Contracts Casebook," *The American University Law Review* 34 (1991): 1064–1140.

41. Flax, *Thinking Fragments*.

42. T. Grillo, "The Mediation Alternative: Process Dangers For Women," *Yale Law Journal* 100, no. 6 (1991): 1545–1611.

43. Northrup, "Uneasy Partnership."

44. Flax, *Thinking Fragments*; C. Weedon, *Feminist Practice And Poststructuralist Theory* (Oxford: Basil Blackwell, 1987).

45. S. Bem, *The Lenses of Gender* (New Haven: Yale University Press, 1992).

46. J. Flax, "Postmodernism and Gender Relations in Feminist Theory," *Signs* 12, no. 4 (1987): 621–43; Weedon, *Feminist Practice.*

47. Bem, *Lenses Of Gender.*

48. Calas and Smircich, "Re-Writing Gender"; Martin, "Deconstructing Organizational Taboos"; Mumby and Putnam, "Bounded Rationality."

49. K. K. Deaux, "From Individual Differences to Social Categories: Analysis of a Decade's Research on Gender," *American Psychologist* 39, no. 2 (1984): 105–16.

50. J. P. Daly, "The Effects on Anger on Negotiations over Mergers and Acquisitions," *Negotiation Journal* 7, no. 1 (1991): 31–39; T. M. Gladwin and R. Kumar, "The Social Psychology of Crisis Bargaining: Toward a Contingency Model" (New York University, 1986).

51. L. L. Putnam, "Challenging the Assumptions of Traditional Approaches to Negotiation," *Negotiation Journal* 10, no. 3 (1994): 337–46; Strauss, *Negotiations.*

52. H. Garfinkel, *Studies in Ethnomethodology* (Englewood Cliffs, N.J.: Prentice Hall, 1967).

53. J. Scott, "Experience," in *Feminists Theorize the Political*, ed. J. Butler and J. Scott (New York: Routledge, Chapman and Hall, 1992), 22–41.

54. This approach is presented as one of several possible alternatives to theorizing negotiation. Models of negotiations as relationships fit certain social situations, while those as dialogue and transformation suit others (Putnam, "Challenging the Assumptions"). The challenge is to envision diversity in approaches, not merely variations on common themes, the state of current theory.

55. D. Bakan, *The Duality Of Human Existence* (Chicago: Rand McNally, 1966).

56. R. Harre, *Personal Being* (Cambridge, Mass.: Harvard University Press, 1984).

57. M. Deutsch, "The Effect of Motivational Orientation upon Trust and Suspicion," *Human Relations* 13, no. 2 (1960): 123–39.

58. Schelling, *Strategy of Conflict.*

59. Fisher, Ury, and Patton, *Getting To YES*; Walton and McKersie, *Labor Negotiations*.

60. Pruitt, *Negotiation Behavior*.

61. J. Z. Rubin, "Some Wise and Mistaken Assumptions about Conflict and Negotiation," in *Negotiation Theory and Practice* (Cambridge, Mass.: Program on Negotiation, 1991), 4.

62. Rubin and Brown, *Psychology of Bargaining*; R. W. Gilkey and L. Greenhalgh, "The Role of Personality in Successful Negotiations," *Negotiation Journal* 2, no. 4 (1986): 245–56; Lewicki, Minton and Saunders, *Negotiations*.

63. Pruitt, *Negotiation Behavior*; J. Z. Rubin, D. Pruitt, and S. H. Kim, *Social Conflict* (New York: McGraw–Hill, 1993).

64. Kahneman and Tversky, "Prospect Theory"; Neale and Bazerman, *Cognition and Rationality*; L. Thompson and R. Hastie, "Judgment Tasks and Biases in Negotiation," in *Research in Negotiation in Organizations*, ed. B.H. Sheppard, M. H. Bazerman and R. J. Lewicki (Greenwich, Conn.: JAI Press, 1990), 2:31–54.

65. P. Carnevale and D. G. Pruitt, "Negotiation and Mediation," *Annual Review of Psychology* 43 (1991): 531–82.

66. Neale and Bazerman, *Cognition and Rationality*.

67. D. M. Kolb, "William Hobgood: Conditioning Parties in Labor Mediation," in *When Talk Works*, ed. D. Kolb and Associates (San Francisco: Jossey Bass, 1994), 149–91.

68. N. Hartsock, "Exchange Theory: Critique from a Feminist Standpoint," in *Current Perspectives in Social Theory* (Greenwich, Conn.: JAI Press, 1985), 6: 57–70.

69. Ibid.

70. J. Halpern, "Friendship's Effects on the Buyer-Seller Relationship" (Cornell University, 1992); R. Kramer, E. Newton, and P. Pommerenke, "Self-Enhancement Biases and Negotiation Judgment: Effects Of Self-Esteem and Mood," *Organizational Behavior and Human Decision Processes* 56, no. 1 (1993): 110–33; Smith and Miller, "Integrative Bargaining."

71. G. Loewenstein, L. Thompson, and M. Bazerman, "Social Utility and Decisionmaking in Interpersonal Contexts," *Journal of Personality and Social Psychology* 47 (1989): 1231–43; Halpern "Buyer-Seller Relationship."

72. R. E. Kramer, E. Newton, and P. Pomerenke, "Self-Enhancement Biases and Negotiator Judgment: Effects of Self-Esteem and Mood," *Organization Behavior and Human Performance* 56 (1993): 110–133.

73. S. R. Wilson, "Face And Facework in Negotiation," in *Communication and Negotiation*, ed. L. L. Putnam and M. E. Roloff (Newbury Park, Calif.: Sage, 1992), 374–406.

74. R. Fisher and S. Brown, *Getting Together* (Boston: Houghton-Miflin, 1988).

75. Northrup, "Uneasy Partnership."

76. E. Goffman, *The Presentation of Self in Everyday Life* (Garden City, N.Y.: Doubleday, 1959).

77. R. Harre, *Personal Being* (Cambridge: Harvard University Press, 1984); J. Fletcher, "Castrating the Feminine Advantage: Feminist Standpoint Research and Management Science," *Journal of Management Inquiry* 3, no. 1 (1993): 74–82.

78. M. E. Roloff and J. M. Jordan, "Achieving Negotiation Goals: The 'Fruits and Foibles' of Planning Ahead," in *Communication and Negotiation*, ed. L. L. Putnam and M. E. Roloff (Newbury Park, Calif.: Sage, 1992), 21–45.

79. J. Butler, *Gender Trouble: Feminism and the Subversion of Identity* (New York: Routledge, 1990).

80. D. M. Kolb and S. Eaton, "What Mrs. Dalloway Knew: Invisible Work in Negotiation." Paper presented at Women's College Coalition Conference, Mt. Holyoke College, 1994.

81. R. Friedman, *Front Stage, Backstage: The Dramatic Structure of Labor Negotiations* (Cambridge: MIT Press, 1994).

82. Cobb, "Empowerment and Mediation."

83. Goffman, *Presentation of Self.*

84. Ibid.

85. R. Kramer and D. Messick, *The Social Context Of Negotiation* (Newbury Park, Calif.: Sage, 1995).

86. Walton and McKersie, *Labor Negotiations*; Mnookin, "Exploration of Barriers."

87. C. McEwen, "Commentary on Research on Dispute Resolution" (Bowdoin College, 1994).

88. J. K. Sebenius, *Negotiating the Law of the Sea* (Cambridge, Mass.: Harvard University Press, 1984); I. W. Zartman, *New Perspectives on International Multilateral Negotiations* (San Francisco: Jossey-Bass, 1994).

89. D. M. Kolb, "Women's Work: Peacemaking behind the Scenes," in *Hidden Conflict in Organizations: Uncovering behind the Scenes Disputes,* ed. D. M. Kolb and J. Bartunek (Newbury Park, Calif.: Sage, 1992), 63–91.

90. Friedman, *Front Stage, Backstage;* H. Ibarra, "Homophily and Differential Returns: Sex Differences in Network Structure and Access in an Advertising Firm," *Administrative Science Quarterly* 37, no. 3 (1993): 422–47; C. Stohl, *Organizational Communication: Connectedness in Action* (Thousand Oaks, Calif.: Sage, 1995).

91. Friedman, *Front Stage, Backstage.*

92. J. Forester, "Beyond Dialogue to Transformative Learning: How Deliberative Rituals Encourage Political Judgment in Community Planning Processes" (Cornell University, 1994).

93. Kolb, "Women's Work."

94. Negotiation analysts might be quick to point out that to talk about interdependence is to weaken oneself by suggesting that one is more dependent on a deal than the other, information that is best strategically withheld (Lax and Sebenius, *Manager as Negotiator*). To think about negotiations within a context of connection is, by implication, to rethink the relationship between information and bargaining power.

95. Cobb, "Empowerment and Mediation."

96. Fisher, Ury, and Patton, *Getting To YES;* Pruitt, *Negotiation Behavior;* Walton and McKersie, *Labor Negotiations.*

97. Sebenius, "Negotiation Analysis."

98. Carnevale and Pruitt, "Negotiation and Mediation," 83.

99. Neale and Bazerman, *Cognition and Rationality.*

100. Schelling, *Strategy of Conflict.*

101. L. Ross and C. Stillinger, "Barriers To Conflict Resolution," *Negotiation Journal* 7, no. 4 (1991): 389–405; Mnookin, "Exploration of Barriers."

102. Neale and Bazerman, *Cognition and Rationality*; Kahneman and Tversky, "Prospect Theory."

103. Kolb and Coolidge, "Her Place at the Table."

104. Greenhalgh and Gilkey, "Sex-Role Differences."

105. Fisher, Ury, and Patton, *Getting to YES.*

106. S. R. Wilson and L. L. Putnam, "Interaction Goals in Negotiations," in *Communication Yearbook*, ed. J. A. Anderson (Newbury Park, Calif.: Sage, 1990), 13:374–406.

107. W. R. Fry, I. J. Firestone, and D. L.Williams, "Negotiation Process and Outcome of Stranger Dyads and Dating Couples: Do Lovers Lose?" *Basic and Applied Social Psychology* 4, no. 1 (1983): 1–16; L. Greenhalgh, "Relationships in Negotiations," *Negotiation Journal* 3, no. 4 (1987): 235–43; Halpern, "Buyer-Seller Relationship."

108. B. R. Brown, "Face-saving and Face-restoration in Negotiation," in *Negotiations: Social Psychological Perspectives,* ed. D. Druckman (Beverly Hills: Sage, 1977), 275–99; Wilson, "Facework in Negotiation."

109. Putnam, "Challenging the Assumptions."

110. Roloff and Jordan, "'Fruits and Foibles'"; Wilson and Putnam, "Interaction Goals in Negotiations."

111. L. L. Putnam, "Bargaining as Organizational Communication," in *Organizational Communication: Traditional Themes and New Directions,* ed. R. D. McPhee and P. K. Thompkins (Beverly Hills: Sage, 1985), 129–48; Roloff and Jordan, "'Fruits and Foibles.'"

112. C. M. Keough, "The Nature and Function of Argument in Organizational Bargaining Research," *Southern Speech Communication Journal* 50, no. 1 (1987): 1–17; L. Putnam, S. R. Wilson and D. Turner, "The Evolution of Policy Arguments in Teachers' Bargaining," *Argumentation* 4 (1990): 129–52.

113. Cobb, "Empowerment and Mediation."

114. L. Mather and B. Yngvesson, "Language, Audience, and the Transformation of Disputes," *Law and Society Review* 15 (1980–81): 757–821.

115. Putnam, "Challenging the Assumptions."

116. Lax and Sebenius, *Manager as Negotiator.*

117. Mather and Yngvesson, "Transformation of Disputes."

118. Ibid.; Putnam, "Integrative And Distributive Bargaining."

119. Kolb and Coolidge, "Her Place at the Table."

120. Cobb, "Empowerment and Mediation"; J. Conley and W. O'Barr, *Rules v. Relationships* (Chicago: University of Chicago Press, 1990); Putnam, "Challenging the Assumptions."

121. Cobb, "Empowerment and Mediation"; Keough, "Organizational Bargaining Research"; Putnam, "Bargaining as Organizational Communication"; Putnam, Wilson, and Turner, "Teachers' Bargaining"; Roloff and Jordan, "'Fruits and Foibles.'"

122. R. Vayrynen, *New Directions in Conflict Theory: Conflict Resolution and Transformation* (Newbury Park, Calif.: Sage, 1991); L. Kriesberg, "Conclusion: Research and Policy Implications," in *Intractable Conflicts and Their Transformation,* ed. K. Kriesberg, T. A. Northrup, and S. J. Thorson (Syracuse, N.Y.: Syracuse University Press, 1989), 210–20.

Epilogue

Relevance and Communication

12

FUTURE PROGRESS IN DISPUTE RESOLUTION
LINKING PRACTICE AND ACADEMIC RESEARCH[1]

Timothy Hedeen

I. Introduction

The present body of research in dispute resolution has grown a great deal since 1981 when James Wall wrote: "[M]ediation, despite its importance and seeming ubiquity, remains understudied, less than understood, and unrefined."[2] A number of the authors in this book have contributed to the growth of our understanding of dispute resolution, with particular attention to work site issues. Preceding chapters have identified various issues for future research to expand our understanding of the field. But while the overall body of research has expanded in both breadth and depth, there remains a dearth of research that is usable by practitioners. To help remedy this situation, this chapter discusses how research can be conducted to make it more practitioner-friendly, thereby assisting work site dispute resolution efforts.

As with many other disciplines, the dispute resolution community looks to the academic world for valuable theoretical, analytical, and practice tools. Predominantly, however, the research in scholarly journals and books is, for lack of a better term, "academic": the research is presented in a language and context that typically requires previous and often extensive knowledge of the professional literature. Sanford Jaffe provides a concise summary of where research stands in relation to practice:

> Dispute resolution is a field in which research is hurrying to catch up with practice. Developments on the legislative, executive, and judicial fronts are generally occurring faster than the research can advance to offer guidance and direction.[3]

This need for timely, relevant research suggests that researchers should consider how they can best provide guidance and direction for practitioners. To provide the necessary ingredients for the informed growth of the field, academic researchers should give more attention to what is studied, as well as *how* and *where* their findings are presented. There is great potential to dovetail the academic interests of scholars and the operational needs of practitioners. This chapter reviews the need for research and then discusses three dimensions that are important if the collective interests of all members of the dispute resolution community are to be linked: identifying the research topics relevant to the needs of practitioners, using research methodologies based in actual practice, and improving the accessibility of research findings to practitioners.

II. Why Research Is Needed

In any field or discipline involving social interaction, research should provide insights into the processes and conduct that constitute effective practice: "The value of research and analysis is to enrich understanding and to provide a sound basis for decision-making."[4] But while there has been a rapid growth of dispute resolution in recent years as a field of practice and an academic discipline, there is so little interaction between practitioners and researchers that practice does not guide research and research does not inform practice. As a consequence, dispute resolution is too young to enjoy such benefits of a long history as a knowledge of tried-and-true strategies of predecessors, lessons from the pitfalls of others, and an awareness of the limits of practice. In addition, many practitioners still operate without the benefit of research to inform and guide their work.

Thus, the field of dispute resolution currently is moving forward on the long and circuitous road of learning by experience, a road where wrong turns and unnecessary detours are too common. The alternative is to link practical learning and academic research to generate research relevant to practice. This approach can eliminate many of the growing pains that are already occurring in the field. One such growing pain is overextending the scope of dispute resolution services; this has already begun as trainers develop programs and take on work they are not prepared to handle.[5] In addition, the reliance on existing models and techniques to address future needs in dispute management systems will surely lead to failed initiatives and stagnation. Research can provide a shorter and straighter road that bypasses many of these pitfalls, but only if it is done with input from and output to the entire dispute resolution community of scholars and practitioners.

III. Research Relevant to Practice

For dispute resolution practitioners, "relevant research" is characterized by at least four traits:

1. It focuses on topics relevant to practice.
2. It uses methods in applied settings, not laboratories.
3. It maintains the rigor of academic standards for research.
4. It develops prescriptive conclusions applicable to practice.

This list is neither exhaustive nor exclusive, but represents the most common criteria voiced by practitioners.

A. *Relevant Topics*

Practitioners and researchers will not always agree on what are appropriate research topics.[6] Yet the development of a research agenda for the field of dispute resolution must grow out of discussions between members of these communities. It is notable that other social science fields also wrestle with this divergence of research interests. In the relatively young field of strategic management, which is considered an applied discipline by many, "concerns have been raised about the practical relevance of business research in general and strategic management in particular."[7] Even among management faculty, a survey elicited a mean response of "somewhat dissatisfied" with "the relevance of academic research to the needs of industry."[8]

Similar sentiments have been related in more established disciplines as well. Former U. S. Secretary of Labor John T. Dunlop has written: "the bulk of academic research in industrial relations and economics in recent years has had very little impact on either public or private policy decisions."[9] He also claims that ". . . fruitful research into labor organization problems has withered and the insights such work could offer to many issues has been lacking." Dunlop concludes that, "a further debilitating consequence is that graduate students and young scholars are in the main disqualified from making contributions to public policy and to the problems of major organizations."[10]

Based on the experiences of other fields, it would appear that dispute resolution has followed a popular course: academics have studied in deep, rigorous, and theoretical directions, while practitioners have remained outside of a research community they see as inaccessible, non-applicable, and uninteresting. This inaccessibility has generated the frequently expressed disdain among nonacademics for intellectual and critical viewpoints. Birkhoff has termed this the "ridicule of 'talking heads.'"[11] She cautions that "practitioners who disregard important research findings will perpetuate ineffective, or worse, unethical practices."[12]

To improve on this state of affairs, academics and practitioners must first explore together the values and needs of each group, and then jointly devise a research agenda for the field. One prominent code of ethics for the field, the 1995 Model Standards of Conduct for Mediators, addresses this directly.[13] One of the standards, "Obligations to the Mediation Process," reads: "Mediators have a duty to improve the practice of mediation." This implies a responsibility to evaluate and to refine the practice of dispute resolution through an ongoing dialogue with those conducting research.

B.   Relevant Methodology

A meeting of the minds must occur with regard to methodology as well, and the outcome should uphold the standards of both groups. Practitioners find great value in research that is conducted on-site for it is this experience that speaks most directly to their work. Due to the abstraction and distance that characterize simulations and laboratory experiments, these methods do not command the confidence of practitioners in the same way that applied research does.

Applied research is done in the workplace or on-site within the practice of dispute resolution. Most applied research methods are integrated into practice whether the research is conducted by an outside researcher or the practitioner involved with an actual dispute resolution process. Research methods such as participant observation, interviewing, and on-site evaluation allow an individual other than the practitioner to conduct the research.[14] Methods of data collection based on the clinical research model, self-evaluation, or surveys can be done by the practitioner. Some of these, such as the clinical model, provide rich data without specialized or time-consuming processes. They build on the regular data collection required as part of the task of resolving a dispute.

From an academic viewpoint, research methods in any setting must be concerned with issues of validity and reliability. There are a variety of both quantitative and qualitative research methods applicable to dispute resolution that handle these concerns satisfactorily. The models of research identified in the preceding paragraph uphold the scholarly research tradition, provided the appropriate method is chosen for the particular issue being studied. Thus, the issue is not a lack of available valid and reliable research methods suitable for use in applied settings. Rather, the situation reflects a disinterest in using many of these methods for at least three reasons. First, on-site research with actual participants is less convenient than on-campus or laboratory studies with simulations or models since it demands that the research not interfere with service delivery. Second, this research generally entails additional time and money due to such factors as travel and coordination with the practitioners' schedules and processes. Finally, on-site research is more difficult to control for purposes of validity and reliability than laboratory-based research.

Practitioners and researchers alike share the interest that any site-based research must not disrupt or harm the services under study. Some of the research methods mentioned above can address this concern, but others remain problematic. For example, a faculty member who conducts multiparty mediations encountered problems when an apprentice conducted on-site observation research:

> Graduate students in the mediation room take notes—they scribble furiously—which makes everybody else in the room hysterically nervous. So rather than the parties in the dispute paying attention to each other, they're paying attention to the graduate student who is taking notes back there.[15]

This illustration also raises two concerns specific to dispute resolution: privacy and confidentiality. To balance these with the need for research is not an easy task. The resulting arrangement must provide thorough detail while remaining unobtrusive to those involved. This question cannot be resolved here, and will benefit from future exchanges both within and across the practitioner and researcher communities.

With the assistance and insight of practitioners, future research can have "relevance with as much rigor as possible" and not "rigor regardless of relevance."[16] Integrative thinking on the part of academics and practitioners will create research projects that adhere to high standards of methodological validity and reliability while being relevant to the needs of practice.

IV. Dissemination and Presentation

The accessibility of research findings, i.e., where and how research advances are published and presented, must be given more attention if practitioners are to be reached more effectively. The "where" of research presentation refers to the media through which it is distributed. To date, this has been through a handful of academic journals and university-based book publishers. While this limited distribution is not inherently problematic, what is more troubling about this arrangement is that it results in a small group of editors—some of whom have little field experience—determining what research gets published.

For example, a colleague recently complained: "There's a lack of sensitivity amongst those who edit journals to what is useful knowledge for practitioners."[17] While this may not be a fair characterization of editors' intent, the result is that many practitioners do not see great value in reading the scholarly literature.

Barriers to the broad dissemination of these journals and books include price and consumer base. The journals are circulated only to individual subscribers and university libraries, and the books travel in similar circles, with the added barrier of high prices.[18] As many practitioners do not have access to libraries that own these materials, and often find the costs of the publications prohibitive, the research in these publications remains largely inaccessible and unused.

Practitioners have not embraced research because many perceive that it is not related to practice, a view that has been "fostered by numerous dry research reports, which indeed offer little insight into practice dilemmas or decisions."[19] The image of the "dry research report" leads us to the "how" of research presentation. The language used by academics to report research findings is often unfamiliar to practitioners. The impact of language differences was experienced firsthand by a conference organizer who sought to bring together researchers and practitioners:

> The practitioners and researchers were not talking the same language. . . . You can't even have the dialogue if they're not talking the same language. There's some problems inherent, [and] a whole bunch of education has to occur before that dialogue is productive.[20]

Because an important by-product of research is education, more attention should be given by the dispute resolution community to communicating in "plain English" so others can understand and use the information. The education needed to bridge the languages and interests of researchers and practitioners is not so great, however: a brief introduction to the tenets, language, and methods of research would adequately prepare a practitioner to better understand academic research. Similarly, a brief introduction to the rules, language, and methods of practice would sufficiently ready an academic researcher to understand practice and to present research findings accessible to practitioners. Such education would demonstrate to each group which of the components are presently shared, and which components need some translation for the benefit of the other community. What today passes for "jargon" in academia and for "shop talk" in mediation centers would become the common lexicon of the field.

V. Conclusions and Implications for Future Research

As several earlier chapters in this book have demonstrated, dispute resolution practitioners at the work site are venturing forth today into uncharted territory in an accelerated fashion. With accessible yet meaningful research findings to assist them, practitioners and policy makers can make prudent and informed choices about the future direction of a field now marked by relatively severe growing pains.

This chapter suggests three major implications for future research to assist practitioners. First, efforts must be made to identify those topics on which academics should focus their research to be helpful to practitioners. One way to do this is to survey practitioners about the topics which would be most useful. For example, for work site dispute resolution issues the practitioner members of professional associations such as the Society of Professionals in Dispute Resolution and the Industrial Relations Research Association could be contacted for this purpose and the findings shared with academic audiences.

Second, while a variety of research techniques must be used to fully understand dispute resolution and dispute management, more work must be done in real-life situations if practice is to be helped by research and vice versa. Academic research designed in cooperation with dispute resolution practitioners at the work site is less likely to be stalled or delayed by the many complications more easily anticipated by those working in the field every day. It also is somewhat less likely to produce compromised findings due to flawed or impractical research designs.

Finally, once a research project is completed, more attention must be given to publishing the findings in "plain English" in practitioner journals in addition to academic publications, as well as presenting the findings at professional conferences heavily attended by practitioners. A research literature that is made more accessible to the practitioner community will have more impact on both the theory and the practice of this dynamic and robust field.

Without the collaborative bridge-building discussed above, dispute resolution research and practice will undoubtedly develop and grow, but in a slower and more halting fashion and with many more mistakes. For workplace dispute resolution systems, these mistakes represent lost opportunities to more effectively manage disputes and to improve productivity through fewer disruptions of work. Through cooperation and coordination among researchers and practitioners, we can build these bridges now rather than continuing to linger on opposite sides of the river.

Notes

1.   The idea for this chapter arose from a presentation entitled "Points of Intersection: Academics and Practitioners in Dispute Resolution," delivered at the 1995 Annual International Conference of the Society of Professionals in Dispute Resolution (SPIDR) in Washington, D.C. The author extends his gratitude to all those who attended this workshop, as much of the dialogue contributed to this chapter. The author would also extend his gratitude to Patrick Coy for his helpful comments and suggestions.

2.   J. A. Wall, "Mediation: An Analysis, Review and Proposed Research," *Journal of Conflict Resolution* 25, no. 1 (1981): 178.

3.   S. Jaffe in *Mediation Research*, ed. K. Kressel and D. G. Pruitt (San Francisco: Jossey-Bass, 1989), xiii.

4.   R. O. Clarke, "Industrial Relations Theory and Practice: A Note," in *Theories and Concepts in Comparative Industrial Relations*, ed. J. Barbash and K. Barbash (Columbia: University of South Carolina Press, 1989), 198.

5.   There is a considerable trend among trainers and programs to deliver services in areas about which they know little. Without consideration of their own shortcomings, many groups are undertaking initiatives far afield of their own strengths. For more on this, see T. Hedeen, "Mediation: Growing Field, Growing Pains," *The Snapshot: Newsletter of the New York State Dispute Resolution Association* (1996).

6.   For example, C. Gopinath and R. C. Hoffman report in "The Relevance of Strategy Research: Practitioner and Academic Viewpoints," *Journal of Management Studies* 32, no. 5 (1995): 582, the results of a survey that asked corporate CEOs and academics to identify the two or three most important strategic issues of critical importance to the success of corporations into the year 2000 and beyond. The three top-ranked issues by CEOs were: (1) managing operations; (2) environmental analysis (government policy, social and economic factors); and (3) global competition/business. In contrast, the issues most highly ranked by academics—and therefore most likely to be researched—were: (1) global competition/business; (2) managing new organizational forms; and (3) strategy implementation.

7.   Ibid., 575.

8.   Ibid., 576.

9.   J. T. Dunlop, "Policy Decisions and Research in Economics and Industrial Relations," *Industrial and Labor Relations Review* 30, no. 3 (1977): 275.

10.   Ibid., 279.

11.   J. Birkhoff, "Marketing Isn't Everything: The Importance of Research in Dispute Resolution," *Society of Professionals in Dispute Resolution News* 19, no. 3 (1995): 1.

12.   Ibid., 12.

13.   The Model Standards of Conduct for Mediators are the product of a joint effort by the American Arbitration Association, the American Bar Association, and the Society of Professionals in Dispute Resolution. The standards also address self-determination, impartiality, competence, confidentiality, and five other areas regarding practice. Each of these broad terms and areas could be explored in future research. This would move the field forward considerably. See *Model Standards of Conduct for Mediators* (Washington, D.C.: American Arbitration Association, American Bar Association and Society of Professionals in Dispute Resolution, 1995).

14.   There are numerous texts on applied research methods, including *Direct Practice Research in Human Service Agencies* by B. Blythe, T. Tripodi and S. Briar (New York: Columbia University Press, 1994). For a broader examination of social research, consult K. D. Bailey, *Methods of Social Research* (New York: The Free Press, 1987) or E. Babbie, *The Practice of Social Research* (Belmont, Calif.: Wadsworth, 1989). One example of research using survey data is T. Hedeen and P. Moses's analysis of community mediation in New York state, based on case records and participant demographics collected through a comprehensive records survey maintained by the state's Community Dispute Resolution Centers Program. See "Alternative Dispute Resolution Participation: Preliminary Analysis of the New York State Community Dispute Resolution Centers Program," *Proceedings of the Twenty-First International Conference,* Toronto, Ontario, October 20-23, 1993 (Washington, D.C.: Society of Professionals in Dispute Resolution, 1993), 249-56.

15.   See note 1 above, quoted from the discussion following the presentation.

16.   R. A. Gordon quoted in Dunlop, "Policy Decisions," 282.

17.   See note 1 above, quoted from the discussion following the presentation.

18. As the director of Onondaga County Dispute Resolution Center, I started a practice of regularly mailing a short annotated bibliography to volunteer mediators. I noticed that of the four books listed on the summer 1995 edition of that bibliography, none was available for under thirty dollars.

19. Blythe, et al., 13.

20. See note 1 above, quoted from the discussion following the presentation.

INDEX